A UNION OF INTERESTS

AMERICAN POLITICAL THOUGHT
edited by
WILSON CAREY McWILLIAMS AND LANCE BANNING

A UNION
OF INTERESTS

Political and Economic Thought in Revolutionary America

Cathy D. Matson
and Peter S. Onuf

 University Press of Kansas

Published by the University Press of Kansas (Lawrence, Kansas 66045), which was organized by the Kansas Board of Regents and is operated and funded by Emporia State University, Fort Hays State University, Kansas State University, Pittsburg State University, the University of Kansas, and Wichita State University

Library of Congress Cataloging-in-Publication Data

Matson, Cathy D., 1951–
    A union of interests : political and economic thought in revolutionary America / Cathy D. Matson and Peter S. Onuf.
       p.   cm. — (American political thought)
    Includes bibliographical references.
    ISBN 0-7006-0417-0 (alk. paper)
    1. Political science—United States—History—18th century.
2. Republicanism—United States—History—18th century. 3. Federal government—United States—History—18th century. 4. Economics—United States—History—18th century. 5. United States—Economic policy—To 1933. 6. United States—Politics and government—Revolution, 1775-1783. 7. United States—Politics and government—1783-1789. I. Onuf, Peter S. II. Title. III. Series.
JA84.U5M29   1990
973.3—dc20
                                             89-16749
                                              CIP

Printed in the United States of America
10 9 8 7 6 5 4 3 2 1

The paper used in this publication meets the minimum requirements of the American National Standard for Permanence of Paper for Printed Library Materials Z39.48-1984.

To Herb Sloan and Ruth Smith

Contents

Preface

In this book we survey the history of American political and economic thought during the republic's founding and formative years. The most exciting recent work on republicanism has helped illuminate the long-neglected but crucial domain of political economy. Our goal in this book is to show how the rapidly changing context of revolutionary American federalism shaped the development of this thinking and how, in turn, changing economic ideas contributed to the reconception and reconstruction of the union.

The exigencies of nation building made extraordinary demands on inherited ways of thinking. In order to grasp the dimensions of the resulting ideological transformation, we have sought to merge the perspectives of the economic historian and the political historian. This effort dates from 1984, when we both lived in Worcester and began to explore common intellectual interests. Some of the preliminary results of our collaboration appeared in a special issue of *American Quarterly* on "Republicanism in the History and Historiography of the United States," edited by Joyce Appleby. Since then we have incurred many individual and institutional debts.

Cathy Matson's research and writing was supported in 1987–88 by a generous grant from the American Council for Learned Societies. Edward Countryman, Paul Gilje, Bill Pencak, J. R. Pole, and R. C. Simmons offered helpful criticism on portions of several chapters. This book includes parts of essays by Matson published in R. C. Simmons and A. E. Dick Howard, eds., *The U.S. Constitution;* Conrad Wright and William Pencak, eds., *New York and the Rise of Capitalism;* and William Pencak and Paul Gilje, eds., *New York in the Age of the Constitution* (see Bibliography for full titles). Matson wishes to thank the University of Tennessee–Knoxville and particularly the History Department for their continuing support. Librarians at the New-York Historical Society, the New York Public Library, the Pennsylvania Historical Society, the American Antiquarian Society, Columbia University, and the Library of Congress were unfailingly helpful. To the librarians at the University of Tennessee who processed innumerable requests for interlibrary loan materials, a very special thank you. The many colleagues at Tennessee who listened to and criticized portions of the book provided a stimulating environment. Anne Mayhew, John Bohstedt, Terry Neale, and David Tandy of the economic history group have given invaluable advice, and Bruce Wheeler will recognize the results of many scholarly exchanges about the period in points of interpretation. But, above all, Cathy Matson wishes to acknowledge John Zomchick for providing a model of intellectual precision and inspiration for the life of the mind. Sarah Matson Zomchick continues to be a source of joy.

Peter Onuf acknowledges the helpful comments of Herman Belz, Ronald Hoffman, Michael Lienesch, Rosemarie Zagarri, and Neil York on various chapters. This book incorporates parts of essays by Onuf in Terence Ball and J. G. A. Pocock, eds., *Conceptual Change and the Constitution;* Herman Belz et al., eds., *To Form a More Perfect Union;* Michael Gillespie and Michael Lienesch, eds., *Ratifying the Constitution;* Herman Wellenreuther, ed., *Essays on the Constitution;* and Neil L. York, ed., *Toward a More Perfect Union.* Onuf conducted much of his research at the American Antiquarian Society in Worcester, during and after he held a National Endowment for the Humanities fellowship there in 1984–85. The AAS staff, under the leadership of Director Marcus McCorison, provided superb support.

Both authors wish to thank Dedman College and the History Department at Southern Methodist University for bringing Matson to Texas at a crucial point in the collaboration. We are particularly grateful to series editors Lance Banning and Carey McWilliams for their encouragement and criticism.

Our book is dedicated, with respect and gratitude, to Herb Sloan and Ruth Smith, good critics and good friends for many years.

Dallas, Texas, and Knoxville, Tennessee   *January 1989*

Introduction

Many of the delegates who gathered in Philadelphia in the summer of 1787 were convinced that the American states were in the throes of a "critical period" and that the Confederation was not long for this world. If the union collapsed, the state governments would quickly move to fill the vacuum of power. The result, advocates of a strong central government predicted, would fulfill Turgot's dark prophecy. In an influential tract widely excerpted in American newspapers in the 1780s, the eminent French economist and statesman warned that if America was to remain "the hope of the world," it must avoid becoming the "image of our Europe, a mass of divided powers contending for territory and commerce."[1] Constitutional reformers charged that the states had already become just such a "mass of divided powers," concluding that the Confederation government was incapable of dealing with a plethora of threatening circumstances at home and abroad.

Repeated failures to amend the Articles of Confederation demonstrated the futility of a gradualist, incremental approach to constitutional reform. Of course, the state governments were bound to resist any change that would jeopardize the sovereign powers secured to them by the Articles. And here was the rub. Most nationalists agreed with James Madison's penetrating analysis in the "Vices of the Political System": the problems of the union were rooted in the turbulent politics of the states and the exaggerated pretensions of their governments.[2] But how could the states ever be induced to sacrifice their rights and interests to a powerful central government? And how could nationalists, whose distaste for the excesses of popular politics was well known—and whose "aristocratic" ambitions were widely suspected—persuade the people to submit to a remote, "consolidated" national regime?

The story of how the framers of the federal Constitution overcame these and other formidable obstacles is the subject of a vast literature. We do not offer a detailed narrative of this history, nor do we attempt to provide a comprehensive synthesis of recent scholarship on the development of revolutionary American political ideology. Scholars have shown how this thought was shaped by specific historical circumstances—for instance, by the crisis of currency finance and revolutionary debts, or by the outbreak of Shays's Rebellion and other agrarian disorders.[3] They have also identified a wide array of influences on American political and economic discourse in the period between the Revolution and the Constitution.[4] Our indebtedness to this scholarship should be apparent.

Americans drew on classical republican, liberal, and jurisprudential traditions, among others, to conceive and construct solutions to the problems they saw themselves confronting in the aftermath of the Revolution. We believe that no one of these discursive traditions should be accorded a decisive, determinative role in the American founding.[5] The framers of the Constitution intended to preserve and perfect the union; our intention therefore is to reconstruct the discourse of American *federalism*. Our contention is that this discourse was grounded in a history of debate over the role of government in the regulation of the economy, a debate that was particularly complex and confusing in revolutionary America because of jurisdictional confusion under the Articles of Confederation. Thus, just as the crisis of the union was defined in economic terms, discussion about the future of the nation's economy was shaped and limited by the division of political authority in the federal union.

The genius of the Federalists was to link ratification of the Constitution with the rapid development of the national economy so as to appeal to the many optimistic and enterprising Americans who hoped to reap the rewards of independence. The Federalists did not, therefore, necessarily embrace a more "liberal" stance than their adversaries on the organization of the American economy. In the ratification debates, "realistic" Federalists asserted that the national government would have to play a strong, positive role in protecting American interests abroad and in promoting expansion and development at home. Meanwhile, a few opponents of a strong national regime argued eloquently for economic freedom and unregulated markets. Yet the opposing parties did *not* generally define themselves according to their enthusiasm for neo-mercantilist, or republican, or liberal prescriptions for the economy. The issue, instead, was one of scope and scale. Should state or federal governments intervene in the economy, and toward what ends? What kind of union would best serve the interests of individual Americans, or of the respective states or regions?

The debates at the Philadelphia Convention and the state ratifying conventions constitute the immediate settings for the conceptual changes we will explore in this book. But changing conceptions of union, state sovereignty, federalism, and the nature of republican government were grounded in more gradual and fundamental transformations in the ways Anglo-Americans thought about private "interest" and the public good. Our plan therefore is to begin in the first chapter with a review of political economic discourse in colonial America, focusing particularly on the idea of interest.

During the century and a half before the American Revolution, the dramatic expansion of the Atlantic economy challenged the traditional premises of political economic thought. New ways of thinking about the relation between private interest and the public good began to emerge, and many colonial merchants and traders found inspiration—and justification—in the new language of economic freedom. Some bold thinkers began to argue that unfettered private exchanges better served the public welfare than did regulation of the economy by distant imperial authorities.

But thinking about economic freedom was still inchoate on the eve of the Revolution. Although many Americans had glimpsed the potential benefits of unregulated private enterprise, their vision lacked a satisfactory theoretical foundation, particularly concerning the relationship of economic freedom and political liberty. Anglo-Americans had not yet elaborated a coherent alternative to a centrally directed political economy, and their claims for individual political or economic rights largely remained embedded in traditional communal contexts. Few Americans were prepared, even in the euphoria of 1776, to argue that the free play of enterprising individuals would itself provide an adequate basis for economic development and social welfare. Despite complaints about specific commercial regulations, American colonists could not easily discount the substantial benefits of membership in the British Empire.

After independence, we suggest in chapter 2, revolutionaries encountered practical, political problems as they attempted to exercise their new economic freedom. The new nation's experiments with unregulated foreign and domestic exchange raised troubling questions about the virtue and patriotism of the American people. Republican moralists inveighed against the anarchy and licentiousness of unbridled self-interest. Even groups that sought greater commercial freedom acknowledged the need for more effective governmental interventions in the economy. Merchants looking for new markets depended on Congress to negotiate favorable trade agreements; land speculators, commercial farmers, and urban artisans all sought the support and sponsorship of state governments in furthering their economic ambitions.

American politicians began to revive mercantilist practices in response to the demands of rising interest groups in the states. But many Americans remained skeptical about their prospects for economic freedom during the 1780s, despite the successes of the new state governments in protecting and promoting economic interests. Continentally minded developers, "projectors," and expansionists were convinced that the imprecise and ambiguous idea of a national interest that supposedly would flow from the implementation of enlightened policies in the states did not, in fact, provide adequate security for their property or support for their enterprises.

The tendency of the states to pursue their own interests at one another's expense—and regardless of common, national interests—was particularly conspicuous in the protracted struggle over the future of the West, our subject in chapter 3. Commentators agreed that development of the vast western hinterland was crucial to America's prosperity and power. But jurisdictional conflict kept the frontiers in an uproar, retarding growth and jeopardizing the union itself. The belated cession of state claims to Congress did not bring peace to the frontiers. As Congress formulated its policy for developing the new national domain, squatters and speculators spread out across the Ohio country and threatened to bring on full-scale war with the native tribes.

Meanwhile, separatists sought to break away from the old states and form new states of their own; some reportedly entered into treasonous negotiations with neighboring imperial powers.

Confusion on the frontiers revealed the inadequacy of uncoordinated and often conflicting state responses to common problems. The state legislatures had gained considerable popular support as they sought to reconstruct the postwar economy; given Congress's failure to act effectively, the states' discriminatory legislation against foreign commerce and efforts to protect infant manufactures and promote internal improvements apparently represented the only hope for recovery. But, as we show in chapter 4, state policies did not satisfy a growing number of influential interests, particularly with the onset of depression in the mid-1780s. At the same time, reform-minded "nationalists" were convinced that the weakness of the union—and the dominant position of the sovereign states—threatened the nation's independence as well as its position in the Atlantic economy.

Frontier disorders and commercial crises convinced nationalists that the Articles of Confederation were inadequate to the exigencies of the union. The authors of the Articles had been determined not to recreate the tyrannical central authority that had driven the colonists to revolution. According to Article II, "each State retains its sovereignty, freedom, and independence": this union would be based on consent, not coercion. The states cooperated well enough to win the war, recognizing the central role of Congress and the Continental Army in vindicating American rights and securing the benefits of self-government. For enthusiastic revolutionaries, union as means converged with union as end: because republican citizens and states were naturally drawn to each other, the elimination of Britain's corrupting rule would usher in a millennium of harmony and peace.

Yet, nationalist reformers insisted, such a voluntaristic and consensual "union" was inadequate to the exigencies of the postwar period. Furthermore, the tendency to think of union in these terms worked against the institution of a more energetic government, capable of enforcing its will across the continent. Instead of sustaining virtuous republican governments, reformers argued that the Articles had encouraged the states to pursue their selfish interests. Opposition to national commercial policy and to the creation and development of a national domain had been justified by invoking the spirit and letter of the Confederation. Constitutional reformers therefore had to seize the high ground from their obstructionist opponents and show that a strong central government was compatible with the genius of American politics. They had to convince voters that the American union would not be destroyed but would instead be made more "perfect" under the proposed Constitution.

But if the defects of the Confederation were easily demonstrated, it was much more difficult for reformers to redefine "union" in a way that would rationalize a radical redistribution of power from the states to the central government. Reformers had to overcome formidable obstacles before they could design and then defend the extended, federal republic. The most obvious were popular loyalty to the states and the pervasive fear that constitutional innovations would jeopardize republican liberty. But reformers also had to overcome their own predispositions against popular government and state authority before they could embrace a federal solution to the nation's problems.

As the Philadelphia Convention approached, these reformers came to recognize that sectional differences also endangered the union. In chapter 5, we assess the impact of growing intersectional conflict and tension on the constitutional reform movement. Proposals for separate unions began to appear in late 1786: perhaps three or four distinct confederations would form the most durable and "natural" alignments of interest among the American states. Even more alarming were contemporaneous rumors that prominent Americans favored establishing a monarchy embracing the entire continent. The juxtaposition of these extreme solutions with the deterioration of congressional government under the Confederation forced constitutional reformers to reconceptualize the federal union.

Chapter 6 reviews the history of the Philadelphia Convention, with a particular focus on the framers' efforts to construct a broadly acceptable federal regime. As they attempted to balance and reconcile state and national authority, the delegates hoped to counter the appeal of monarchist and disunionist proposals. The proposed system would secure the acknowledged benefits of monarchy by establishing an "energetic" central government; it would also protect the distinct sectional interests that disunionist proposals had brought to the fore. The initial challenge to the delegates was to persuade one another that a national republic could harmonize and promote diverse interests effectively and energetically. They also had to accommodate the claims of the respective states, and here again, political and organizational imperatives played a crucial role. However committed they might have been to curtailing state powers, the delegates came to Philadelphia as representatives of the respective states. Yet the impact of state particularism, like the monarchist and sectionalist impulses also present in the Convention, was offset by the delegates' commitment to national constitutional reform. American federalism was indeed the product of the multiple roles the delegates forced one another to play—as advocates of both state and sectional rights and interests—in their collective quest for an energetic, republican national government.

As they scanned the political horizon in the period before the Philadelphia Convention, constitutional reformers focused on the collapse of popular virtue and the corruption of republican government in the states. But for many of them these original concerns were soon supplanted. Once delegates began to consider federal-state relations in terms of specific local and regional interests, the creation of a powerful, consolidated national regime no longer seemed the panacea for all of America's political ills. Nationalists thus discovered the virtues of federalism; they came to see that not only was creating a workable balance between central and state authority politically expedient, it would also provide the best security for their own rights and interests.

The federal system designed at the Philadelphia Convention thus acknowledged and perpetuated a plurality of distinctive jurisdictional and political economic interests in the extended American republic. At the same time, consciousness of these distinctions raised larger questions about the union: what was the point of such elaborate precautions and guarantees if Americans had no common interests? Antifederalists exploited such concerns, as we show in our discussion of the ratification debates in chapter 7. Federalists replied that the proposed Constitution would serve a wide array of distinctive interests, even as those interests were subsumed in a broadly inclusive and harmonious union. Thus, while emphasizing interstate conflict, domestic disorders, and American weakness in foreign affairs, Federalists also articulated a more positive conception of a national interest.

Drawing on the visionary projections of spokesmen for territorial expansion and economic development, reformers promised that different interests would become reconciled in a dynamic and expanding national economy. Such optimism about America's prospects provided the conceptual background for the articulation and defense of specific interests at the Philadelphia Convention and for the Federalists' subsequent claims that their Constitution would promote national prosperity and power without jeopardizing individual liberties or states' rights.[6]

By appropriating the language of expansion and development, the Federalists were simultaneously able to appeal to cosmopolitan nationalists who had long thought in continental terms and to the great mass of "middling" Americans. Federalists promised that their system would protect and promote the proliferating interests of enterprising citizens, thus countering Antifederalist charges that reformers meant to erect an elitist, aristocratic regime on the ruins of republican liberty in the states. Instead, Federalists argued, their union would extend the scope of economic opportunity opened up by independence and fostered by the state governments.

Antifederalists were not hostile to economic development. Many opponents of the Constitution welcomed the salutary effects of banking, promotional, and protective legislation, convinced that economic energies could best be mobilized in myriad local and regional settings. But the Antifederalists' solicitude for local interests and state sovereignty—and their anxieties about the potential abuse of centralized power—constituted a major liability during the ratification debates. The temptation to associate the defense of individual liberties and responsive local governments with traditional republican precepts proved irresistible to many Antifederalists. However, Antifederalist appeals to revolutionary republicanism and state patriotism gave their opponents the rhetorical advantage. Federalists could plausibly—if often inaccurately—assert that Antifederalists were hostile to a free and developing economy. The anticommercial bias of classical republicanism and its celebration of small, homogeneous polities were, Federalists said, incompatible with America's expanding and prosperous republican empire. The separate states had proven inadequate to the needs of many of their citizens, who now required the protection and support of a more energetic, extended republic. Enterprise would flourish among a truly republican people, Federalists claimed, and the development of mutually supporting interests would preserve and strengthen the union.

In chapter 8 we show how ratification of the Constitution gave rise to an initial burst of enthusiasm about the prospects of the American political economy.[7] In the new federal republic, optimists declared, old forms of property would be secure while boundless new opportunities would open before an enterprising people. In a bold reformulation of traditional thinking about virtue and luxury consumption, a few visionary theorists even suggested that the new nation's rising wealth was compatible with its devotion to republican principles. This was possible, they suggested, because in an extended republic, or "empire of liberty," the collective energies of a free people would transform the bounties of nature through productive labor. Luxury therefore need no longer be associated with excessive importation and conspicuous consumption but could be seen as just reward for the enterprise of myriad small producers. The rise of American luxury was also identified with subduing the vast hinterland. According to the prevailing wisdom, manufactures would develop in semirural areas, close to commercial agriculture, and in urban centers where craftsmen would be protected from ruinous European competition.

Federalists exulted in the promise of economic development. As the new nation gained strength from the simultaneous growth of agriculture, manufactures, and trade, the United States would take their rightful place in the family of nations. Yet, as the first Washington administration began to formulate policy, it soon became clear that the Federalists' "union of interests" was at least problematic, if not altogether imaginary. As our epilogue suggests, partisan conflicts in the 1790s called into question Federalist promises about the future of American political economy. Treasury Secretary Alexander Hamilton's financial program proved controversial, even among Federalists. Hamilton's attempts to conflate the interests of the government with those of aggressive investors—especially in large-scale manufacturing enterprises—offended many segments of the citizenry and gave a major impetus to the Democratic-Republican opposition.

Federalist promises remained unfulfilled. But the idea of a natural union of interests—among republican states and among enterprising citizens—would continue to exercise a powerful influence in American political and economic thought.

1
Interest and Ideology in Revolutionary America

As they approached independence, Americans had no clear conception of the role government should play in regulating their economic life. Revolutionary leaders who called on fellow citizens to sacrifice private interests and devote themselves to the common cause invoked traditional "republican," or corporatist, notions of political economy that had inspired generations of Anglo-American oppositionists. Entrenched colonial elites, anxious to defend their status and power against radical innovations in imperial governance, naturally found republican ideas attractive. Republicanism also exercised a powerful appeal among the large numbers of Americans in the cities and the countryside who resisted the disruption of traditional economic and political relations.[1]

The deeply conservative thrust of the resistance movement is apparent in popular political discourse. Yet colonists' claims to historic English rights and their calls for the restoration of the old imperial order disguise significant "liberal," or progressive, tendencies in American political economic thought. After all, colonial merchants who sought to dismantle, or at least neutralize, the regulatory apparatus of British mercantilism had helped bring on the imperial crisis. For many Americans—including groups not directly affected by enforcement of the navigation acts—the belief that the Revolution would eliminate all arbitrary political restraints on individual economic freedom constituted its decisive appeal.

In historiographical retrospect, the contradictory tendencies in American revolutionary thought and practice appear striking. At one extreme, proto-liberal free traders sought to release private interest from all public restraint; at the other, traditionalist, "classical" republicans would suppress any privatistic, self-aggrandizing

11

impulses that jeopardized the public good. In theory, the only common ground between advocates of the two positions was their shared antipathy to the kind of governmental structures associated with British imperial rule. In practice, however, revolutionary Americans were eminently capable of sustaining ostensibly contradictory premises and of shifting from one position to another as circumstances dictated.[2] And theoretical predispositions notwithstanding, the new state governments were soon forced to adopt policies that interfered more extensively in the American economy than the hated British mercantilist system itself. Revolutionaries may have sought to promote individual economic and political freedom, but the exigencies of the war necessarily led to the dramatic expansion of public authority over the lives of private citizens.

In this chapter we will trace the development of the various strands of political economic thought available to Americans as they set about creating their new republican order. We will show how indistinct these lines of thought often proved to be, as Englishmen and Americans confronted and sought to master the transformation of the Atlantic economy. Indeed, this conceptual confusion reached a climax in revolutionary America.

REPUBLICANISM

The view of political economy articulated by classical republican theorists at the time of the American Revolution was founded upon the premise that political right and personal virtue flowed from the ownership of hereditary and transmissible land. In a virtuous republic, the majority of proprietors enjoyed a "happy mediocrity" through the ownership of modest freeholds. These landholdings guaranteed personal independence and autonomy, thus providing the material conditions for an orderly society governed by reason and self-restraint. Unencumbered title was a primary basis of social order as well as of individual rights; to lose title was to lose one's personal identity and political liberty.[3]

Given these assumptions, republican theorists found the related implications of "interest" deeply disturbing. Interest was potentially dangerous to the health of a republic, whether it was the pecuniary interest taken in loaning money or the private interest of individuals or groups. In the first sense, interest represented claims, rights, and bonds of obligation that could compromise personal independence and traditional authority. To meet this threat, republicans often favored rigorous restraints on usury and high-interest loans, as well as on more modern forms of stockjobbing. In the second sense, interest suggested loyalties and commitments distinct from, and at least potentially opposed to, those of the larger community. This kind of interest could create an anticommunity of credit and debt or fragment existing communal bonds. In either case, excessive self-interest—the blatant disregard of social obligations—jeopardized social order.[4]

Republican ideology acquired new vitality in response to the efflorescence of interest and interest groups in the late seventeenth and eighteenth centuries. In the broadest sense, republicanism was a critique of the financial and administrative changes following the Glorious Revolution and an idealization of a traditional, static agricultural economy in which freeholders did not depend on credit at interest or risk their property in speculative enterprises. Merchants and manufacturers could not survive without borrowing: banks, annuities, war loans, flexible interest rates, and international networks of credit were the lifeblood of commerce. But traditionalists warned that as the British Empire grew—and its "limbs rotted of interest"—there would be a corresponding weakening of the body politic.[5]

Debates over foreign policy exacerbated differences in the views of landed and commercial classes. Republicans identified the new commercial interests with Court Whigs who had supposedly fomented and financed the interimperial rivalries that had kept Britain involved in four long and costly wars during the eighteenth century. By Queen Anne's War (1702–13), critics of the new order had become increasingly shrill. Although country gentlemen dominated Parliament, their influence over national policy diminished as they confronted new financial institutions, commercial interests, and political factions that extended to the farthest reaches of the empire. With the return to peace in 1713, the government negotiated a controversial trade agreement with the long-standing imperial rival, France—according to the opposition, a land of lace, brandy, and the wooden shoes of peasant poverty. Thereafter the Walpolean faction rose to consolidate the emerging economic order. It was in this context that "interest" took on the invidious meanings that survived in oppositionist rhetoric until and beyond the American Revolution.

The landed classes were not uniformly hostile to the rise of commercial interests. Proponents of traditional political right and obligation rarely opposed commerce and manufacturing as such. Instead, they were troubled by the association between commerce and warfare—and higher land taxes—and by political factionalism and the corruption of the House of Commons through patronage. Similarly, although many oppositionists benefited from the expansion of credit, they warned against the dangers of a large, permanent public debt and of the risks of speculative ventures long-term loans made possible.

From the republican perspective, the new potential for economic and political excess jeopardized public virtue. The web of market relations grew so complicated that unfamiliar buyers and sellers were encouraged to take every possible advantage of each other. Merchants gambled on the unpredictable values of goods; they were continually tempted to commit "fraud upon strangers."[6] Relations based upon credit were irrational and fitful, and the merchant who followed an interest defined in such insubstantial terms could hardly be master of his own economic behavior. Rational as his daily choices might be, the dangers to which he exposed his character by relying on the vagaries of credit and the ploys and subterfuges of competitors seemed to preclude the emergence of a permanent, substantial commercial interest that could support and advance the general welfare.

Many Americans agreed that the claims of reason, justice, and patriotism could be endangered by the pursuit of exotic goods in distant markets. As a New Yorker put it, virtuous citizens should seek "the firm Bank that constantly secures us [from] the impetuous Raging of that turbulent Sea of Passions which incessantly dash against the Frame of human Nature."[7] Certainly, another writer added, "there is such a bewitching Charm in Self-Interest, that the Mind, intoxicated by this delusive Syren, is generally impervious to Truth and Reason. . . . A Man's personal Advantage gives so strange a Biass to his Reason, that he perceives not his own Injustice."[8] Like their English counterparts, American critics of commerce attributed the dangers of excessive self-interest to a "thirst after luxury" imports. Following their own selfish impulses, American traders would divert staples to foreign nations in return for costly "superfluities," "artificialities," and "unnaturall" goods. Not only would such trade do little to satisfy the colonists' legitimate needs, insisted critics, it would also deprive British producers of valuable markets.[9] Said William Livingston, "That Luxury is the Harbinger of a dying State, is a Truth too obvious to require the Formality of Proof."[10] Unless colonists curbed their "habitual Tea-drinking," one form of luxury consumption which "so universally prevail[ed],"[11] there was a real danger that "we [might] Eat our selves."[12] The extensive distribution of imported commodities amounted to a "prodigious increase of American luxury"—such "an inseparable attendant on an increase of riches" that a merchant "must suit [his] cargo to the taste of customers; and not to old-fashioned notions of parsimony of former days."[13] In short, "Private Interest"—the gratification of an individual's appetites—was no more than a "dirty Shell" unless restrained by society.[14]

Republican warnings about the corrupting influence of commerce and the dangers of self-interest did not simply express the concerns of classes excluded from new sources of wealth and power. In fact, many spokesmen for the republican position, in Britain and in America, were well situated to reap the benefits of the new economic order. Their concern was with speculative bubbles, luxury consumption, political factionalism, and corruption. But by invoking an idealized traditional political economy, oppositionists helped throw the new regime of commercial interests into bold relief. Their contribution was to clarify the equivocal character of these new interests and to force mercantilists to formulate new definitions of the national interest.[15]

MERCANTILISM:
THE NEW STRUCTURE OF INTEREST

Mercantilist exponents of imperial expansion discarded many of the key assumptions of traditional political theory that continued to inform republican critiques of the new commercial order. For them, society was not characterized by organic fixity; political space was not delimited by the estates of the landed classes. The boundaries of empire could be extended by the exercise of military power and successful commercial competition. Private trading ventures were particularly important because they provided new commercial connections that helped overcome scarcity, poverty, and unemployment.[16]

In 1691 Dudley North set forth a basic mercantilist premise: "The whole World as to Trade, is but one Nation or People, and therein Nations are as Persons."[17] Commerce brought interested parties together on a world scale, making it possible to satisfy an ever greater range of needs. Obviously, wrote Carew Reynel, "riches are the convenience of the nation," and "people . . . [its] strength, pleasure and glory"; but, he added, "trade preserves both."[18] Other writers pointed up the implications of this logic: "Trade and commerce are the pillars of prosperity and safety to England," according to one;[19] "its neglect," another concluded, "will be England's ruin and confusion."[20] But none matched Daniel Defoe's passion for trade, "the life of the nation, the soul of its felicity, the spring of its wealth, the support of its greatness. . . . ([I]f it should sink) the whole fabric must fall, the body politic would sicken and languish, its power decline, and the figure it makes in the world grow by degrees contemptibly mean."[21] For these writers, "liberty" was defined not by an enduring relationship with the land but as the freedom to take risks and accumulate mobile wealth. The idea of interest was more and more frequently invoked by mercantilists to describe enlightened private behavior that produced beneficial results for the entire community.

American traders eagerly embraced the mercantilist justifications for the pursuit of self-interest. One merchant conceded that "every Man ought to promote the Prosperity of his Country, from a sublimer Motive than his private Advantage," but concluded that it was "extremely difficult, for the best of Men, to divest themselves of Self-Interest."[22] Another explained that sometimes interest "Connects People, who are intire Strangers" or "separates those who had the strongest natural Connections."[23] But most Americans recognized that, in some form, "interest . . . governs all the world."[24]

According to the mercantilist account, the aggregate of personal fortunes and public treasure constituted the wealth of a nation. And no interest was so crucial to promoting national wealth and welfare as the "merchant interest." Merchants served the nation by venturing into a world that was usually at war and always infested by pirates, deceitful debtors, and ruthless competitors. As a result, the traditional conception of commercial enterprise as a means of "fraud upon strangers" began to give way to approval of the exchange of "refinements" which enriched and civilized the national community.

The merchant interest was the leading sector in advancing national wealth and power. As Richard Campbell explained, the "honest gain" of the merchant "returns more than he carried out, adds so much to the National Riches and Capital Stock of the Kingdom." "Wealth and Plenty follow him . . . and Public Credit increases."[25] Even Commonwealth writers such as Joseph Addison, with their well-known reservations about the impact of commerce on society, recognized the important role played by merchants: "There are not more useful Members in a Commonwealth than Merchants. They knit Mankind together in a mutual Intercourse of good Offices, [and] distribute the Gifts of Nature."[26] Moreover, the general prosperity that flowed from the rapid circulation of commercial wealth was the real basis for the "independence" and "virtue" to which landowners had previously made sole claim. "The lasting prosperity of the landed interest," said staunch mercantilist Malachy Postlethwayt, "depends upon foreign commerce" and the "well-grounded knowledge of political arithemetick" that secured a favorable balance of trade.[27]

Given the great contributions commercial interests made to the national welfare, mercantilists argued that it was crucial to direct regulatory policies not to the restraint of domestic commerce but to balancing international trade in Britain's favor. They concluded that exploiting the "exhorbitant Appetites" of foreign consumers for British goods represented the best means of promoting Britain's interest. Because there were global limits to the wealth for which trading nations competed, national treasure—and private fortunes—depended on a favorable ratio of exports over imports. Thus, as late as 1750, Joseph Harris believed that there was "but a certain proportion of trade" and "a limit to the vent and consumption of all sorts of commodities."[28] It followed, wrote Matthew Decker, that "if the Exports of Britain exceeded its Imports, Foreigners must pay the balance in Treasure and the Nations grow Rich." Such an advantageous balance would obtain only if foreigners developed a taste for British exports.[29] By the same logic, Britons should refrain—or be restrained—from excessive consumption of imports.

The mercantilists' conception of commercial liberty privileged new forms and uses of property while reorienting state policy toward exploiting new and unpredictable opportunities abroad. In promoting "balance," mercantilist writers emphasized the need for state support of commercial interests. Securing interest through a system of "artificial legislashun" was not new to the early modern world, but it gained momentum—and more elaborate theoretical justification—during the eighteenth century. When commercial policies failed to maintain a favorable balance of trade or to permit merchants to advance their private interests, it was easy to blame political factionalism rather than economic causes beyond state control. The regime of interest flourished as private enterprises and state power converged.[30]

By the early eighteenth century, Britain's growing prosperity and power enabled economists to turn their attention to domestic material consumption and to consider the advantages of exchanges within the empire.[31] In its basic sense, consumption referred to the satisfaction of material needs and desires. The passion to consume could stimulate socially useful activity, commentators asserted, as long as it did not distort or displace individual reason and responsibility. Even in the seventeenth century, economists suggested that "the exhorbitant Appetites of Men" were "the main spur to Trade . . . Industry and Ingenuity" "when nothing else will incline them."[32] As Nicholas Barbon explained, "It is not Necessity that causeth the Consumption. Nature may be Satisfied with little; but it is the wants of the Mind, Fashion and the desire of Novelties and Things Scarce that causeth Trade."[33] These accounts reflected changing attitudes toward luxury consumption. "Trade," wrote Charles Davenant in 1692, "brings in that wealth which introduces luxury," a presumably pernicious result. But, considering "the posture and condition of other countries . . . it is become with us a necessary evil."[34] Yet, if for mercantilists the necessity of luxury consumption was becoming clearer, its "evil" was rapidly attenuating.

The successes of self-interested merchants in the international economy and the resulting array of goods available to consumers showed that commerce could give shape and purpose to the "perpetual restless ambition" of the great mass of the people "to raise themselves." Because of commerce, consumers gained access to "more of life's necessitous goods," not to mention the less "necessitous arts and manufactures" that satisfied "fashion" and "mere opinion."[35] Indeed, many items once considered luxuries were now thought to be a "salve upon our great appetites." Properly regulated, luxury imports could elevate and civilize English consumers while satisfying their baser impulses; foreign trade could introduce "refinements," "arts," and "politeness."[36]

The growth of consumer demand and new definitions of individual "needs" were the keys to a prosperous modern economy. Joseph Addison endorsed the expanding scope of consumption: "Nature indeed furnishes us with the bare Necessities of Life, but Traffick gives us a great Variety of what is Useful . . . Convenient and Ornamental." Commerce, although not essential for sustaining life itself, was requisite for civilized comfort.[37] John Trenchard and Thomas Gordon, who, like Addison, scorned stockjobbers and the "monied interest," shared his opinion that commerce brought "civilized virtues" and "politeness."[38]

Mercantilist writers agreed that the growing wealth and power of the empire were fueled by the rapid circulation and consumption of goods. Regulations and prohibitions could guarantee an orderly system of trade while curbing excesses and imbalances in consumption patterns. Within this regulated framework, the reciprocal interests of merchants and their customers converged with the national interest. Coincidentally, by regulating the flow of imports, the mercantilist system could check the deleterious consequences of luxury consumption on private character.

Anglo-American readers could trace the emerging rationale for interest and consumption through the works of eminent philosophers as well as those of polemical writers. Acknowledging the dangers of unbounded acquisitiveness for political and social order, John Locke in his "Second Treatise" argued that the most pernicious effects of competitive self-interest could be controlled by a voluntary compact among free individuals to form a commonwealth. Political authority would coordinate and secure the multiplicity of interests while self-regarding individuals would restrain themselves in order to protect their property. Thus, Locke liberated "ceaseless, perpetual motion" only to seek its proper limits. It was his confidence in the ability of interested individuals to control and coordinate their appetites and interests that set him apart from less optimistic critics of the new order.[39]

David Hume's 1752 essays represent a further, important step in the legitimation of interest. He justified the "love of gain" and consumption of the world's bounty, while downplaying resulting political factionalism and cyclical economic crises. Although mild forms of mercantile regulation might be necessary to protect and encourage "infant interests," they should not be allowed to restrain individual initiative. Hume's attempt to establish lawful patterns in economic phenomena brought him to the verge of a conception of a self-correcting economy. He thought that if there were a "general agreement" about the "benefits of luxury," the community should be prepared for alternating periods of high prices and interest rates, scarcities and gluts. It was in the long-term general interest to ride out these temporary disturbances.[40] More than most of his contemporaries, Hume emphasized the connection of interest to personal agency rather than institutional restraint. A ruler's responsibility "aims only at possibilities" rather than constant intervention. Hume's economic analysis led him to one of the most far-reaching and authoritative endorsements of expanding consumption prior to the American Revolution.

Yet Hume's endorsement of interest and consumption paled next to the polemical productions of merchants and publicists who chafed at what they considered excessive regulation. "Freedom" in trade was never far below the surface of their rhetoric. Even in the seventeenth century, groups of merchants throughout the empire appealed for relief from commercial duties or exemption from regulation on the grounds that restriction was harmful to the national welfare as well as to their personal interests. The continuing influence of "free trade" among the Dutch provided one influential model for commercial success. Particularly after 1713, when the focus of British mercantile rivalry shifted from the Dutch to the French and Spanish, commercial propagandists repeatedly extolled the benefits of the "hollander free trade."[41] Many American traders found these arguments attractive.

FREE TRADE

The leading premise of mercantilist colonial policy was that national greatness depended on encouraging vigorous trade—and consumption—throughout the empire. Spokesmen for colonial commercial interests recognized the advantages of this trade for their clients, endorsing the mercantilist axiom that "we are all linked in a Chain of Dependence on each other, & when properly regulated, by the most prudential Laws, form a beautiful Whole, having within ourselves the rich Sources of an active Commerce & diffusive Happiness throughout."[42]

American merchants had a vested interest in imperial prosperity and power. But the success of the mercantile system could not completely disguise the subordinate, dependent status of the colonies. When mercantilist writers considered the colonial relation, it became clear that there would be no "balance" of power and plenty within the empire. "The very nature of colonies," Postlethwayt explained, was "that they ought to have no culture or arts, wherein to rival the arts and culture of their parent country." Nor could colonies "in justice consume foreign commodities, with an equivalent for which their mother country consents to supply them," or "sell to foreigners, such of their commodities as their mother country consents to receive."[43] Throughout the colonial period, mercantilists asserted their right to enjoy a "monopoly" of colonial consumption.[44]

Though the full implications of these claims were felt only late in the colonial period, local conditions from the outset of settlement led many Americans to question mercantilist premises. A number of particular cases strongly suggested that "to sett Trade Free" was the "wisest course." "Liberalitye with respect to duties and the items of our traffick" would present new opportunities to trade in southern Europe and the foreign West Indies.[45] Finding the goods and markets which brought the best prices was not always compatible with trade regulations dictated by distant authorities; bounties to promote production of new staples might be useful, but prohibitions on other exports could pose considerable hardships. It was "the Interest of the City and Country to Lay no Duties," as one New York pamphleteer put it.[46] Regulations, another said, were a mere "Solecism in Trade, and the Bane of Industry." Since "Self-Interest is the grand Principle of all Human Actions," the best encouragement was "Liberty" in commerce.[47]

Demands for relief from regulations that sought to establish specific patterns of production and exchange in the empire could be linked to proposals for colonial manufactures. Colonial critics of mercantile regulations under the navigation system complained that limits on exports denied American commercial farmers reliable markets and were thus detrimental to imperial as well as colonial prosperity. By the 1730s, advocates of manufactures in the northern port cities began to argue that increased local production of hemp, potash, iron goods, hats, and other items would be the best remedy for the colonies' commercial woes. Royal governors and their allies dismissed such thinking as visionary and impractical: "the main bent" of colonial farmers was "to produce grain," they insisted, and this was their "natural" and proper role in the imperial economy.[48] For the time being, of course, mercantilists had little to fear. Capital shortages and high labor costs precluded any significant reorientation of the colonial economies, however much enterprising merchants and entrepreneurs chafed at imperial commercial regulations. But the idea that the development of home manufactures would enable Americans to achieve a more favorable position in the Atlantic economy remained compelling.

By the 1750s, free trade advocates moved beyond such prudential—and narrowly self-interested—concerns to argue for the expansive potential of unregulated trade. The Seven Years' War provided diverse chances to enter commerce or enhance existing connections. Colonial economies were now relatively mature and diversified: paper money experiments had proved useful in circulating domestic commodities and easing debts; urban centers drew a wide range of necessities from their expanding hinterlands; and accumulated capital and skills even permitted the founding of a few, pioneering manufacturing enterprises. Yet in the depression of the mid-1760s, Americans portrayed themselves as victims of misguided policies. "Why is the trade of the colonies more circumscribed than the trade of Britain?" a Boston writer asked; "Can any one tell me why trade, commerce, arts, sciences, & manufactures, should not be as free for an American as for a European?"[49] From this perspective, "freedom" was coming not only to mean the absence of political interference but also to suggest the positive value of seeking "a free and open trade with all the powers of Europe."[50]

Free trade arguments became increasingly popular in the late colonial period. Even more than mercantilists who, by definition, were committed to regulation and restraint, free traders celebrated the beneficent effects of interest and consumption. Acquiring and consuming more of the world's commodities made many Americans impatient with all restraints on commerce. Paternal political authority—now manifested in the "fickel opinions" of mercantilist policymakers—stifled the rage for new items of consumption. The free traders offered a powerful critique of imperial politics as well as an appealing alternative to commercial restraint: merchants, more than politicians, were true public servants, because they alone could satisfy the diverse needs and desires of the consuming public. "Former rarities" and the "infinite number of other curiosities" they had brought to America were the free traders' proud contribution to the welfare of their countrymen.[51]

According to free trade logic, elimination of artificial political obstructions between the original production and ultimate acquisition and consumption of the world's wealth would create a truly "natural economy." Some free traders even anticipated Adam Smith's argument for the inevitable social redistribution of wealth. A New Yorker thus dismissed the threat of a dynamic economy to social order: "The private interests and passions of men naturally lead them to divide and distribute the stock of society, among all the different employments . . . as nearly as possible in the proportion which is most agreeable to the interest of the whole society."[52] In effect, the common interest would be promoted by the uninhibited play of private interests in the marketplace.

While such arguments gained considerable public sympathy for the free trade position, they were obviously intended to justify blatantly self-interested behavior. Unlike mercantilist "fair traders" who accepted the constraints of political authority, smugglers—the most colorful and conspicuous exponents of free trade in practice—did not scruple to defy imperial law in order to provide commodities to avid colonial consumers. To advance their illicit interests, smugglers "made the mode" for such goods as lemons, spices, fine apparel, and snuff into "necessity," thereby earning broad popular support for their "insubordination."[53]

Even before there was a higher cause around which to rally—the constitutional liberty and national interest of the American people—independent traders taught Americans how to defend their new habits of consumption. The right to consume suggested, in turn, an emerging idea of the common interest fundamentally at odds with mercantilist imperialism. The aggregate of individual interests was not merely the "public welfare" but "America's interest"; the foreigner was not only French and Spanish but British as well. Such was the meaning of the outcry of adversely affected colonial merchants who complained that the Tea Act of May 1773 gave an undue "monopoly interest" to the British East India Company; American smugglers and foreign traders feared that "we should soon have found our trade in the hands of foreigners"—that is, British merchants.[54] Moreover, unrestrained pursuit of forbidden commodities in foreign markets was elevated to a private right: "Every man has a natural right to exchange his property with whom he pleases and where he can make the most advantage of it." Therefore, recent British policy jeopardized private rights at the same time that it demonstrated the common disadvantages faced by American interests in the imperial economy.[55]

Free traders could claim to serve the public by providing access to the world's circulating goods at low prices and without artificial limitations. They helped push Americans one more step away from traditional conceptions of political economy. But the free traders' facile identification of private and public interest was hard to defend during wartime, when interimperial rivalries fractured world markets and when sacrifices (of private interests) were obviously necessary. By definition, free traders were hostile to legislative restraint; they sought access to market opportunities regardless of state policy. Thus they responded to the exigencies of war and attempts to enforce mercantile regulation with undeviating determination to serve their own interests, even if this meant trading with the enemy or ignoring customary price levels. To their critics—including many of their erstwhile customers—free traders were excessively passionate in the pursuit of self-interest and represented the very antithesis of the virtuous, self-denying patriotism that the war demanded.

Close observers in Britain had not failed to register alarm that the opportunities of the Seven Years' War and postwar period had "given rise to A NEW SYSTEM OF INTERESTS" which "opened a new channel of business; and brought into operation a new Concatenation of powers" antithetical to an orderly mercantile economy.[56] Officials in America generally agreed that merchants, especially in the "Illicit Trade," "abhor every limitation of Trade and Duty on it, and therefore gladly go into every measure whereby thay hope to have Trade free."[57] By 1770 large numbers of American merchants withdrew from their own nonimportation agreements with the claim that they were "starving on the slender Meals of Patriotism."[58]

Writers and policymakers on both sides of the Atlantic called attention to the self-serving character of free trade arguments. Yet these ideas reflected important changes in imperial relations after 1750 and enabled Americans to clarify their relationship to imperial authority. When Parliament responded to the "new system of interests" in America with a spate of reform measures, there was still further reason to question mercantilist precepts. Some American merchants began to associate mercantilism more with oppression than with opportunity.[59] In the words of one noted merchant leader, mercantilism was no more than a "glaring monument" to "the all-grasping nature of unlimited power," not the model of power and plenty in a system of orchestrated interests. The opposite of virtue and liberty, the empire was designed to serve the narrow "interest of a selfish European island."[60]

The far-reaching effects of economic liberty on the colonists' material welfare and political loyalties also spurred considerable discussion in Britain. William Pitt, Lord Shelburne, and Edmund Burke doubted the wisdom of restraining the colonists who "naturally seek the vent of goods which satisfied private interest."[61] Perhaps, as the London *Public Advertiser* noted, Britain wrongfully asked for "a pitiful Pittance in the Form of a Tax," when it could "with a Good-Will, obtain Millions by fair Commerce."[62] By the eve of the Revolution, London merchants who formerly allied their interests with American traders were far less inclined to exert pressure on Parliament to remove distasteful legislation. The Londoners felt "America's free trade parties" would not be satisfied with reform and would "never rest till they have obtained a free trade with all the world."[63]

Although the nonimportation movements of 1765, 1768, and 1770 required colonists to forego levels of consumption to which they had been accustomed, this was the sort of "sacrifice" that many merchants, eager for relief from overpurchasing and swollen inventories, welcomed. But the Continental Association of 1774 set forth a plan for nonexportation and nonconsumption, thus banning "every species of extravagance and dissipation."[64] Indeed, patriot leaders may have demanded, as John Murrin suggests, "an extraordinary excess of virtue."[65] Price controls and local enforcement committees were part of the new machinery of public virtue, as were a new series of prohibitions on trade to the lucrative West Indies markets. Merchants, concerned about their own dwindling opportunities, warned that these new regulations could become so excessive that they would impoverish the new nation and undercut the Revolution.

They implored patriot leaders to reconcile their calls for virtuous self-sacrifice with the imperatives of financing and managing the war effort. In 1775 John Jay proposed to modify the Association agreement so that well-placed smugglers could acquire ammunition and salt for the army from West Indian and Dutch markets; later that year he noted that "we have more to expect from the enterprise, activity, and industry of private adventurers, than from the lukewarmness of assemblies."[66] Many Americans were forced to agree, however reluctantly, that "trade flourishes best, when it is free."[67] Within months of setting up the commissary and paymaster departments, Congress was inundated with proposals from former merchants whose businesses (they claimed) were now all but defunct because of the Association and whose "thirst after interest" steered them toward the prospects of business in the interior. "Projectors" came forward with plans to start ironworks, construct barracks, hire wagons, requisition supplies, raise sheep for wool and salted meat rations, and distill substitutes for rum. When Congress turned reluctantly to the private contract system in 1779, almost all the recipients were former successful wholesale merchants from northern cities.[68]

LIBERTY AND VIRTUE

The prospects for realizing a substantial degree of economic liberty under the banner of free trade were tempered by republican calls for sacrifice of private interest to the public good. Yet the balance between liberty and virtue was precarious. By the 1760s some Americans were inspired by the general hum of discussion about economic freedom to envision the possibility of individuals pursuing their diverse interests in a self-governing polity. In this way radical economic liberals helped shape the goals of the American resistance movement. But their ideas were never adopted in unqualified form. In their efforts to force the British Parliament to repeal obnoxious trade legislation, the nonimportation movements not only called for republican self-restraint and moral regeneration but also promised increased domestic production and access to new foreign markets. For economic liberals enraptured by these prospects, self-restraint was only a temporary necessity. Their greater objective was to alter the imperial political economy in ways that would create new opportunities for risk taking and profits. The sacrifices required by the resistance movement would prepare the way for domestic manufactures and internal improvements. Nonimportation also promised a benign future of free exchange which inspired Americans of middling means to challenge the traditional order as they pursued their own economic and social ambitions.[69]

The early months of the Revolution opened up a wide range of activities for traders and shopkeepers of the interior. The exigencies of mobilization provoked huge private debts in paper obligations and introduced new consumer goods to farmers and frontier families. By 1776 much of the self-restraint promoted during the nonimportation movements gave way to the promise of unfettered private enterprise at all levels of society. Commerce, in the American interior as well as on the world's oceans, was the most obvious way to wealth. In the hinterlands of the new states, merchants and farmers enjoyed new opportunities to trade with the moving armies, extended their networks of debt and paper currency to the breaking point, discovered new profits in engrossing supplies or inflating prices, and expanded their horizons beyond local markets to meet the bulging demand of the militias. As a result, it became increasingly difficult to reconcile the rhetoric of self-restraint and the dream of creating a classically virtuous republic with the reality and promise of unfettered private enterprise.[70]

Yet if the economic imperatives of war saved Americans from an excess of virtuous self-denial, they also clarified the limits of free trade. Although free trade had given Americans a ''taste for refinements'' and images of a bountiful future, a Smithian congeries of interested individuals competing in the marketplace could not adequately articulate or implement revolutionary goals. Certainly the problems of raising and provisioning an army, currency inflation, and flagging spirits in both civilian and military sectors after the first year of formal warfare all called into question whether Americans had enough virtue to eradicate—or at least control—corruption, venality, and luxury. Too much "freedom" seemed to threaten the success of the Revolution.[71]

A wide range of critics—including conservative Whigs as well as radical republicans—thus challenged enterprising Americans to sharpen their justifications of interest and consumption. The demands of the war deflected merchants from their traditional role of promoting transatlantic trade and prosperity. Though merchants still had a vital role to play in securing political liberty, they would have to subordinate their activities to the common cause. Southern congressmen such as John Rutledge, Richard Henry Lee, and Samuel Chase well understood that military victory and political independence were necessary preconditions for the development of the American economy: they could not be achieved without a widespread willingness to sacrifice immediate and particular interests. Revolutionary leaders persuasively argued in the years from 1775 to 1777 that unbridled self-interest would subvert military mobilization and civilian morale.

Yet patriotic appeals for public sacrifice enjoyed mixed success at best. The wartime stimulus to key sectors of the economy illuminated the growing gap between the rhetoric of self-restraint and the reality of economic opportunity.[72] Neo-mercantilist price controls and trade regulations conspicuously failed to restrain enterprising Americans from exploiting unprecedented chances to produce and supply needed goods. The dilemma was clear to all who would confront it: enforce a regime of virtue to sustain the war effort, at the risk of destroying the material foundations of the nascent republic; or permit commercial interests the freedom they had sought from mercantilist regulation, while jeopardizing a public spirit of self-sacrifice and disinterestedness. These questions were never far below the surface during the revolutionary era, even when attention focused on political and constitutional issues.

The ideological resolution of this dilemma was to suggest that by being virtuous now Americans could be prosperous in the future. Temporary restraints on consumption were made more palatable when they were linked to the idea of an emergent American interest: nonimportation offered the prospect of American self-sufficiency outside of the British Empire. If patriotism called for denial and sacrifice, it also called forth ringing affirmations of the possibilities of material development. Ambitious plans for American expansion took shape in proposals by "enlightened societies" for the promotion of "useful arts and manufactures" for mining, spinning, and many other "industrious endeavors." New manufactures, together with the westward expansion of settlement and trade, promised unprecedented abundance. In such visions, Americans justified their privations and anticipated just rewards for their virtue.[73]

The combined force of wartime emergency and republican ideology led to an Americanization of political economic thinking. The great task for revolutionary political economists was to realign agricultural, commercial, and manufacturing interests so that they reinforced one another and sustained the new political order. As a result, and notwithstanding the wisdom of the free traders, commerce was subjected to neo-mercantilist restraints: Americans demonstrated a willingness to employ state power to promote integrated and balanced economic development. At the same time, economists stressed the commercial character of agriculture, recognizing the primacy of agricultural production for domestic and international markets in sustaining American prosperity. Their identification and equalization of interests (agriculture was described as a form of manufacturing) prompted a shift in emphasis from consumption to production in thinking about the new nation's economic prospects. Since consumption, at least luxury consumption, had always been problematic for republicans, the focus on production helped reconcile a dynamic economy with republican values. The pursuit of interest when conceived as productive activity could be assimilated with hard work and other traditional virtues. The broader conception of related, productive interests thus tended to reintegrate economy and polity in American thinking.

American revolutionaries groped toward a new conception of political economy. Colonial writers had frequently emphasized the continent's tremendous potential for economic development: "Nature has furnished us with every Thing for our Advantage, and we only want Frugality and Industry to make us Opulent."[74] By 1775 some commentators believed that America's natural endowments were sufficient to "bid defiance to the whole world."[75] America could become "a whole empire," "and it may be extended farther and farther to the utmost ends of the earth, and yet continue firmly compacted."[76] During the revolutionary era even more Americans embraced this optimistic vision of their collective destiny.

At first revolutionaries did not foresee a significant role for government in stimulating enterprise and developing the continent's vast natural endowments. They believed that the success of the war effort itself depended more on the patriotism of myriad citizens than on authoritative political structures. But as the pressures of a protracted war led to political divisions and popular demoralization, the revolutionaries' faith in economic freedom was sorely tested. The state governments began to set restraints on private initiatives in order to protect and promote local interests in a hostile international environment. At first these policies were sufficiently successful to gain wide, if not universal, support. But changing economic and political circumstances after the conclusion of the Revolutionary War alienated growing numbers from the plethora of new regulations. If some Americans called on their state governments to regulate trade and encourage development, others sought to eliminate these "artificial" political barriers to private economic opportunity. During the 1780s, American political economy was shaped by these conflicting expectations.

2
State Governments and the Economy, 1776–1785

For many Americans, the Revolution promised to expand the scope of their overseas trade. Great merchants such as Robert Morris rose to the occasion. "There never has been so fair an opportunity for making a large fortune since I have been conversant in the world," Morris wrote in 1776.[1] The future of the entire nation looked bright to those who believed that trade would "regulate itself" in the common interest. "We now have a free trade with all the world," David Ramsay exulted in 1778. As a result, "the wealth of Europe, Asia, and Africa, will flow in upon America: Our trade will no longer be confined by the selfish regulations of an avaricious step-dame, but [will] follow wherever interest leads the way."[2] When the fighting was over, peace negotiator John Jay continued to predict that "the whole world will be open to us, and we shall be at liberty to purchase from those who will sell on the best terms and to sell to those who will give us the best prices."[3]

After the war was won, many Americans anticipated an era of economic autonomy and commercial prosperity. In 1783 John Adams expressed the hope that Britain's "jealousy of American ships, seamen, carrying trade, and naval power" would not result in renewed mercantilist restraints on American commerce. But, continued Adams, if Americans were denied complete reciprocity, especially in the West Indies, then Congress must "attach herself more closely to France." That country's policy of "free ports and no odious discriminations" was more compatible with American liberty.[4] James Madison, Benjamin Rush, Pelatiah Webster, and Thomas Paine also added their optimistic voices to the international free trade chorus.[5]

31

During the early years of the war, agitation for free trade was translated into a program for America's economic future that had broad appeal. The sweeping change in consumer "taste" which preceded and developed alongside the movement for independence played a crucial role in this conceptual development. By invoking the language of political rights and envisioning a new regime that would faithfully promote the people's "true interests," revolutionaries lifted conventional grievances about thwarted economic opportunities under imperial rule to a higher, more universal plane. For the most sanguine revolutionaries, political freedom was the key to a process of economic development that would enrich all Americans. Economic freedom thus became meaningful to a wide array of Americans, including farmers who wanted to sell their commodities in more competitive markets, enterprising speculators who clamored for access to unappropriated frontier lands, and mechanics and artisans who believed that market forces would raise their wages and increase demand for their products.

Enthusiastic proponents of domestic economic freedom promised that the release of private energies in the marketplace would serve the interests of all Americans. They identified this economic freedom with "liberty," or the right of individual citizens to share equally in the opportunities and responsibilities of their new republics. Tangible benefits for specific groups of merchants, small traders, and agriculturalists—and later, manufacturers—were aligned with the "universal self-interest" of individuals and thus with claims to "liberty and freedom of the most extreme sort."[6] Governor Jonathan Trumbull of Connecticut believed that "all restraints on trade are grievances, that a free intercourse and trade among the citizens of the United States tendeth to their mutual advantage."[7] Thus, arguments for international and domestic economic liberty converged as northern merchants scurried to exploit old and new channels of trade. A vocal group of West Indies smugglers and reexporters sought to avoid onerous European commercial regulations, and inland farmers became convinced that they could only make a decent living if they were free to seek the best prices for their surpluses. A farmer in Lancaster declared in 1777 that "the Shops are full of Goods, and every Body busy, so that you would think yourself in a Sea port town whose Trade was open," that is, free.[8] Humbler retailers and shopkeepers also advocated free exchanges as widespread citizen involvement in the war effort stimulated participation in domestic markets and reinforced popular claims to share in the new economic freedom. They eagerly seized opportunities to deregulate prices and wages and to free domestic trade from laws and customs that fixed the quality of goods, the times of sales, and the limits of allowable debt. Philadelphia artisans echoed the new refrain in 1779 when they said that "trade should be as free as air, uninterrupted as the tides. . . . [I]t will ever return of itself, sufficiently near to a proper level . . . if . . . injudicious attempts to regulate it are not interposed."[9]

But many Americans greeted such bold formulations with skepticism. By the end of the war, misgivings about the prospects for economic freedom had become widespread. A weak Congress appeared powerless to expand the scope of international free trade by negotiating favorable agreements with foreign powers. Meanwhile, conservative commentators warned that the uninhibited play of private interests threatened to wreak havoc in the domestic economy. Traditional arguments for limiting individual acquisitiveness in the name of virtue or prudence thus seemed increasingly timely and relevant.[10] Although most republicans believed that the pursuit of self-interest, properly directed, could contribute to the common wealth and welfare, they also recognized the dangers of selfishness and factiousness. Private interest could unleash unruly energies that would subvert order and stability in the states and in the Confederation as a whole; interest groups—or factions—were all too prone to appropriate the inspiring language of economic freedom to mask their narrow, selfish ambitions.

The latent tension between virtue and interest in republican ideology during the Revolution became manifest in the struggles over the distribution of authority, particularly concerning the regulation of commerce, that characterized Confederation politics. Conservative, cosmopolitan republicans who worried about the new nation's "respectability" abroad and its ability to preserve order at home rejected the new meanings of economic liberty and provided the impetus for constitutional reform in the 1780s.

CONGRESSIONAL DIVISIONS

Arguments about economic freedom drew attention to the divergent objectives among leading revolutionaries and in American society generally. They also highlighted divisions among congressional delegates from 1777 to 1779. Many revolutionary leaders favored opening American ports to all the world, reciprocity with the new nation's trading partners, and no controls on prices, wages, or profits. Future nationalists such as Benjamin Rush and Gouverneur Morris argued that effective controls were impossible in modern economies where only the agreement of parties in the marketplace established "the justice of the exchange." Real problems developed when, at the behest of the "debtor interest," governments issued paper currency that could not sustain its nominal value, so subverting rational exchanges.[11] Other congressmen revealed their own distinctive interests when they emphasized the centrality of international commerce and the potential harm of port regulations and price controls by the states.[12]

Richard Henry Lee, John Adams, Elbridge Gerry, Joseph Hawley, Roger Sherman, and George Wythe proclaimed their fealty to free trade principles in a 1776 resolution and again in a Model Treaty that proposed "reciprocal and equal advantages" of "a free trade . . . with all nations." They also depended on merchants' private credit and loans to promote the common cause.[13] During the course of debate, several delegates endorsed petitions for open ports that they thought would facilitate the development of ties on an equal, reciprocal basis.[14] Benjamin Franklin and John Adams warned that without free access to the American trade, European powers might be tempted to interfere in America's domestic politics. Commerce itself would obviate national differences and establish lasting foundations of reciprocity without entanglements.[15]

In keeping with the goals of the Model Treaty, many leading revolutionaries argued that America's free trade regime ultimately should include even Britain itself. Until the states found new outlets for agricultural surpluses, the old channels of exchange would secure the best prices—as long as merchants ignored their political differences and treated each other as commercial equals. Reports of impending peace negotiations inspired new optimism among those who looked forward to the day when ports would be "open to all the world upon equal terms."[16]

Some congressmen advocated greater freedom for American merchants overseas while promoting protectionist policies and restraints on trade at home. Another group of delegates, sensitive to widespread popular agitation for greater economic freedom, recognized the potential for conflict between international free traders and smaller merchants, farmers, and domestic consumers. These delegates doubted that foreign powers would treat the American states with the magnanimity anticipated by free traders. There was also good reason to suspect that some congressional proponents of international free trade were motivated by selfish interests. The profitable activities of Robert Morris, Silas Deane, and their associates raised serious questions about the proper relationship between private commerce and the public good. Excessive reliance on free trade and private enterprise left Congress at the mercy of merchant speculators who charged exorbitant, unregulated prices for commercial services and goods. Finally, the wealthy merchants who benefited from doing business with and for Congress were notoriously hostile to the state paper notes and currency systems that had proven so useful to so many Americans.[17] Henry Laurens charged that many international wholesalers made "patriotism the stalking horse to their private interests." Roger Sherman and John Armstrong agreed.[18]

The greatest danger, these and other congressional critics warned, was that undue emphasis on the prospects of worldwide free trade would distract attention from the exigencies of war and the new nation's vulnerable international situation, both of which made limited commercial regulations essential. Some congressmen also thought that the states should be the guardians of economic freedom properly defined and regulated. The state governments were better equipped to check the excesses of private profit seeking and the tendencies toward dangerous liaisons with foreign nations. The states could also respond more flexibly to the changing requirements of a war stretching across many distinct regions.[19]

As long as calls for virtuous self-sacrifice remained compelling and congressmen continued to defer to the authority of the states, disagreement over economic policy in Congress remained muted. Whether delegates emphasized the centrality of international commerce and foreign relations or insisted on the primacy of diverse, local interests in the domestic economy, they all agreed that the Revolution required a greater sense of public obligation and a willingness to sacrifice private interests. Congressmen feared that pervasive private profit seeking (in their own ranks as well as in society at large) would unleash anarchy and licentiousness—the manifest, material expression of destructive, antisocial "passions." Congress thus appealed to the sovereign states to suppress those insidious elements which, "in repugnance to every principle of public virtue and humanity, [and] instigated by the lust of avarice," were "assiduously endeavouring, by every means of oppression, sharping, and extortion, to accumulate enormous gain to themselves" at the expense of the poor and dependent inhabitants.[20]

Republican moralists argued that when private interests combined to form collectives of interest in parties or factions, selfishness gained a wider and more dangerous scope and influence. During the imperial crisis, these warnings had been directed primarily at the old colonial elites and had helped inspire broad popular participation in the movement for independence and the war which followed. Now, republican language could be aimed either at "interested" factions in the patriot leadership or at the "expectant capitalists"—the humbler farmers and traders, particularly in the interior, who sought to rise in station and reap the benefits of economic freedom promised by the Revolution. Republican commentators feared that the poor example set by some congressmen would encourage the popular "rage to loose the ties which bind us in orderly commerce": the pursuit of selfish interest by rural entrepreneurs, they claimed, was too often justified in the "name of liberty." Even worse, the idealized republican yeoman too often proved to be among the most rapacious and greedy patriots, not the most virtuous.[21]

The difficulties of defining the proper limits of economic freedom became apparent when observers focused on the currency and debt questions raised by wartime mobilization. Although few Americans questioned the necessity of paper currency, republican commentators were quick to underscore potential dangers and abuses of an "artificial" medium of exchange. At first republican strictures generally were addressed to the "little men"—the misguided farmers and small traders—who failed to appreciate the dangers of private debt or paper money inflation.[22] By 1779, however, critics were also railing against the prominent revolutionaries who exploited the "excessive liberalitye of commerce" for their private advantage; these speculative and financial wizards were often likened to the "mushroom gentlemen," the bankers, brokers, and banditti who flourished during England's financial revolution. Private enterprise—at least among these suspect groups—frequently led to "licentiousness," "peculation," "greed," "fraud," and general "deceit against the government and the public good." The Revolution required more self-denial and greater solicitude for the public welfare. But, as one self-styled republican proclaimed, it was doubtful whether Americans had "sufficient virtue to support their liberty." So long as Americans pursued their selfish interests heedless of all moral and political obligation, there seemed to be little hope of achieving the "happy mediocrity" of property in James Harrington's influential prescription for Oceana.[23]

STATE REGULATION

Before 1779, the central government was ill equipped to respond effectively to republican warnings about the dangers of unrestricted economic freedom. Helpless to collect the requisitions and tax funds it needed, Congress made an early decision to recognize de facto localism by turning many of the tasks of supply and revenue collection over to the states. As a result, the most important struggles over the direction of revolutionary political economy took place at the state level. Interest groups vied for influence in the legislatures where, depending on the political and rhetorical situation, they invoked "liberal" arguments for greater economic freedom or "republican" arguments for state regulation of international trade and domestic private enterprise. This clash of interests and ideas spurred a fundamental reconceptualization of American political economy.

Anglo-Americans were no strangers to domestic economic regulation. By 1750 the colonial legislatures had long experience collecting their own revenues, taxing citizens, operating land banks and paper currencies, distributing land and arguing over deeds, contracts, and riparian rights, and regulating the flow of inhabitants and goods within their boundaries. The colonial assemblies jealously defended these privileges against attempts to form an intercolonial union at Albany in 1754 and against Parliament's threats to destroy them throughout the imperial crisis. It seemed only proper that Congress recognize the states' jurisdictional autonomy and confirm their claims to independent regulation. In late 1777, Congress urged the states to experiment with price and wage fixing; although these efforts might lead to "laws unworthy the character of infant republics," they had nevertheless "become necessary to supply the defect of public virtue, and to correct the vices of some of her sons."[24]

Economic legislation passed in many of the northern states from 1777 to 1779 followed similar lines, and its advocates espoused familiar intellectual rationales. Seeking to restrain the "excessive influx of commerce," the state governments began to formulate their own importation, exportation, and commercial taxation laws; fix prices and wages; prevent forestalling; limit profits to 25 percent to 40 percent; embargo exports of necessary foodstuffs; and requisition their citizens for supplies to continue the fighting.[25] The interventionist stance of state governments that could claim broad popular support led to significant limitations on economic liberty. Commercial farmers, merchant exporters, and military suppliers were drawn by the promise, but frustrated by the elusiveness, of freer exchanges. Unlike the more fortunate public creditors and commissary officials, these groups were threatened with bankruptcy when they lost their "usual channels of trade." Farmers complained that embargoes deprived them of markets while commissaries ruthlessly seized their grain to sell to the army at exorbitant prices. State officials also fixed prices of foodstuffs and services at unacceptably low levels. Exporters were equally incensed by wartime embargoes and requisitions and by the inability of state governments to keep foreign ports open to American trade. Neither farmers nor exporters could see any benefits in the depreciating state and continental certificates they were forced to receive from army departments for their services and goods.

Responding to pressure from these groups, some state governments sought to alleviate their wartime fiscal crises through paper currency issues. But citizens refused to pay the taxes that would retire this currency. Open hostility to tax collectors continued well into 1779, forcing some states to give up the loathsome levies. By 1781 a majority of the northern state governments had accommodated the most pressing demands of commercial farmers and other enterprising citizens who sought to exploit the new economic opportunities opened up by the war.[26]

For nonagriculturalists opportunities were uneven. With rumors of impending peace "the floodgates of commerce were opened." But very soon city warehouses were filled to overflowing and the remaining British war specie and other "natural means of remittance" were siphoned off to pay the first debts due to foreign creditors.[27] For many American merchants, the benefits of international commerce began to seem illusory. Despite considerable success in attempts to reestablish old colonial commercial ties, it soon became clear that American exports would fail to offset the vast importation of British manufactures. This trade imbalance was exacerbated by the activities of British auctioneers and factors who took up residence in American cities and threatened to drive native importers out of business.[28] Unscrupulous British merchants were also charged with dumping "fripperies" and "superfluities" on Americans, tempting them with wasteful luxuries.[29] Their agents acted as "overseers" of American trade: "Our business is inspected, and scarsely a house in London but has one among us whose whole employ is to trace us through every labyrinth of our business." When an American merchant approached failure, the foreign agent bought him out; when Americans developed new manufactures, the attentive resident foreigner imported cheap British equivalents to undersell them.[30] In the South, British agents purchased tobacco and rice that they then sold in northern cities at extravagant markups, returning to their captive markets in the South with northern and British manufactures.[31]

To merchants caught up in a web of private indebtedness, the outstanding loans of state and national governments were particularly irksome. As local interest groups scrambled for influence in the legislatures, major creditors grew restive about the ability of the state governments to fulfill their financial obligations. Importers warned that their own failing credit would have disastrous repercussions for retailers and shopkeepers: postwar prospects for economic recovery and growth would collapse into anarchy.[32]

Yet many merchants and traders agreed with spokesmen for the "agrarian interest" that Congress could not be expected to defray revolutionary financial obligations and restore American credit. Congress had in fact been negotiating additional foreign loans, thus violating a classical republican injunction against foreign indebtedness and the political dependencies it created. Some northern merchants connected this reliance on foreign loans with simultaneous efforts to reintegrate wealthy ex-Loyalists. In the early postwar scrambles to reestablish credit and markets, congressional "nationalists" seemed all too willing to sacrifice the interests of patriotic American merchants by welcoming returning Loyalists and by failing to regulate the commercial activities of British agents and factors in the northern cities. Meanwhile, Congress dallied over crucial treaty negotiations with the British that the merchants hoped would secure favorable terms for Americans in the transatlantic trade and so promote general prosperity.[33] Instead, the final draft of the peace treaty, approved on January 14, 1784, called on the states to return the estates of ex-Loyalists and stipulated that there be "no lawful impediment to the recovery of the full value in sterling money, of all bona fide debts."[34] Many New England merchants and tradesmen, said Jeremy Belknap, "flew into a passion" against this violation of revolutionary republican commitments.[35] In Virginia, George Mason reported that people everywhere were asking, "if we are now to pay the Debts due to British Merchants, what have we been fighting for all this while?" Through rioting, petitions, and legal actions, patriots asserted their rights to exclude former enemies permanently and to deny Congress authority over the thirteen sovereign republics.[36]

Disenchantment with congressional financial and commercial policy and popular opposition to its conciliatory stance toward the Loyalists drove significant numbers of commercially oriented Americans to look to the state legislatures for effective support and protection during the early 1780s. Neither unfettered free enterprise nor *ad hoc*, piecemeal wage-and-price controls were acceptable. Instead, merchants and domestic traders sought more systematic state intervention under more stable political conditions. Perhaps, they reasoned, a separate state revenue could best provide for repayment of worthy creditors while maximizing their own influence over economic policy; by serving the private interests of Americans who had financed the Revolution, the states would also secure economic independence for themselves. Proponents of state intervention suggested that independence from foreign entanglements and independence from distant congressional power were related imperatives, equally essential to American liberty.

As a result of these developments, Congress's February 1781 plan to establish "a permanent Fund to support the national Credit and cement more effectually the common Interest of the United States" was greeted with skepticism.[37] Other things being equal, the proposed 5 percent impost on all American imports might have won the support of farmers who wished to avoid real estate taxes. Because it promised to defray the interest, if not the principal, of postwar federal debts to domestic creditors, it also might have received significant merchant support. But the absence of any provision for state control over the collection and distribution of impost revenues guaranteed the proposal's defeat.[38]

A renewed request in 1783 met similar resistance in the state legislatures.[39] No state wanted to enlarge congressional powers if other states stood to gain disproportionate advantages; many state leaders also expressed fears of the dangerous implications of losing control of the purse and sword. No, said Richard Henry Lee, the national impost was "too early, and too strong an attempt to over leap those fences, established by the Confederation to secure the liberties of the respective States."[40] Fearful of future challenges to state independence, Silas Deane urged leaders to "liquidate, and apportion the public debt, without loss of time, and let each state take its proportion, and manage its own revenues. The great object with Congress is to make a common purse or treasury to be supplied by imposts, duties, etc. . . . independent of the several Legislatures." If the assemblies "are wise and mean to be in fact independent," Deane concluded, "they will never submit to a system which will prove as fatal in its consequences" as Congress's 1783 revenue plan.[41]

Six states enacted their own imposts. Pennsylvania's impost made significant strides toward defraying state and federal financial obligations to the large number of wealthy and middling security-holders in the state.[42] In Massachusetts and New York, impost revenues repaid loans from private citizens, portions of congressional requisitions, and revolutionary war pay certificates in the hands of commercial farmers and war suppliers.[43] In addition, some states began to assume the federal government's responsibility for certain securities and bills of credit floated during the war. They issued large amounts of paper money to serve both as a circulating medium and as a fund to pay state taxes. Portions of these emissions were designated to pay individual creditors the interest and principal on federal certificates which, in turn, were accepted in payment of taxes—and thereby retired from circulation—or exchanged for new state certificates less prone to rapid devaluation. Optimists in New York and Connecticut hoped to see their states become the creditors of Congress.[44]

Even short of that goal, state imposts and assumption of the debts had important consequences. Some northern legislatures succeeded in gaining the confidence of influential public creditors and thus fragmented potential support for national revenue proposals. The state legislatures fostered alliances between agricultural and commercial interests by effectively balancing solicitude for creditors with a popular commitment to paper money. State assumption neither repudiated the debt nor depreciated it into oblivion with too much paper money—both typical "agrarian debtor" strategies—nor did it pay the debts with specie, as "merchant creditors" typically demanded.[45]

Through mid-1784, there was considerable agreement that the states' impost systems benefited "all the honest buyers and sellers" while giving due notice to the "stockjobbers and landjobbers" that "no new tyranny" would be tolerated, whether it originated in Congress or in private cabals.[46] Farmers attributed their improving fortunes to the "favorable situation" of being "left free" of export duties and land taxes which might have been "drained into a consolidated union" if Congress had succeeded with the national impost. At the same time, citizens of modest means in both urban and rural areas could be confident that the state legislatures would adhere to republican principles when compelled to impose trade regulations.[47]

STATE RETALIATION AND PROTECTIONISM

At first, many West Indies provisioners were more hesitant about supporting state imposts than were dry goods importers. Their traffic was often doubly taxed, first as exports from the French or British islands and then as American imports. The "dishonest smuggler" who saw imposts as "barriers which are so easily broken over" would benefit from higher duties at the expense of honest merchants who had to sell at higher prices and consumers everywhere who had to buy inferior commodities.[48] Faced with illicit commercial competition, many West Indies provisioners at first argued that trade should be made freer, not be further encumbered, in order to guarantee "natural harmony" among buyers and sellers.[49]

In 1784, however, the West Indies interest abruptly abandoned this position and began to press for active intervention by the states. Even before the articles of peace were signed, debate in Britain over its commercial relations with the new nation portended grave consequences for American Caribbean traders. William Pitt and Edmund Burke argued that "principles of reciprocal benefit" should govern British policy. "While there is an immense extent of unoccupied territory to attract the inhabitants to agriculture," Burke explained, the Americans "will not be able to rival us in manufactures."[50] But hard-liners were intent on subordinating the American trade to British interests and opposed mutually beneficial commercial relations. Lord Sheffield insisted that because the Americans would have to import British manufactures, Parliament could lay whatever limitations on the West Indies trade it deemed necessary for its own interests; meanwhile, Canadian and Nova Scotian merchants could send ample supplies of wheat and fish to the islands. By controlling the Mississippi River, Britain could dominate the American interior, a vast, fertile region far removed from the Atlantic states. The United States were incapable of preserving their extended territorial claims or of pursuing coherent and viable commercial policies. "[E]ach state," wrote Sheffield, "has reserved every power relative to imports, exports, prohibitions, duties, etc., to itself," which would always leave Britain well situated to negotiate commercial terms or, if necessary, apply force.[51]

West Indies merchants and planters, joined by grain exporters in the northern states and Maryland, insisted that Britain and Canada would never adequately supply West Indian demand. British wheat rotted en route, and few British merchants would accept rum or sugar for the return voyage when specie was in short supply. Only North Americans would transport grain of high quality, quickly, and take West Indies rum and molasses in partial payment. More seriously, Sheffield's polemical opponents argued, the Americans' independence from "the old channels" of British manufactures and credit would ultimately promote American economic development.[52] If the British refused to give their former colonists "a more liberal mode of commerce," Americans and West Indians would "take their freedom" into their own hands.[53]

The hard-liners won the debate, and the first of many prohibitive barriers against American commerce with British possessions was enacted July 2, 1783. American provisions could only be carried to the British islands in British vessels; the importation of American salted meats was absolutely forbidden. British merchants paid steeper duties on exports to the United States than to other places.[54] By mid-1785, additional legislation placed heavy duties on American shipments of rice, tobacco, and naval stores to Britain. Fish and whale oil, two of New England's primary exports, were excluded from British ports. Grain exports from Pennsylvania and New York to Britain were all but halted in 1785, and exports to the West Indies were drastically reduced through 1787 due to gluts and falling prices.[55]

American outrage was immediate and loud.[56] Grain exporters and commercial farmers in the "bread states" depended on West Indies markets. New England and the southern states could not absorb their surpluses and would not offer prices as high as those traditionally paid by West Indies planters. Prescient observers warned that alliances between farmers and merchants would erode under the British prohibitions, as farmers who agreed to deal with British carriers raised their prices and discriminatory regulations forced honest traders to become smugglers.[57] Worst of all, the British were monopolizing the Philadelphia and New York export trade.[58] Importers were also distressed at the loss of specie through remittances to British firms.[59] New England merchants could no longer depend on the freight charges between the West Indies and London and would soon lose most of their market for ship sales.[60] Not only were shipments of New England fish and whale oil vastly diminished by late 1784, the region's distillers and peltry exporters also began to report bankruptcies.[61] Southern commerce, cut off from old connections to the West Indies, also suffered from the rapidly decreasing capacity of northern traders to transport staples and deliver manufactured items. At Williamsburg and Charleston, shipping was "null" because of "ruinous machinations" in Parliament.[62] John Jay, John Adams, and Stephen Higginson spoke for many northern provisions exporters when they decried the Orders in Council and British refusal to negotiate a commercial treaty on reciprocal terms. Americans, they said, would be driven into the arms of other foreign powers.[63] James Madison believed that the British regulations "robbed us of our trade with the West Indies."[64]

By 1785, confidence in the states' abilities to respond capably to British discrimination was waning and some exporters, importers, manufacturers, commercial farmers, and state creditors began to support efforts to expand Congress's powers.[65] Despite this growing skepticism, however, the state governments proceeded to retaliate against the British Orders in Council and endeavored to protect domestic manufactures, thereby bolstering the credibility and popularity they had already gained through imposts and debt assumption. This commercial retaliation effectively conceded the impossibility of free trade among the American states and the wider world: the goal of securing reciprocity through commercial alliances now seemed unattainable. It was essential to make Europeans take the American states seriously. The states thus sought to give their merchants competitive advantages against foreign rivals. In 1784 and 1785, nine states added steeper duties on British goods entering their ports. Duties ranged from 5 percent—the amount set in the proposed national impost—to 25 percent; Rhode Island established a treble duty on British goods.[66]

Through mid-1785, farmers and merchant exporters, and their friends in the assemblies, argued that commercial retaliation was their sole defense against powerful economic adversaries. Rufus King reported that "the states are more and more embracing the notion that they must rely on themselves rather than upon alliances or treaties with foreign powers."[67] King and other nationalists watched with trepidation as the individual states made increasingly popular responses to British hostility.

Commercial discrimination was linked to domestic investment as merchants sought safe harbors for surplus capital and commercial farmers and entrepreneurs promoted the rapid development of the interior. The Revolution had given an impetus toward self-sufficiency and numerous modest, although often abortive, experiments in manufacturing. With former sources of finished goods cut off by the war and with the prospect of new markets in rapidly developing frontier regions, many Americans saw the great potential for manufacturing and internal commerce. Northerners looked toward the southern states for new markets, and both sections looked west. By 1784, a "manufacturing interest," including many merchants and wealthy mechanics, enlisted the support of artisans and commercial farmers for a program of improvements and protectionism. Held together by their need for active government support, manufacturers and their allies insisted that the states should play a leading role in securing the benefits of economic freedom. In New York, for example, manufacturers appealed to the state legislature for tariffs on imported commodities they wished to produce and market themselves; domestic production would create jobs for industrious workers and stem the flow of specie to European rivals. The lists of prohibited imports grew in New York, Pennsylvania, Massachusetts, New Hampshire, and Virginia. By 1786, merchants, mechanics, and artisans in Massachusetts had pressured the legislature to ban the importation of fifty-eight commodities; the list included not only "luxuries and extravagance" but "necessities" which the state's own producers wanted to protect.[68] Protectionist legislation in several states excluded imports defined as luxuries, taxed competing products, and abetted initiatives for many "useful manufactures."[69] Commentators began to realize the tremendous consequences of this turn to domestic productivity. As a Maryland writer put the case for protectionism, "We can only become opulent, respectable, and truly independent, by checking the progress of enervating luxury, and encouraging the useful, industrial and meritorious mechanics of America by a tax on foreign manufactures, so as to disable them from undercutting us at our own market."[70]

Newspaper essayists could draw equally on the discourses of republican liberty and of economic freedom to justify protectionist measures that would unleash the expansive potential of the American economy. In five states, protectionism was combined with nonimportation movements reminiscent of colonial boycotts; while producers and politicians would do all in their power to "encourage . . . the manufactures and produce of this country," consumers were enjoined to relinquish funeral luxuries, raise more sheep for making woolens, and respect legislation that regulated local fairs and weekly markets.[71] Associations of tradesmen and manufacturers in many states vowed to charge "moderate" or "fair" prices for American-made goods and expressed the "sincere hope" that citizens would consume them despite their initially inferior quality.[72] No longer motivated merely to weather slumps and specie shortages or to serve a few special interests, the alliances of productive interests across class and wealth lines emphasized the abundance of the interior, labor power in the cities, and consumer demand for a wide array of new products. Mechanics' associations, improvement societies, and labor combinations would all link their fortunes to manufactures.[73] Manufacturers began to associate their new urban productive capabilities with both commercial agriculture in the West and merchants' new markets in non-British international trade.[74] Foreign goods and foreign merchants would play only a secondary role in an American system that secured the liberty of complementary interests under the benign protection of local and state governments.[75]

Internal improvements would help coordinate these complementary interests. In Pennsylvania, development-minded promoters advocated state aid to "the inland navigation of the state": "Repairing and improving the public roads" would "promote the ease and commodious transportation of the *country produce* to and from this city." Domestic manufactures of cloth also came in from the countryside in meager lots, so involving the majority of small producers and consumers. The state assembly saw the advantages of promoting domestic manufactures. "Although the fabricks and manufactures of Europe and other foreign ports . . . may be afforded at cheaper rates than they can be made here, yet good policy and regard to the well-being of divers useful and industrious citizens" required protective tariffs that would benefit the interior as much as coastal cities.[76]

STATES IN THE ASCENDANT

The political and economic dislocations of the war and postwar periods subverted grandiose visions of free trade in a world of peaceful nations bound by the global exchange of necessary commodities. On a more modest scale, these conditions also seemed to jeopardize the promise of free exchange and private profit for the great mass of ordinary Americans. While national leaders became increasingly doubtful about the prospects for international reciprocity and frustrated by their inability to concert a coherent commercial policy, interest groups looked to the sovereign states for protection and relief, implicitly acknowledging the practical limits to economic liberalism at home and abroad.

Debtors of all classes; groups united in their determination to develop the interior or to exclude returning Loyalists, auctioneers, landlords, and usurers from their formerly dominant positions in the northern cities; and those who sought to consolidate commercial advantages gained during the war—all hoped the state governments would foster national productivity and prosperity through moderate taxation and import regulations. Testimonials to the new nation's natural bounty thus could be linked to—and modified by—obeisance to the "natural rights" of the "sovereign people" in the separate states to regulate economic life. Land speculators and proponents of internal improvements argued that enlightened land and development policies would promote a better distribution of population and wealth between coastal regions and a rapidly expanding hinterland. In the North, optimists threw their support behind measures for state assumption of revolutionary debts, levies on domestic and international commerce to enhance state revenues, temporary monopolies to foster the development of transportation routes and of new inventions that would advance commercial agriculture, government protection of a "free interior," and state support for new enterprises, ship-building, and the immigration of skilled labor.[77]

Optimism about the prospects for economic freedom under the aegis of the states depended on the legislatures' responsiveness to these emergent interest groups. The successes of state economic policies in turn seemed to enhance the outlook for an economy of equilibrating sections, perhaps along the lines suggested by David Hume in his prescriptions for an international network of exchange. Increasingly, commentary on the American economy shifted from the activity of the self-regarding or self-sufficient individual to "productive" and "industrious" collectives of small producers with their overlapping and interlocking relationships.[78] Growing awareness of the domestic interior and its vast potential for development was crucial to this new conception of American political economy. The states' success in enacting regulatory and retaliatory measures set the stage for rethinking economic policy by promoting new alignments of interest groups.

But there were limits to the scope and appeal of a vision of the American economy centered on harmonious trade relations among sovereign states, protected from the depredations of foreign rivals and the dangerous designs of the speculators and financiers who favored political and economic centralization. A workable definition of economic freedom in America depended on clarifying the ambiguous relationships of the states with each other and of the states collectively with the world at large. The state-centered political economy of the Confederation years was too fragmented and defensive—and too ambivalent in its simultaneous appeal to classical republican and emergent liberal premises—to permit a clear, continental vision of the new nation's future greatness. And growing numbers of influential Americans became convinced that the very survival of the state republics hinged on thinking and acting continentally.

Although James Madison set forth the most famous rationale for the "extended republic" in his *Federalist* No. 10, his reasoning was anticipated by many Americans who reflected on political economy over the 1780s. The invention of American federalism was the achievement of politicians and commentators who confronted the ideological limitations of the conventional prescriptions offered both by classical republicans and by advocates of economic freedom. But only when new and more inclusive interest group coalitions began to promote development did it become possible to conceive of a dynamic national political economy.

The realignment of interests in the critical period before the Philadelphia Convention and the framers' political inventions were preceded by initiatives in the states to shape the future American political economy, many of which enjoyed broad popular support and a considerable measure of success. Thus, although the movement for greater congressional authority gained support over the 1780s, the achievements of the state governments in furthering the interests of their constituents represented a formidable obstacle to nationalist reformers. Skeptical Americans had to be persuaded that the reconstitution of the union would inaugurate a new era of regional interdependency and national prosperity.

3
Interstate Conflict and the Expansion of the Union

If wartime dislocations led Americans to doubt one another's—and even their own—virtue, the drafting and ratification of the Confederation justified equivalent skepticism about the motives and interests of the states. In pursuit of their interests, the states appeared willing to jeopardize the common cause and subvert the union: "state jealousy"—the hostile competition for relative advantage—endangered American independence and therefore constituted a much more immediate and pressing threat to the success of America's republican experiment than did the defective character of particular republicans.

Pitting large "landed" states against their small, "landless" neighbors, the western lands controversy exemplified the chronic hostility and suspicion that imperiled the common cause. Both blocs were convinced that their adversaries intended to use the central government to promote their particular interests. The result was to exaggerate state claims and diminish the power of the union: the landed states insisted on their territorial integrity, resisting all efforts to circumscribe their boundaries; and the landless states demanded an equal vote in Congress, regardless of disparities in size and population. Both principles—territorial integrity and state equality—were incorporated in the Articles of Confederation, thus guaranteeing that controversies between states and between sections would continue to immobilize Congress.

An ominous corollary that was a direct result of these conflicts was the union's failure to expand during the Confederation years, despite the rapid growth of frontier settlements and widespread agitation for the recognition or creation of new states. Opposition to new states revealed the prevailing sense that the separate states were naturally antagonistic. As James Madison concluded, in-

creasing the number of states in the union would unleash centrifugal tendencies that might ultimately destroy the "Machine"
of continental government.[1] The future of the "extended republic" depended on the ability of the union to expand, but its
apparent propensity was instead to contract: on the eve of the
Constitutional Convention, many commentators predicted the
division of the union into separate regional confederations.

The same nationalists warned that Americans could not afford
to allow their republican experiment to run this apparently
disastrous course. By exaggerating unnatural and artificial state
interests, the Articles subverted the union. The enmity of "sovereign" states made Americans foreigners to one another and
thus threatened to Europeanize American politics; the imminent
collapse of the union represented a standing invitation to European powers to interfere in American affairs and thereby reverse
the outcome of the Revolution. Congress's inability to formulate
an effective national trade policy exposed the states to commercial
depredations. Meanwhile, uncertain conditions on the frontiers
prompted settlers to seek alliances with their British or Spanish
neighbors. The common element in all these warnings was a
pervasive suspicion about the potential misuse of state power, by
old and new states alike. The reformers' controversial conclusion
was that the broad powers of the separate state republics under
the Articles of Confederation constituted the chief threat to
republican government in America.

THE ARTICLES OF CONFEDERATION

"The best political writers," most notably Montesquieu, warned
that republican government could not survive in large states.[2] But
the ideological preference for small states was tempered by the
realization that the Americans would have to preserve their
independence in a world of great, despotic powers.[3] How could
they do this without sacrificing the liberty, equality, and independence of their small, republican states? The solution was to form a
Confederation, founded on and dedicated to upholding the sovereignty of its member states. By confederating, Vattel wrote in his
Law of Nations, republics could counter the power of large,
despotic regimes.[4] English radical Richard Price hoped "that by

such means universal peace may be produced and all war ex-cluded from the world."⁵

Americans who sought to combine the advantages of local self-government with viable provisions for collective security saw the United States as an exemplary international organization. When Congress was debating an early draft of the Articles of Confederation in July 1776, John Witherspoon, president of the College of New Jersey, located the American union in a progressive world-historical scheme: "It is but little above two hundred years since that enlarged system called the balance of power, took place. . . . [It] is a greater step from the former disunited and hostile situation of kingdoms and states, to their present condition, than it would be from their present condition to a state of more perfect and lasting union."⁶ In Witherspoon's conception of world history and of the American Confederation, states were constants. "Progress" was measured by their ability to perfect arrangements among themselves for sustaining collective "security and peace." Therefore, it was imperative that the founders of the Confederation harmonize conflicting rights and interests before attempting to establish a "perpetual union."⁷ But the result of these efforts was protracted impasse. Just as residual loyalty to George III had delayed independence, the momentous implications of the Con-federation for the future of the states—and the world—proved an impediment to action. The failure of the states to confederate when they declared their independence assured that the goal of the Revolution for most Americans would be to preserve their states' rights: union would be a means of securing state sovereignty.

It remained to be seen if the American states would behave differently than their European counterparts. Many commen-tators, in Europe and America, were skeptical. The apparent inability of the states to band together, notwithstanding the demands of the war, was disheartening; their evident determina-tion to promote their own rights and interests did not bode well for the future, even if American arms should triumph. The history of the Articles tested the Americans' faith in the capacity of their new republics to achieve an enlightened accommodation with one another and so transcend the sordid imperatives of power politics. During the prolonged drafting process, John Rutledge of South Carolina began to wonder if the states could ever come to terms; "we have made such a devil of it already."⁸

The states negotiated their union under desperate pressure. "Nothing but Present danger will ever make us all Agree," wrote New Jersey delegate Abraham Clark in August 1776, "and I sometimes even fear that will be insufficient."[9] Yet if the "Present danger" worked toward union, it also promoted the expression of local interests. Taking advantage of the wartime crisis, state leaders insisted on concessions from other states. When provoked by Congress's apparent unwillingness to uphold their essential rights or interests, they hinted that their states might abandon the war effort. Given the importance of preserving the union and showing a common front to friends and foes, congressmen took such warnings to heart. Successive drafts of the Articles therefore diluted congressional authority and secured states' rights. Not surprisingly, few congressmen could muster enthusiasm for the Confederation that was finally forwarded to the states for their approval in October 1777.[10] The document also met a cool reception in the state legislatures, and because Maryland refused to ratify, the government of the union was forced to carry on without constitutional authority until the war was nearly over.

Compromises on taxation, representation, and land claims gave everyone something to dislike in the Articles. No one pretended that the Confederation adequately reconciled conflicting state and sectional interests: if anything, the structure of the new union exacerbated mutual suspicions. Although most congressmen agreed in theory with Charles Carroll that they would have to rise above the "little and partial interests" of their own states, the drafting process made them jealous defenders of local rights and thus jeopardized larger, more general interests, if not fundamental principles.[11] Some provisions clearly represented expedient, political concessions to groups with leverage in Congress: thus the small states threatened not to confederate unless they were guaranteed equal voting power. Delegates from large states, such as John Adams of Massachusetts, were bitterly opposed to such a guarantee, insisting that representation proportional to population was alone "equitable" and that "an equal vote for the small states will endanger the larger."[12] For Adams, the compromise of principle seemed all the more glaring and dangerous in a document that purported to found a "perpetual" union.

Because political compromises and concessions were so conspicuous in the completed Articles, ratification did not retard—

and may even have hastened—the rapid deterioration of Congress as an effective governing body. From 1781 on, nationalist proponents of a stronger central government emphasized defects in the Articles as they campaigned for amendments to give Congress greater control over commerce and an independent revenue. By early 1787, Henry Knox spoke for a growing number of Americans who were convinced that "the poor Federal government is sick almost unto death."[13]

STATE EQUALITY

When the Articles were being drafted, the apparent determination of the large, landed states to hold on to their extensive western claims reinforced the small states' insistence on state equality in Congress.[14] John Witherspoon's vision of the United States as an enlightened international system, or "federal union," reflected his determination to guarantee the survival of New Jersey and other small states. Considered as corporate entities, the small states had as much to lose as the large: "In questions of war" they were "as much interested" and "therefore should vote equally." Though Witherspoon conceded that "equality of representation was an excellent principle," he insisted that "nothing relating to individuals could ever come before Congress; nothing but what would respect colonies."[15] A confederation not premised on state equality would invite the larger states to extend their power.[16]

Concerns about the unequal size of the states persisted despite Congress's capitulation to the small states on the representation issue in the draft of the Articles sent out to the states. The argument for equal voting was based on the assumption that the large states would exploit their superior voting power under a scheme of proportional representation to oppress their small neighbors. Yet, if this was a plausible prediction of large-state behavior, it followed that *any* inequality or imbalance in the union would jeopardize the smaller and weaker states. The protracted struggle over the large states' western claims thus reinforced a prevailing tendency to apply European ideas about international relations to the American state system.

Small-state spokesmen suggested that the large states were, in their determination to gain the upper hand over their neighbors, no different from European nations. Republican government, however inestimable its benefits for the citizens within the various states, apparently did not have any significant positive impact on relations *among* the states. The large states' resistance to territorial equalization revealed their apparent determination to exercise their superior power over their neighbors. "The great inequality now existing, and which is likely to increase, between the different states was a very unfavourable circumstance" for the stability of the union, the French financier Turgot wrote in 1778. The propensity of the larger states to seek "extended dominion"—to make themselves even larger—entailed grave risks to their republican character. Turgot urged the Americans to establish a better balance "in laying out future states."[17]

The conventional thinking about state behavior encapsulated in the balance-of-power concept provided a standard to measure the large states' supposed contempt for fundamental republican principles and their disregard for the interests of the union as a whole. These concerns were most fully developed by Marylanders in their extended campaign against Virginia's western claims. Marylanders complained that they were obliged to share the costs of securing the West, by contributing their "blood and treasure" to the revolutionary cause, while being excluded from its benefits. The defense of the large states' territorial pretensions constituted a drain on the resources of the entire nation, but when America's enemies were finally subdued and law and order reigned on the frontiers, the fertile western lands would be a limitless source of revenue—for the large states. It was "contrary to all principles of equity on which a Confederation ought to be founded," the Maryland House charged in 1778, that the small, landless states "should be burthened with very heavy expense for the subduing and guarantying immense tracts of country, when they are to have no share of the monies arising from the sale of lands."[18]

Maryland's brief against the landed states was outlined in legislative instructions laid before Congress in 1779.[19] After enlisting the small states in their campaign to establish control over the West, the large states would inevitably predominate. Preponderant wealth and power would lead large states "to oppress by open force their less wealthy and less powerful neighbors" or cause "the depopulation, and consequently the impoverishment" of the small states. The Maryland instructions suggested that union depended on a balance of state power that was threatened by their disparate prospects for economic development. When the nominal equality of the states under the Articles no longer disguised or inhibited these disparities—and when the populous states claimed that equal state voting violated the right of their citizens to be "equally" represented—the union would collapse. Then the large states would strike out on their own, annexing their small neighbors or forcing them to join regional confederations on unequal terms.[20]

State equality, broadly defined, would sustain a stable balance of power across the continent that would enable Americans to defend and promote their common interests. The American union therefore constituted an improvement on the European state system only to the extent that the states respected one another's sovereignty and equality and sought to achieve a more perfect balance of power. "Among confederated republics," a Boston newspaper writer explained, "the safety and harmony of the whole, depends on a proper equality in the several individuals. The state therefore that wishes to extend its territory to a great degree beyond that of others, is an enemy to the union."[21]

Small-state warnings about the behavior of large states in an imbalanced union undercut conventional claims about the peaceful character of republics and their natural harmony with one another. This skepticism was easily extended to the motives of private citizens. If republics, like other states, were bound to exploit their relative advantages, republican citizens were equally likely to consider their own interests in supporting, or failing to support, their state governments. The loyalty of republican citizens was voluntary and contingent: "People are now to be governed by clear perceptions, not blind attachments."[22]

Small-state leaders had good reason to fear that self-interest would produce factions in their own states that would favor closer alliance or even amalgamation with adjacent large states: merchants would seek commercial concessions; land speculators, access to undeveloped public lands; and taxpayers, relief. In 1786, a writer in the *Connecticut Courant* showed how calculations based on interest jeopardized small-state sovereignty. Doubtful that the people of Connecticut would be willing or able to resort to violent measures to protect their interests—for instance, by seizing the port of New York—"Yankee Doodle" thought his state should "apply to the State of New-York to take us into their government, and to be part of it—then we shall reap every advantage of the impost and waste lands, and be as benefited as if we were to extend our government over them."[23]

TERRITORIAL INTEGRITY

The western lands controversy also led large-state leaders to suspect the motives of their small-state counterparts and thus to discount the influence of republicanism on interstate relations. For Virginians, any challenge to their state's charter claims threatened its very existence as a state. They sought to preserve Virginia's territorial integrity against encroachments by private land companies or by the small states that tried to assert Congress's jurisdiction.[24]

Virginians did not fear any direct assault on their claims by Maryland and the other small landless states. The immediate danger came from the Indiana Company and other groups of "landmongers": by combining forces and distributing shares in influential quarters, the companies were able to mount formidable campaigns to validate their titles, first in Virginia and later in Congress. When the western claims question reached Congress, Virginians vehemently resisted any interference in what they insisted was a matter of domestic policy. "Should Congress assume a jurisdiction," predicted George Mason in a Remonstrance he drafted for the Virginia Assembly in 1779, it would "subvert the sovereignty and government of any one or more of the United States, and establish in Congress a power which in process of time must degenerate into intolerable despotism." Because the survival of the union depended on securing the sovereign states' essential rights and interests, Congress had to be kept from "arrogating" dangerous, "despotic" powers to itself.[25]

Although Virginian rhetoric focused on the prospective menace of a strong central government, its objective was to expose and discredit the machinations of the small-state delegations in Congress. Insisting that they simply sought to uphold the vital principles of territorial integrity and states' rights—and denying any interested motives in preserving their extraordinary advantages over their small neighbors—the Virginians claimed that their "enemies" would go to any lengths to gratify their "envy" and "avidity."[26] The small states—not Virginia and the other large states—were guided by the outmoded maxims of balance-of-power politics. First, the small states forged an alliance among themselves to counteract discrepancies in size and power; then, by gaining control over Congress—and this was only possible because of the fundamentally inequitable provision for equal state voting in the Articles—they conspired to seize Virginia's western lands under the pretense of promoting the "national" interest. But this campaign against large-state claims was all the more insidious because the small American states disguised their illicit ambitions by claiming to act in the name of all the states—including Virginia. The landless-state bloc constituted a partial alliance that sought to pervert the government of the union to its selfish ends.

For defenders of large-state claims, challenges to their territorial rights showed that the small American states, despite their republican governments, responded to the same considerations of interest and relative advantage that dictated policy in the Old World. Of course, the disproportion between the American states should be of no consequence: republican Virginia had nothing to gain by attacking its small neighbors. Yet, if the small states failed to recognize this and used the machinery of the Confederation to redress the supposed imbalance of power, Virginians had no choice but to resist. Frustrated by Congress's unwillingness to compromise the western lands issue on the generous terms set forth in the 1781 offer to cede the trans-Ohio region, some Virginians thought their state should abandon the union altogether.[27]

Virginians suspected that small-state policy was determined by the land companies.[28] This malign influence explained why Maryland did not approve the Articles and sought to extort an extensive, unconditional western claims cession from Virginia. When Virginia did make an offer, under the condition that Congress also invalidate company titles, "members within and without doors" combined to oppose it: they claimed that the terms were "improper" and that the "quantity ceded is not enough." But it was clear to Richard Henry Lee that "personal interests, and political views—Toryism, British interest, and Land-jobbing views" best explained Congress's chilly response to Virginia's proposal.[29] Would these petty private interests cause Congress to lose sight of the substantial benefits Virginia now offered the American people? Theodorick Bland, at least, was hopeful that the delegates would be shamed into compliance, whatever their personal motives: "The Covert manoeuvers of the land Jobbing Companies are so well known, that few of their abettors will be hardy enough to oppose [the cession] in its fullest lattitude."[30]

Bland's optimism proved unjustified. The landless-state coalition controlled Congress until late 1783, and the western claims question remained effectively stalemated. During this period, Virginians continued to complain about the companies' insidious influence in the landless states and in Congress. In fact, they suggested, there was no real distinction between Congress and the companies; the prospect of giving "all our country to private companies" in the nominal form of a cession to the United States "is insufferable."[31] The Virginia delegation still hoped that Congress would come to acceptable terms if the land-jobbers were forced into the open. They compiled lists of company shareholders in Congress and in neighboring states. Arthur Lee was convinced that "the publication of the names" of these "Adventurers" would "greatly lessen their influence."[32] Accordingly, in April 1782 Lee and Bland offered a resolution that "previous to any determination" on the western claims, every delegate be required to "declare whether he is, or is not personally interested directly or indirectly in the claims" of any of the companies. Congress's failure to endorse this "purifying declaration" was conclusive confirmation of its corruption.[33]

Virginians could derive several lessons from the western lands controversy. In their corporate capacity, the small states evidently honored the precepts of Old World power politics in seeking to curb the territorial claims of the large landed states. The inordinate influence of private speculators—particularly in Maryland, New Jersey, and Pennsylvania—explained why these republican states pursued such antirepublican policies. Here, indeed, skepticism about the impact of republican government on the behavior of states and the character of the union converged with growing doubts about the capacity of the American states to curb the excesses of factiousness and self-interest. The small states did not behave in a republican fashion because their governments were so vulnerable to private influence.

The Virginians' fear that "the ceded lands may be converted to private, instead of public purposes" therefore was not only an indictment of Congress's intentions and of the small states' pernicious policies.[34] In suggesting that popularly elected officials could so blatantly disregard the true interests of their constituents and of the American people generally in order to promote their own selfish interests, the Virginians also betrayed a deeper and more corrosive mistrust about the future of republican government in America.

NEW STATES

The expansion of the union represented the ultimate test of American republicanism. If, in fact, republics were peaceful and were bound to each other by common principles and interests, there should have been no limit to the number of new states that could be drawn into the American orbit. A true confederation would preserve peace among its members while protecting them all against hostile powers; by increasing the power of the union— and by preempting potential enemies—expansion would enhance collective security. These were the advantages, cited by "peace planners" and other proponents of federalism, that Americans hoped to enjoy under the Articles of Confederation. Americans enthusiastically predicted that their system would rapidly spread across the continent, ultimately inspiring the oppressed peoples of Europe to follow their lead.[35]

Yet the vision of an expanding union of republics was not easily realized. The admission of new states inevitably would alter the balance of power in the union. As long as the existing states retained their territorial monopoly and the United States remained "landless," new states could only come into being through the division of the large, landed states. Even with the creation of the national domain in 1784, old-state leaders feared that the admission of new members would dilute their power and influence in the union. Although in theory the states should not have been concerned about their relative power, radical discrepancies in size and population ensured that Americans would continue to find traditional balance-of-power ideas compelling.

According to Article XI of the Confederation, "Canada acceding to this confederation, and joining in the measures of the United States, shall be admitted into, and entitled to all the advantages of this Union: but no other colony shall be admitted into the same, unless such admission be agreed to by nine States." Because Canada or any "other colony" was by definition *outside* the area presently claimed by the thirteen states, Article XI took on the character of a belligerent manifesto: American expansion was defined in relation to the claims of imperial powers, particularly Britain. But the formation of new states *within* the vast domain claimed by the United States and secured by the Treaty of Paris in 1783 faced insuperable constitutional obstacles. As Congress repeatedly declared, the American union was premised on the territorial monopoly of its original members: "No State shall be deprived of territory for the benefit of the United States" (Article IX).[36] The admission of any new state (as opposed to foreign colony) would be an amendment to the Articles that would have to be "confirmed by the Legislatures of every State"—including the state out of which it was formed.

Given the failure of existing colonies to join the union, the only possibility of adding new states was through the division of the old states. Proposals for expansion of the union through state division were both inspired and defeated by the unequal size of the old states. As settlement spread into frontier areas of the large states, the "unwieldiness of our present governments in extent of territory" became increasingly apparent; therefore separations "must sooner or later take place."[37] But inequality in the sizes of the existing states meant that they stood to gain or lose unequally in any renegotiation of boundaries. And the Articles of Confederation tended to institutionalize the jurisdictional status quo by enabling small groups of states or even individual states to check hostile policy initiatives and thus preserve their relative advantage.[38]

Although the Virginia cession of 1784 promised to initiate a new epoch in interstate relations, old concerns were not easily laid to rest. Hoping to rectify the still vast disproportion among the states, small-state congressmen pressed for further cessions.[39] The "small states appear to wish for every facility to lessen the larger ones," the Virginia delegates complained.[40] Nor did the creation of a national domain through cessions from the landed states mean that Congress was prepared to welcome additions to the union, notwithstanding the language of its territorial government ordinance of April 23, 1784. Because the ordinance described boundaries for new states throughout the West, including territory not yet ceded to Congress, separatists across the continent were led to believe that Congress was now ready to welcome new members. "The Continental Congress, by their resolves, invite us" to separate from North Carolina, leaders of the new state of Franklin proclaimed.[41] But the cessions left existing frontier settlements, the most eligible candidates for statehood, under old-state control. In subsequent years, congressmen retreated from the grand design of 1784, which provided for the entire trans-Appalachian region, and devoted their efforts to planning for new "states" in the unsettled Northwest.

By raising the specter of frontier anarchy, the 1784 government ordinance probably delayed the addition of new states to the union. Separatism, that "epidemic . . . Spirit of making new States," seemed tantamount to disunion and therefore the most dangerous form of factionalism in an extended republic.[42] Of course, separatists denied they were factious, claiming instead that the oppressive rule of the old states distorted and deflected loyalties and interests naturally inclined toward the union. Writers from western Virginia thus suggested that the multiplication (and division) of the states would strengthen the union: "An increase of states in the federal union will conduce to the strength and dignity of that union, just as our increase of individual citizens will increase the strength and dignity of a state."[43] "Nature" (in the form of impassable mountains and great distances) decreed the division of the large states. A Franklinite concluded that "Nature"—not factiousness—"has separated us" from North Carolina.[44] When boundaries were adjusted accordingly, new-state proponents concluded, factional conflict would cease.

By insisting on the inevitability of conflict between the old states and their frontier settlements, however, separatists inadvertently raised questions about the survival of the union. Would the union be more harmonious when these conflicting interests were represented in separate states capable of pursuing independent policies? Opponents of separatism did not think so. They charged that self-proclaimed new states would be founded in factionalism, beginning with internal divisions over the statehood question, and would spread discord throughout the union. Conflicts between old and new states over boundaries and property rights would simply widen the sphere of jurisdictional conflicts that already stretched the bonds of union to the breaking point. If the frontier settlements were really so naturally distinct from the older settlements to the east, there was no hope for the union. Many contemporaries agreed with Rufus King that "no paper engagements" could preserve the connection between East and West.[45]

Antiseparatists such as King explicitly challenged the political character of frontier settlers and questioned their capacity for self-government. In their view, unruly and "licentious" frontiersmen sought statehood in order to pursue their selfish interests at the public expense, thereby jeopardizing the general welfare and even the survival of the union.[46] Large-state leaders saw separatism as yet another assault by land speculators—now disguising themselves as liberty-loving republicans—on their states' territorial rights. Congress's unwillingness to take a strong stand against separatism in turn reinforced old suspicions about small-state motives. The small states were so "jealous of the growing power of the largest governments" that they would "do anything . . . to bring them nearer to an equality with their neighbours."[47]

Although separatists could appeal to basic republican values in promoting their claims to "independence," their agitation was increasingly identified with the centrifugal forces threatening the union. In turn, attacks on the motives of new-state proponents and of their abettors in Congress represented the most forthright challenge to the special character of republican statehood in America in the period leading up to the Philadelphia Convention. If antiseparatist characterizations were apt, the addition of new states would be disastrous. Yet it was also apparent that the failure of the union to expand would endanger the future of republican government in America.

FRONTIER ANARCHY

The new nation's disunited status and its precarious international situation made frontier anarchy seem particularly ominous in the 1780s. The struggle for economic and political advantage in the West represented a sure recipe for "savagism," "barbarism," and the loss of valuable population and resources from the "civilized"

East. Subsistence farmers and those who suffered during the mid-decade depression; middling urban residents who could not survive the rising prices and heavy taxation caused by interstate jealousies; speculators and traders reeling from the hard times resulting from international discrimination in money markets and commodities—all might contribute to a flood of disaffected immigrants into the interior.[48]

In July 1784, Spain closed the lower Mississippi to American traffic and asserted its jurisdiction over much of the territory between Georgia and the river. Convinced that free navigation was crucial to the commercial development of the transmontane hinterland, southern planters who eyed opportunities for expansion joined with western settlers in seeking to open the river and, if possible, to remove the Spanish from the region altogether. But negotiations between John Jay and Don Diego de Gardoqui in 1785 proved disappointing, particularly to southerners. Under the terms of their proposed agreement, Spain would remain in control of the Mississippi for twenty-five years; meanwhile, the two countries would open a direct trade that presumably would benefit northern shippers. At no time before 1786 were intersectional relations so badly strained. Nor did the Jay-Gardoqui talks gain much respect for Congress, under whose auspices they were conducted and then abruptly terminated.

Alienated by Congress's inability to open the navigation of the Mississippi, westerners threatened to leave the union and seek protection—and profits—elsewhere. They did not hesitate to exploit eastern anxieties about their political volatility and "savage" character. The history of the Tartars demonstrated the effectiveness of an "army of savages," a North Carolinian wrote. "I do not say that we are already become savages," he added, but the warning was clear:

> Every one of us has appetites or habits which he brought with him from a distant place. We have lived in maritime countries, and have tasted the benefits of commerce. . . . We must therefore be allowed to export our produce, for when a whole nation has a passion which is not fitted to their situation, they will infallibly strive to alter their situation. If the liberty of trading is not given us, we must take it.[49]

The absence of workable government in the West would compel settlers to savage measures *because* their tastes and interests were civilized. French settlers in the Illinois country thus complained about being left "in a state of nature, without law, government or protection."[50]

If the United States could not establish law and order and secure the region's economic interests, warned a Louisville writer, "our allegiance will be thrown off, and some other power applied to." When westerners shipped goods to New Orleans, the Spanish confiscated them or forced Americans to sell them at ruinously low prices. Westerners were in danger of becoming Spanish vassals, and if Congress did not support their interests, they would have to take matters into their own hands.[51] Some frontier people were determined to "drive the Spaniards" from the Mississippi; perhaps the British would come to their aid. Other westerners would "talk very strongly of becoming Spanish subjects."[52] In any event, streams of settlers resolved to enjoy the new land's legendary bounty. "Do you think to prevent the emigration from a barren country loaded with taxes and impoverished with debts," one of them asked, "to the most luxurious soil in the world?"[53]

The new nation's imperial neighbors seemed ready to stimulate and exploit frontier discontent. Prominent Kentuckians opened communication with the Spanish, while "favorable proposals" were reportedly offered by Britain.[54] The British were "busy on our frontiers," fomenting Indian wars;[55] they had reopened negotiations with the Vermonters[56] and were even supposed to be plotting with the Shaysites in Massachusetts.[57] Virginia congressman Edward Carrington was convinced *"that great Britain will be in readiness to improve any advantage which our derangements may present for regaining her lost dominions."*[58] Congressmen's fears about British counterrevolutionary designs were compounded by the tendency of frontier people to press for recognition of their individual and collective rights. Antiseparatist commentators warned that new state movements played into British hands, raising "their hopes that they may hereafter gain, by divisions among ourselves, that dominion their tyranny and arms have lost."[59] A division of Massachusetts would "throw" the people of Maine "into the arms of Great Britain," either as a new colony or "as an addition to the province of Nova Scotia."[60]

Negotiations between self-proclaimed new states and foreign powers represented the opening wedge for the Europeanization of American politics. The danger was not that the frontiers remained in an absolute "state of nature" but rather that spontaneous new political formations inadequately attached to the union would spin completely out of control. America would thus be drawn into European wars, George Washington warned, unless "there is energy enough in the Government to keep our people within proper bounds."[61] The anarchy of weak and disconnected new states would recreate the savagery of European politics on the American frontier—without the moderating effects of a traditional balance of power among well-established states. Political instability would lead to chronic warfare among whites as well as between whites and Indians. Here, in the nightmarish prospect of counterrevolution, the worst of both worlds met: the savagery of sovereign states would unleash the savagery of licentious settlers in their natural state.

The West was more than a strategic liability to the new nation. Just as many Americans recognized the inevitability of neocolonial dependency and subservience to "European systems" in America's commercial weakness and disjointed trade policies, they could see the implications of disunion prefigured in the anarchy of western politics. With the loss of the West, America would fulfill Turgot's dark prophecy. Reenacting European history, the American states would become "a mass of divided powers contending for territory and commerce and continually cementing the slavery of the people with their own blood."[62]

4
Commercial Crises and Regional Development

Nationalists who were concerned about controversies over the western lands also expressed grave reservations about the country's vulnerability in international trade. Early attempts to secure open ports and commercial reciprocity with European nations failed. After 1783, dreams of "perfect freedom" were further compromised by British discrimination against Americans in the northern fisheries and the West Indies.[1] In a series of Orders in Council, the British government reinstituted mercantile restraints on the provisions, tobacco, and naval stores trade, dashing the hopes of merchants in the northern states for lucrative trade links with the British Caribbean.[2] Some nationalists, most notably Alexander Hamilton, feared that the new restrictions would destroy the "natural channels" of trade between the United States and Britain. Others emphasized the deleterious impact of British discrimination on American interests throughout the Atlantic economy: American trade with southern Europe and the foreign West Indies had always depended on primary links with now-forbidden British markets. Most commentators agreed on the necessity of a uniform American response to the Orders in Council. But because they represented such a wide array of local and regional interests, congressmen were unable to reach consensus on the best means to secure the new nation's commercial interests.[3]

Nationalists were convinced that congressional impasse over commercial policy was a function of fundamental flaws in the organization of the union under the Articles of Confederation. American developments appeared to bear out the suggestions of writers such as David Hume and Josiah Tucker that trade patterns ultimately adapted to political boundaries.[4] The alignment of specific local interests with potentially hostile state governments could lead to dangerous and debilitating conflicts. The states retained sufficient "sovereign" power to block any measure that appeared to jeopardize their particular rights and interests. Meanwhile, with Congress powerless to act, the states were forced to take the policy initiative. But thirteen different commercial policies were worse than useless, John Adams ruefully concluded. "Our commerce has returned to its old channels," Adams wrote in 1784, "and . . . it can follow in no other" so long as the states remained disunited. As a result, Britain could feel "sure of the American commerce."[5]

WORLD TRADE

Critics of the new nation's "disunited" commercial policy believed that American prosperity depended on eliminating as many artificial barriers to trade as possible. But the sovereign states' control over commerce threatened the new nation's prospects by putting the United States on an "unequal footing . . . with other nations" and stirring up "mutual disgusts and alienation amongst the several members of the [American] Empire."[6] "While we have no national system of commerce," "Common Sense" wrote in late 1783, "the British will govern our trade."[7] A group of Philadelphia merchants later complained that without effective national regulation of commerce, "we are at this time under the effects of European systems."[8] Just as the revolutionaries had driven out the hordes of parasitic British placemen who preyed on the colonies before independence, it was now "indispensible" to reject the "agents" and "emissaries" of British merchant houses.[9] To many suspicious observers, it was apparent that the British meant to subjugate their former colonies by flooding them with exports while barring American traders from lucrative West Indian markets. Such "unequal" trade relations would reduce the Americans to a colonial condition. In theory, a British writer explained, commerce "is the imports and exports of different countries for *mutual advantage*"; "any other [i.e., unequal] commercial connections must be ruinous to one part or the other."[10]

The states could only avoid European domination by taking "speedy and decisive measures" to encourage industry and coordinate trade policy. Otherwise, a New York writer warned, "our citizens will not even be what they have been since the late war, the *factors* of foreign merchants; we will sink to the same state with the coasts of Africa or India, where the whole trade is in the hands of foreigners—where foreigners are everything, and the natives nothing."[11] It was absurd to "call ourselves free and independent states!" Thomas Dawes of Massachusetts exclaimed. "We are independent of each other, but we are slaves to Europe."[12]

How could the United States best avoid a degrading dependence on European powers? Agrarian theorists in Europe and America urged the new nation to avoid commerce, or at least foreign trade, altogether. "Everything will be ruined if ever your trade becomes a favourite object," one French writer predicted.[13] "As you have our vices," cautioned Abbé de Mably, "you will soon have our politics."[14] But many Americans who recognized the dangers of foreign trade on unequal terms believed a vigorous internal trade would "help to bind the States together" and secure the new nation's economic independence.[15] The self-sufficiency that could "render us truly independent" of Europe would depend on promoting American manufactures.[16] "For an independent nation, to depend wholly on the supply of others, for their cloathing and every other manufacture, is quite a political solecism; such a people may please themselves with sounds, and their independence like a child's rattle, may tickle their fancy."[17] But if enterprising Americans were free to exploit the continent's abundant natural resources, real economic independence would be within reach.

Even Thomas Jefferson recognized that his countrymen had a "decided taste for navigation and commerce" and would not be confined to agriculture, whatever its advantages in theory.[18] "Commercial republicans" such as St. George Tucker sought to dispel the "prejudices" of those who "consider commerce as a bane":

The establishment of our independence calls upon us to act with the provident circumspection and foresight of a nation laying the foundation of its future character. Our views should be extended far beyond those narrow limits, which were rigidly prescribed to us while dependent colonies. The only means by which nations can rise into consequence, are, by their arms, or by their commerce.[19]

Americans could either prepare for war or promote uniform trade policies: they could not avoid the choice by remaining in splendid isolation. Misguided efforts to turn away from the world simply invited Old World powers to exploit the resulting power vacuum. Instead of advancing the progress of commerce and civilization, Americans would be regressing to a more barbaric and warlike stage of development. The institution of a national system of trade, on the other hand, accorded with the "genius" of an enterprising, commercial people who sought to avoid Old World entanglements. Tench Coxe, a leading exponent of economic expansion, called for improvements in agriculture and "internal navigation" that would "bring into action the dormant powers of nature." But the crucial component in Coxe's vision was the development of American manufactures, the best guarantee of "real independence."[20]

COMMERCIAL REVERSALS AND STATE JEALOUSIES

Nationalists blamed their inability to secure reciprocal trade relations with European nations on the weakness of the national government under the Articles of Confederation. They feared that Congress's failure to regulate and promote commerce would lead to a dramatic expansion of state power that would jeopardize republican liberty in the states as well as national prosperity. By 1784 the state governments began to retaliate against British discrimination with their own discriminatory legislation; at the same time, they sought to spur economic recovery through paper currency emissions and the assumption of the war debts. Coalitions of commercial farmers, international traders, and debt holders formed in the legislatures to promote increasingly autonomous—and potentially antagonistic—state economic policies. Yet nationalists were convinced that the states, acting on their own, were more likely to be drawn into conflicts with one another than to improve their commercial situation. Speaking of the states' retaliatory commercial regulations, Pelatiah Webster thought it "a sad omen to find among the first effects of independence, greater restraints and abridgements of natural liberty, than ever we felt under the government we have lately renounced and shaken off.'' Misguided state policies threatened "freedom of trade, or unrestrained liberty of the subject to hold or dispose of his property as he pleases.''[21]

Although nationalists could not yet offer a viable alternative, support for independent state policies proved highly variable under changing economic conditions.[22] After the onset of a commercial depression in 1785, alliances among particular interest groups that had supported aggressive state policies began to fracture. Growing numbers of citizens became convinced that state interventions in the economy compromised their "natural liberty," as optimism about the prospects for rapid economic recovery gave way to mounting concern over the impact of gluts, auction sales, higher rents, and specie flight.[23] "The scarcity of money is beyond your conception," James Warren wrote from Massachusetts to John Adams.[24] As a result, private indebtedness had risen to "alarming proportions."[25] By late 1785, the British Orders in Council had drastically reduced legal trade to the West Indies. In Massachusetts, molasses and sugar imports were "at a very low Ebb and still declining," but "every branch of [that trade] is very much embarrassed."[26] Grain shipments intended for the West Indies accumulated in New York City warehouses, so depriving international traders of essential remittances and bills of exchange.[27]

Stephen Higginson warned that the distresses of shipbuilders, importers, and manufacturers would affect other interests: "Those who have imported largely from the British are generally in distressed circumstances. . . . [T]he distresses of those people must, and will, be communicated to others who are connected with them in Business; and this connection is so extensive, as to affect a great part of those who are engaged in Trade."[28] State efforts to protect infant manufactures would continue to win the loyalty of many mechanics and small investors. But state governments failed to offer significant support to merchants seeking additional investment opportunities in manufacturing. Although agricultural export prices began to rise again by 1786, prices of manufactures such as sugar, barrelled salted meat, and snuff continued to decline until 1788. Prices of iron goods and textiles fluctuated until the time of the ratification controversy, when they began to increase steadily. Particularly wherever duties on the imports of sugar, molasses, and tobacco were high, distilling, refining, and snuff manufacturing became costly enough to drive out established concerns, resulting in bankruptcies and unemployment.[29] Only five New York distilleries were in business in 1786, compared to twelve in 1774.[30] In Boston, distillers were reputedly "at a stand."[31]

Many observers continued to insist that "foreign obstructions," including Loyalist factors and commission agents, were responsible for America's economic distress. But there was mounting disaffection with state management of the economy as well. Dislocations resulting from the depression illuminated intrastate regional and class tensions which the state governments were ill equipped to resolve. Paper currency emissions, for example, answered the needs of many inland farmers and shopkeepers but offered little consolation to retailers and wholesalers who required specie for international remittances.[32] Nor would mechanics and manufacturers remain satisfied with state impost policies and discriminatory duties against foreign goods. Such measures might be effective in a rising economy, but they could do little to halt the waves of bankruptcies in depressed cities such as Baltimore, Philadelphia, and New York.[33] Long credit had been stretched to the breaking point by late 1785 as commercial farmers and "country buyers" were dunned by dry goods importers for myriad small debts. Peter Colt, Jeremiah Wadsworth's agent in Hartford, decided that "trusting" small debtors "never was nor ever will be so good as the goods themselves. . . . I would keep them till they were rotten before I would [give] credit in these bad times."[34] Once state policies began to "annihilate commerce," a newspaper writer added, they would "effectually ruin the landed interest by sinking the value of lands."[35]

Although class tensions continued to preoccupy nationalists, they were most concerned about interstate conflicts over trade issues. To a large extent, state policies were determined by the presence or absence of dominant regional ports. Legislators in New Jersey and Delaware, states without such ports, established free ports and free-floating grain prices while they simultaneously discouraged the flow of raw materials to manufacturers in states which assessed heavy taxes on "foreign"—or out-of-state—commodities.[36] These initiatives had enjoyed some success, at least in the region around Wilmington where numerous flour mills and a vigorous shipping industry flourished, despite the proximity of Philadelphia. But the failure of state economic policies in Rhode Island was as disturbing to nationalists as their apparent success in Delaware. By 1785, Providence merchants believed they were virtually barred from trade with Massachusetts and New York because of prohibitively high state duties.[37]

Nationalists in Connecticut, New Jersey, and Delaware hoped that the bewildering array of new state legislation would be supplanted by more uniform congressional control over imposts and protective legislation. In the meantime, however, they sought equally state-interested arrangements. In order to escape the commercial domination of their prosperous neighbors in New York, Pennsylvania, and Massachusetts, they entered into a variety of cooperative arrangements with British shippers. The regrettable result was to invite "excessive" numbers of British agents into the secondary ports while prompting the "exodus of our best mercantile interests" to the larger, commercially dominant cities.[38]

Merchants and domestic traders in New York City, Philadelphia, and Boston were equally quick to blame policymakers in other states for the deterioration of interstate trade relations. The relatively low duties assessed in the smaller northern ports gave "unfair advantage" to "lesser men." Protective legislation which sought to put small producers and manufacturers in New York, Pennsylvania, and Massachusetts "on a prosperous footing" was undercut by the difficulty of securing raw materials and goods for export from nearby states. The consequence was that exporters could not compete with their British counterparts for the trade of the southern states, nor could manufacturers resist the onslaught of British imports.[39]

But merchants in the dominant port cities acted no less selfishly than their less well-situated neighbors in promoting their own particular interests. New Yorkers continued a long-term policy of embargoing wheat and flour exports in order to raise their prices above those in Connecticut and New Jersey.[40] Since 1784, New York had extended the double duty on British imports to goods destined for out-of-state customers. In early 1785 the legislature imposed an additional 5 percent tax on all commodities imported from other states for sale to New Yorkers.[41] Not surprisingly, such "Approbrius, indecent" schemes provoked the ire of commentators in neighboring states.[42] But efforts to break New York's control of regional commerce proved unsuccessful; in Connecticut, for instance, ill-fated attempts to attract British carriers to New Haven and New London were condemned by merchants across the state. Merchants in smaller ports throughout the region continued to gather agricultural surpluses from the countryside for transshipment to New York; most return voyages also passed through that port.[43]

"Continentally-minded" nationalists became convinced that jealousies between states with strong ports and states with weak ports, or between northern and southern states, would negate hopes for self-sufficiency both within and among the states. By erecting their own retaliatory barriers to British commerce, the American states simply perpetuated conflicts among themselves and began to resemble the petty, warring kingdoms of Europe. Alexander Hamilton asserted that commerce, under the present, chaotic organization of the union, did not "soften the manners of men" but instead fomented "ruinous contentions." The state governments had created a "system of commercial polity" in which each state sought "to secure exclusive benefits to their own citizens." By blocking the channels in which the national economy would naturally flourish, these regulations were detrimental both to the general interests of all Americans and the particular interests of leading citizens in every state.[44] The "broils among the states," John Jay concluded, seemed destined to infinite permutations; they all "have an aversion to each other."[45] Fisher Ames expressed his exasperation with interstate discriminations in characteristically extravagant but revealing language: "The King of New York levied imposts upon New Jersey and Connecticut, and the nobles of Virginia bore with impatience their tributary dependence upon Baltimore and Philadelphia. Our discontents were fermenting into civil war."[46]

Hamilton cited contests between New York and its weaker neighbors, Connecticut and New Jersey, as conspicuous examples of how interstate rivalries locked them into persistent economic chaos. *"Independent sovereignties consulting a distinct interest"* enacted "interfering and unneighbourly regulations" that threatened the union. Some states had pursued particular advantages to the detriment of others, which "would naturally lead to out-rages." One uniform policy for the region's imports, said Hamilton, would go a long way toward meliorating this conflict.[47]

Commentators in all parts of the country came to similar conclusions. Critics conceded that Massachusetts might have had ample justification for its restraints on British trade but concluded that the encouragement to that trade offered by New Hampshire and Connecticut rendered those restraints nugatory and jeopardized the economic well-being of the entire region.[48] Similarly, leading statesmen in Virginia and Maryland agreed that their long-standing competition for the fruits of western development was detrimental to both states and that regional cooperation was imperative.[49] In North Carolina, Hugh Williamson deplored the high duties which diverted imports through Virginia and South Carolina and encouraged smuggling across state boundaries.[50] And, because of different schedules of import duties, South Carolinians and Georgians could anticipate that commercial conflict would add fuel to their traditional rivalry.[51]

For nationalists, a particularly ominous sign of the states' failures was the sudden increase in smuggling. Smugglers imported goods at prices American consumers found irresistible, despite their growing private indebtedness. As a result, attempts by state legislatures to curtail luxury imports proved unavailing: illegal tea, coffee, cocoa, and spirits continued to flood urban markets.[52] Evading both British and American duties, smugglers conducted a thriving trade between Nova Scotia, Massachusetts, and the West Indies that drove many legitimate merchants out of business. The same smugglers sent American lumber to the islands as a Nova Scotian, not New England, product.[53] Official reports indicated that provisions from the northern states were more likely to enter the British islands illegally than legally.[54] For a decade after the Revolution, North American smugglers received 40 percent more for fish sent unlawfully to the French West Indies than their legitimate counterparts could expect to receive in protected British ports.[55]

Discriminatory duties also promoted smuggling across state borders in the interior. British agents in Virginia and Delaware hired wagoners to carry goods overland to Baltimore, even though that city's port duties were relatively low. New Yorkers noted that their long and tortuous shoreline made it "impossible to prevent smuggling . . . unless such a number of Custom House Officers were employed as might become . . . disgusting and oppressive to the inhabitants."[56] Commercial discrimination also had the effect of discouraging immigration, "the thing most wanted in this country," while fostering "monopolies, the thing to be avoided."[57]

TOWARD PHILADELPHIA

Nationalists were not entirely without hope. By 1786, they noted with satisfaction that the anarchic state of American commerce was driving increasing numbers of their countrymen into their camp.[58] Rufus King was sure that "eminent" citizens across the continent appreciated the seriousness of the depression and would agree that Congress must have sufficient power to regulate the nation's trade.[59] A groundswell of discontent had begun to rise along the seaboard that would splinter economic interests within the states and compel some association along interstate, class, and occupational lines.

Interests not strongly represented in the state legislatures from 1785 to 1787, or disenchanted with policies they had once supported, began to echo nationalist criticisms of interstate rivalries. State governments, they charged, pandered too much to the "agrarian interest," "the paper money interest," and the "petty traders and hucksters" of the interior. Meanwhile, commercial and manufacturing interests in the cities did not get their fair share of posts and perquisites.[60] As a result of such grievances, new nationalist-oriented coalitions of "merchants and traders" or of "merchants and manufacturers" emerged in the major cities. In Philadelphia, one such group warned that "the intercourse of the States [is] liable to be perplexed and injured by various and discordant regulations . . . at the expense of the general welfare." What was required was a "unity of councils, in the great Representative Body of the United States."[61] New York merchants repeated this sentiment: "You cannot perceive, that although the late treaty with Britain has given the name of peace, yet we in fact are called on to wage a *variegated war*" of state against state, states against Congress, and states against other nations.[62] "Pro-Bono Republicae" of Philadelphia believed it was "a very *ridiculous idea*, that every State should enjoy a power of regulating its trade, for every State has a *separate* interest to pursue, and thus different regulations will always clash."[63] A writer in Maryland agreed that if "each state is laying duties on the trade of its neighbours, our commerce cannot be reduced to a system, and our profits must be uncertain."[64]

A great outpouring of newspaper essays and petitions called for an organized national trade policy. In New Haven, Portsmouth, and Newburyport, merchants argued that commercial negotiations with foreign powers could only succeed at the national level.[65] New York City and Boston merchants and tradesmen agitated for an organized response to British regulations: perhaps a new nonconsumption agreement would unite Americans in virtuous self-sacrifice while spurring domestic production.[66] Massachusetts importers and retailers warned Congress that "the exertions of individual cities, or even states, without the support of the whole confederacy, will be inefficacious." "Nothing short of vesting Congress with full powers to regulate the internal as well as the external commerce of all the states, can reach the mischiefs we complain of." At the same time, they added, citizens should be encouraged to refrain from "every idle amusement and expensive foppery" as first steps toward "restor[ing] our virtue."[67] Philadelphia merchants decided that the "jealousy of some of the states" precluded any effective retaliation against Britain while threatening to impoverish American port cities. More regard "to [the] national interest" would "get the better of that jealous spirit."[68]

Since May 1782, nationalists had called on the states to give Congress authority to coordinate commercial policy.[69] Prominent American statesmen such as Jefferson, Madison, Hamilton, John Adams, and Gouverneur Morris had, to varying degrees, abandoned their hopes for open ports and commercial reciprocity with other nations and had watched in dismay as the "disunited states" moved to the brink of disaster. Adams therefore applauded efforts in and out of Congress to establish an authority "competent to the protection of commerce"; otherwise, "our foreign commerce must decline, and eventually be annihilated."[70] Jefferson was convinced that in order to abolish lingering "state jealousies," Americans must "cultivate the idea of our being one nation" and make the "interests of the states . . . joint in every possible instance."[71] In somewhat stronger language, "Harrington'' (Benjamin Rush) argued that the American states would only be able to ''preserve perpetual peace with the nations of Europe'' by the ''terror'' of their collected power.[72]

Yet, despite growing support for a stronger central government, nationalists still had to overcome formidable opposition. Virginian Richard Henry Lee, a future Antifederalist, looked on suspiciously as commercial interests sought more unified control over trade. Echoing classic free trade arguments, Lee insisted that ''the free nature and genius of commerce abhors and shuns restraint, and that in young commercial states, to embarrass trade with heavy imposts or other clogs, is effectually to demolish it.''[73] In addition, proposals for enlarging Congress's commerce powers had generated little enthusiasm when forwarded to the state legislatures in 1784, 1785, and 1786.[74] Too many ''eminent Americans'' continued to cling to their ''local attachments.''[75] Massachusetts representatives feared ''an exertion of the friends of aristocracy'' in Congress.[76] For their part, southerners suspected that the ''northern interest'' wanted to choke off their supply of British manufactures in order to replace them with expensive and shoddy northern substitutes.[77] And Rhode Islanders and North Carolinians were unimpressed with nationalist arguments that the elimination of interstate rivalries would boost trade in secondary commercial centers; they protested against measures they thought would bar them from exporting American goods in British vessels.[78]

Perhaps the greatest obstacle to union, however, was the now well-entrenched popular commitment to economic freedom and the pursuit of private interest. Clearly, nationalists could no longer invoke the language of republican virtue, in its traditional meanings, as they sought to galvanize a viable response to the excesses of state sovereignty. At the same time, however, they could hardly embrace the dissenting legacy of experiments in economic autonomy—whether of individuals within the polity or of the nation in the world. After all, nationalists believed that the unregulated play of interests among thirteen more-or-less sovereign states had brought the union to the brink of disaster more than once since the onset of the Revolution. The central task for nationalist reformers, then, was to convince their opponents that economic freedom was illusory and that interstate jealousies in their myriad forms subverted every state's welfare. Nationalists again argued, as they had with respect to jurisdictional issues, that a stronger central government was the best guarantor of the states' true interests.

But nationalists could not rely on negative arguments alone. To be successful, they had to develop a coherent economic program that responded to the demands of innumerable old and new interest groups. Therefore, even as they emphasized the self-destructive propensities of the sovereign states, reformers promised that a stronger union would promote manufacturing and internal development. If, as Madison suggested, "most of our political evils, may be traced to our commercial ones," it was also true that the alliance of "commercial and manufacturing interests" offered the best prospect for a durable union.[79] From this emerging perspective, international commercial discrimination, interstate rivalries, and disorder on the frontiers represented a complex of interdependent problems that could be addressed effectively only by an "energetic" continental government. Against the many dangerous centrifugal tendencies they cited, reformers posited a true national interest, subsuming and mediating all interests in the union. Nationalists thus linked their political goals to the bold economic visions of the expansionists and projectors, who saw the development of the West and the promotion of interregional and international commerce as the way to ensure the nation's future prosperity and power.

Sales of western lands, made possible only by the creation of a national domain under congressional control, would help defray the revolutionary debt and promote commercialization of the frontier.[80] A national impost of 5 percent, equally levied on all the states, would also enrich congressional coffers that repaid war debts while dissipating tension among jealous states. Banks and other urban institutions would help boost commodities exchange, money transactions, entrepreneurship and invention, charity relief, education, and a host of services. Mandates for uniform quality and transport of agricultural goods, uniform tender laws, and perhaps even a uniform currency would undermine discriminatory interstate laws. Once they were solvent, the states would be able to build roads and canals, thus encouraging sober and industrious settlers to bring commerce and civilization to the frontiers. International commerce would revive in the East as agricultural surpluses streamed in from the West; manufacturers would successfully promote their American productions in the budding local markets along internal waterways.[81]

The pieces of this elaborate economic puzzle emerged in nationalist writings over the 1780s. The projections of western entrepreneurs, global traders, and rising manufacturers began to merge in a vision of coordinated national development. Their advocacy of regional interdependence and the rapid growth of the continental economy guided notions of interest further toward the ideal liberal synthesis of a public good founded on the pursuit of private material success. But it was the nationalist reformers who best articulated the possibilities of combining all interests into a harmonious whole.[82]

The economic dislocations of the mid-1780s were crucial to the realignment and reconception of interests. Although coastal merchants, retailers, and manufacturers despaired of effective regulation or protection by the state governments, the possibility of instituting a strong national regime seemed doubtful at best. As a result, discontented groups began to press for action at the regional level, either as a first step toward national reform or as the best attainable alternative. Representatives from Virginia and Maryland thus met at Mount Vernon in mid-1785 to hammer out their differences. The Mount Vernon commissioners then proposed that delegations from all the states convene at Annapolis in 1786 to consider general commercial concerns. The poorly attended Annapolis meeting in turn prepared the way for the Constitutional Convention at Philadelphia.[83]

Interstate cooperation in the Chesapeake region provided another impetus toward national constitutional reform. By beginning at this level, nationalists could also appeal to enterprising merchants and speculators attracted to regional development. Developers sought to "increase the internal trade" of their states by promoting "the ease and commodious transportation of . . . country produce to and from" exporting cities.[84] Their internal improvement schemes reflected competition between cities and regions for commercial supremacy: entrepreneurs in Alexandria and other Chesapeake ports thus established the Potomac Company in order to develop a navigable pathway into the interior and wrest the western trade away from Philadelphia; Baltimoreans also sought to contest Philadelphia's traditional dominance in the mid-Atlantic export economy by extending their city's trade links to the north and west.[85]

Advocates of regional development were not necessarily nationalists: they naturally were sensitive to the possibility that a strong central government might better secure or promote the interests of *other* regions. Yet if such biases could be avoided, regionalists and nationalists did share important common ground. First, they agreed that the separate state governments could not adequately accommodate the economic interests and ambitions of the American people. The idea of economic development expressed this conclusion in more positive, optimistic terms: with properly constituted governments—on the regional or national level—the American people would reap the greatest possible benefits of "economic freedom." Development would foster common interests in a prosperous, interdependent, and dynamic economy.

Regionalists glimpsed these prospects for economic development on a relatively modest and, perhaps, more realistic scale. The great furor over the navigation of the Mississippi illuminated and exacerbated deep-seated intersectional tensions.[86] On the eve of the Philadelphia Convention, Americans might well ask if there really were, or ever would be, any "natural" bonds of interest between North and South, or between East and West. But the critical contribution of development rhetoric, even when aimed at promoting the interests of one city or region at the expense of others, was an expansive and dynamic conception of the American economy. By appropriating this rhetoric, constitutional reformers could extend the physical boundaries—and imaginative limits—of interest.

5
Union or Disunion?

From 1785 to 1787, proponents of national economic development were joined by merchants and manufacturers throughout the country in disparaging state particularism and calling on Congress to regulate trade. At the same time, however, many Americans were concerned that one section might use a stronger national government to advance its interests at the expense of the other sections. Thus, although leading politicians across the country were united in bemoaning the excesses of the states, their growing awareness of distinctive regional interests threatened to preclude any coordinated response to the looming "crisis."

"The necessities and opposite interests of the constituent states, brook no delay nor doubt," a Philadelphia writer warned in 1785. But Congress seemed incapable of responding to their demands. As a result, southerners, westerners, and northerners would take matters into their own hands and the union would be destroyed.

> Will the southern provinces, when in proper cultivation, wait the finger of Congress to point out markets for them?—Will the back settlers, adventurers and traders wait and languish upon a Spanish negociation, to give them the use of the Mississippi's stream, that washes their plantations? Will the eastern and northern states listen to the restrictions and prohibitions of Congress . . . ?[1]

Congress had to accommodate these distinctive, sometimes opposing sectional interests, if it hoped to preserve its own authority. Nationalists could deplore as artificial the local interests that had flourished under state sponsorship and impeded the development of more inclusive interests. But sectional interests were based on more durable and "natural" economic differences. In theory, this array of interests—if they could be harmonized—would provide the foundation of American prosperity and power. Yet, many Americans began to fear that the Confederation Congress was incapable of serving one set of interests without sacrificing another. The result was a deepening ambivalence about the desirability of a strong national government: intersectional conflict suggested that perhaps the idea of union itself was unnatural.

SEPARATE UNIONS

The movement for national constitutional reform illuminated the problematic relationship between conceptions of the national interest and the growing sense of distinctive sectional interests. When nationalists derided the imbecility of Congress under the Articles, they identified their own private interests with the national interest. But frustration with congressional impotence led some of these nationalists to betray sectional biases. A Boston correspondent thus wondered how long we are "to continue in our present inglorious acquiesence in the shameful resistance that some of the states persist in, against federal and national measures?" He chafed at the "paltry politics, weak jealousy," and "local interests" of the middle states, concluding with a widely reprinted proposal that New England form a "new and stronger union" of its own.[2]

By the time of the Constitutional Convention, the belief that the United States ultimately might divide into three or more separate confederacies was widespread. The conventional projection was that the northern, middle, and southern states would form separate unions; some saw the new states to the west constituting yet another union. In 1781, Alexander Hamilton predicted such a division in his *Continentalist* series: the "vanity and self importance" of "some of the larger states" might lead them "to place themselves at the head of particular confederacies independent of the general one."[3] Many British writers were convinced that the union would collapse after the war, including Richard Champion, who anticipated that "three great Republicks" eventually would emerge.[4]

Postwar developments made such predictions seem increasingly plausible. Beginning in 1784, sectional divisions became more apparent in congressional debates over commercial policy, leading many commentators to conclude that intersectional differences were intractable. Richard Henry Lee warned that congressional power over commerce would enable northern interests to create "a most pernicious and destructive Monopoly" that "would be dangerous in the extreme to the 5 Southern or Staple States."[5] As if to justify such concerns, northerner Rufus King boasted that the "eight northern states" would act in concert to promote their common interests.[6] By late 1786, with northerners and southerners bitterly divided over John Jay's proposal to cede American navigation rights in the Mississippi, talk about disunion was pervasive. Writing from New York, Congressman James Monroe told his Virginia correspondents that northerners wanted "to break up the settlements on the western waters" and "have even sought a dismemberm[en]t to the Potowmack."[7] Many southerners blamed northern commercial interests for Jay's ill-fated treaty and became convinced that their states would be better off on their own.[8]

Failing in their efforts to institute a national commercial policy—and to ratify Jay's treaty—northerners also became disgusted with Congress. As a result, proposals to break up the union attracted considerable interest, even among "respectable" folk who had formerly sought to strengthen congressional authority. As they grew increasingly despondent about the prospects of ever being able to establish a more energetic central government, these erstwhile nationalists may have seen more perfect regional unions as the only alternative. Pennsylvanian Benjamin Rush, a prominent nationalist, thus wrote Richard Price in England that "some of our enlightened men" had begun to "despair of a more complete union of the States in Congress" and were proposing to divide the union in three: "These confederacies they say will be united by nature, by interest, and by manners, and consequently they will be safe, agreeable and durable."[9] Clearly Rush thought these "enlightened men" were not misled by narrow conceptions of local interest. It was precisely because they could take a broad view, considering "nature" and "manners" as well as "interests," that Rush's friends concluded that the United States comprised three incipient nationalities. In the event of disunion, the New Yorker "Lycurgus" wrote, "the religion, manners, customs, exports, imports and general interest" of each section would be "the same"; this "unanimity would render us secure at home, and respected abroad, and promote agriculture, manufactures, and commerce."[10]

Why should respectable nationalists flirt with disunionism? Some may have considered implementation of a coherent commercial policy on the regional level preferable to continuing inaction by Congress. Others may have believed that strong regional unions could restrain the "democratic despotism" of the states.[11] Efforts to draft new state constitutions that could secure property and guarantee order had either been stymied or had achieved only partial success. In Pennsylvania, republican opponents of the state constitution hoped a new national constitution would, as Rush later put it, "overset our state dung cart."[12] But there was no necessary connection between restraining the excesses of the states and creating a strong national union. When Rush wrote Price, the chances of revising the Articles looked slim, making the institution of new governments on the regional level correspondingly attractive.

Not surprisingly, many of the separate confederacy proposals circulating on the eve of the Convention sought to subordinate the states to more powerful unions. Although "Lycurgus" believed the states could preserve "the same sovereignty and internal jurisdiction" they now enjoyed, most disunionists recognized the need to curb state particularism. A Boston writer linked disunion with a regional redefinition of federal-state relations that he hoped would ultimately lead to national constitutional reform. He thought it high time "to form a new and stronger union," but the work would be best begun by instituting "a new Congress, as the Representative of the nation of New-England," leaving the other states "to pursue their own imbecile and disjointed ways" until they learned "experimentally" the value of supporting a properly constituted union.[13] "Reason," writing in New York, had even less patience with the states: state sovereignty was the fundamental defect of American politics. Because "there can only be one sovereignty in a government," he wrote, the "notion . . . of a government by confederation between several independent States, and each retaining its sovereignty, must be abandoned, and with it every attempt to amend the present Articles of

Confederation." But separate regional confederations, he suggested, violated political logic as much as the existing Confederation and would fall prey to the same centrifugal tendencies. The solution was to "distribute the States into three republics," thereby simultaneously dissolving the union and amalgamating the separate states.[14]

Southerners also looked to regional unions for protection against untrammeled state power. "The doctrine of three Confederacies, or great Republics, has it's advocates here," Madison learned from a Virginia correspondent in August 1787. At least one prominent Virginian who embraced this doctrine had called for the "extinction of State legislatures" within each new union.[15] Madison himself favored neither the abolition of the states nor the break-up of the union, but given his low esteem for the Henryite majority in the Virginia assembly, he would not find it surprising that some "enlightened men" thought new regional unions would solve their problems.[16]

There was considerable ambiguity about what to call these proposed regional governments. The use of the word "republic," in apposition to or in lieu of "confederation," strongly suggests that disunionists generally did not contemplate creating regional replicas of the existing union. No one would have claimed that the national government under the Articles was "republican," and this defect had always given the states' defiance of Congress an aura of legitimacy. But designating the sectional confederations "republics" would clearly establish their primacy over the states they included, a usage that anticipated the Federalists' bold application of "popular sovereignty" to legitimize the radical reallocation of power between the states and the national government.[17]

EXTENDING THE REPUBLIC

On the eve of the Philadelphia Convention, many Americans—including future Federalists as well as Antifederalists—shared misgivings about the size of the American union. According to the conventional wisdom, a large state could only be preserved by despotic authority. Suspicious republicans thus detected monarchical tendencies in efforts to reinvigorate Congress and thereby transform the union into a consolidated state. Anxieties about incipient despotism were fueled by rumors that many prominent Americans favored the reestablishment of monarchical government.[18]

The monarchical revival grew out of the same frustration and desperation that led so many Americans to anticipate the break-up of the union. Exasperated by repeated failures to enlarge Congress's powers, "many, very many wish to see an emperor at the head of our nation."[19] Without an effective national government, the union would fall apart and the new nation would soon be at the mercy of foreign predators. George Washington thought there had to be "lodged somewhere a power which will pervade the whole union in as energetic manner, as the Authority of the State Governments extend over the several States." Recognizing that the union itself had to become a "state," Americans asked themselves what kind of government would be most appropriate. Some concluded that monarchy alone could sustain "energetic" government across the continent. Some "respectable characters," reported Washington, "speak of a monarchical form . . . without horror."[20]

Historians have paid too little attention to the spread of monarchist sentiment or to proposals for the division of the union that circulated before the delegates convened in Philadelphia. By then many Americans had become convinced of the "imbecility" of the existing union as well as of the inadequacies of the states; some, in turn, saw the creation of a continental monarchy or a division of the union as the only plausible alternatives. The convention had to create "an efficient federal government," David Ramsay wrote Jefferson in April 1787, or "I fear that the end of the matter will be an American monarch or three or more confederacies."[21] If forced to choose between those alternatives, many "respectable characters" would agree with an anonymous "gentleman in Virginia" who "reprobate[d] the idea of a division of the States": "My opinion is, that America would be happier under the government of France, or the present Empress of Russia, than be divided according to that malevolent suggestion."[22] But Madison thought the "bulk of the people" would resist monarchy: they "will probably prefer the lesser evil of a partition of the Union into three more practicable and energetic governments."[23]

Monarchists could argue that the best form of government for the union was an open question but that if there was a latent form in the existing system—although this might be doubted—it was probably monarchical. Congress had exercised many of the British king's prerogatives, most notably over war and peace.[24] Furthermore, an American monarchy would be constitutionally limited and thus compatible with the preservation of republican government in the states. Monarchists suggested that what was best for the states might not be best for the continent as a whole. Even good republicans like James Wilson had to concede that the "extent" of the United States "*seems* to require the vigour of Monarchy."[25] Hamilton simply did not think "a Republican Govt. could be established over so great an extent." "The British Govt. was the best in the world," he told the delegates at Philadelphia, and he "doubted much whether any thing short of it would do in America."[26]

But most nationalists knew that monarchical schemes could not gain the broad popular approval so essential to the legitimacy of any new regime in America. The challenge was to create more energetic governments without abandoning republican forms. Perhaps this could only be done on the regional level: separate unions might avoid the dangers of large size—the tendency of large states to succumb to despotism—while curbing the democratic excesses characteristic of small states. At the same time, these unions would accommodate fundamental differences of sectional interest. Nationalist reformers might not doubt that there was a true national interest, but they were increasingly doubtful that other Americans could recognize it. They feared that a union that attempted to embrace such self-consciously hostile interests was doomed to factional paralysis. Regional unions would at least facilitate a harmony of interests over fairly extended spheres, while precluding the debilitating conflicts of interest that fostered anarchy and shattered the unity of small republics.

The brief flirtation of some frustrated reformers with the idea of separate unions can be seen as a crucial step toward conceptualizing the extended republic. Disunionists did not directly challenge the conventional idea that there were limits to the size of republics. "Reason" thus acknowledged the "difficulty" of representing and reconciling "the national concerns of a people so numerous, with a territory so extensive," concluding that the executive arm would have to be strengthened to an extent incompatible "with the principles of a democratic form."[27] "All political writers of eminence agree," wrote "Lycurgus"—as did many Antifederalists after him—"that a republic should not comprehend a large territory."[28] In the *Spirit of the Laws,* Montesquieu asserted that the survival of a republic depended on an active, virtuous citizenry, leading American readers such as "Lycurgus" to infer that their states were already much too large. But disunionists waived Montesquieu's authority when they invoked the new language of interest. The boundaries of the American republics, they insisted, should reflect the natural limits of distinct regional economies. The states were thus too small, not too large: state governments obstructed the formulation and implementation of policy on behalf of the larger, regional interest.

Although they were not yet prepared to dispute the long-standing precept that a "state" as large as the union could only be governed despotically, some commentators did suggest that the "more practicable and energetic" regional unions could still be republics. Meanwhile, they warned that the tendency of individual states to claim sovereign powers jeopardized their republican character.[29] The preservation of republican government depended on instituting a more effective union that could guarantee peace among the states and protect them from foreign powers. Reformers usually had the British model in mind when they advocated more energetic central administration, but they knew that most of the people had no stomach for another king. The result of this impasse—the apparently hopeless task of striking the delicate and precarious balance between monarchical and republican principles and reconciling energy and liberty on a continental scale—was to make separate unions seem a tenable option.

Disunion proposals thus prepared the way for the Federalists' reconceptualization of the American union. The first task in this project was to sever republican government from its exclusive association with the states. Perhaps, disunionists suggested, new regional unions would better support republican government; perhaps, Federalists later argued, republican government could be extended over the entire continent. Equally crucial in this conceptual transformation was the notion that shared economic interests constituted the most durable bonds of union in the proposed regional republics. Disunion proposals acknowledged the limits of distinct, presumably hostile sectional interests. But the language of interest could also be deployed on behalf of continental union. The challenge for nationalists was to demonstrate the interdependency of sectional interests while defining an inclusive, transcendent national interest.

RECONCEPTUALIZING THE UNION

Many Americans remained satisfied with their state governments during the so-called critical period. Warnings about the dangers of disunion seemed most compelling to the already converted, including those who had begun to consider proposals for creating regional confederations—the most obvious and immediate threat to union. If such "respectable," reform-minded Americans were now convinced of the primacy of sectional interests, how could efforts to create a strong national government possibly command broad popular support?

Nationalist reformers were accustomed to the obstructionist tactics of the sovereign states, but the rise of intersectional tensions presented them with new political and conceptual dilemmas. With many of their old allies rallying behind sectionalist banners or at least wavering in their loyalties, reformers could no longer sustain their long-standing assumption that misguided state policies represented the only significant obstacles to defining and promoting the national interest. As a result, the reformers' criticisms of the states' sovereign pretensions rang increasingly hollow: if, in fact, conflicts of interest among Americans were natural and not merely the by-product of interstate jealousies, any proposal to shift power away from the states had to be treated with skepticism and caution.

But sectional controversy ultimately served the reformers' cause. First, it made some dramatic transformation of American politics seem likely: if changes were in any case inevitable, reformers could more easily portray themselves as republican constitutionalists who sought to prevent, rather than promote, dangerous "innovations." Second, sectional tensions enabled reformers to overcome their obsession with state sovereignty and even to project a positive role for the states in a new national constitution: sectionalism helped nationalists see the virtues of federalism. But perhaps most important, by raising questions about the very existence of national interests, sectionalism forced reformers to articulate a new, inclusive conception of interest that could justify a continuing national union.

Nationalists drew on an emerging discourse of economic expansion and development in articulating a broadly appealing vision of America's future. Development-minded writers were not necessarily nationalists: some supported state-sponsored programs for stimulating growth; others advocated interstate cooperation on a regional level. But the premises of their arguments—that governments played a crucial role in advancing enterprise and that interdependent local or regional interests would all benefit from development—seemed equally applicable to the national economy. The great achievement of the new nationalist political economy was to combine the traditional idea that similarly situated groups across the nation shared common interests with the developers' belief in the interdependency of distinct, apparently opposed groups. That international traders in all the states would benefit from national commercial regulation was obvious enough, but a conceptual breakthrough was necessary before Americans could believe that a nationally directed political economy would also serve the interests of manufacturers, inland traders, and farmers great and small.

This reconceptualization was facilitated by a shift in focus from consumption to production in accounts of the nation's economic prospects. The new emphasis on production suggested that the pursuit of interest was no longer merely the appropriation of natural resources for private use or the circulation of existing wealth. Enterprising producers created new values in which the larger community ultimately shared. Wealth was both the just reward of productive enterprise and, functioning as capital, the means of creating more wealth. Advocates of the new gospel insisted that the American economy would quickly rebound if commerce and manufacturing were properly encouraged. Economic growth was essential to the progress of civilization. As Philadelphian William Barton wrote in 1786, "A CIVILIZED nation, without commerce is a solecism in politics."[30] Such logic anticipated the utilitarian calculus: commercial prosperity produced a "happy people," capable of satisfying "civilized wants."[31] With commerce defined in this way it was easier to conceive of a productive domestic economy of imperial proportions.

Proponents of commercial development recognized that their view of wealth and interest defied conventional republican wisdom, and they responded to misgivings about selfishness and luxury by attacking the fundamental premises of orthodox thinking. Virtue, defined as the negation of self-interest in behalf of the public good, may have been essential to the survival of primitive agricultural communities before the dawning age of reason and commerce. But, Barton explained, "the wants, fears, nay the very nature of man, necessarily constitute him a social animal." The development of commerce was an expression of this social nature. Political economists such as Barton therefore proposed to substitute a scheme of progressive historical development for the traditional republican cycles of growth and decay. Thus, while republican theorists privileged past over present by idealizing a golden age when material conditions best supported a virtuous— and static—citizenry, the new economists looked forward to an increasingly bountiful future premised on the pursuit of private interests.

Development-minded writers of the 1780s began their historical accounts with a dark age of natural barbarism, not the golden age favored by republican theorists. Although the earliest men were unrestrained by society, they did not enjoy true liberty. Lacking objects toward which to direct and develop their will, "savages" were left enslaved by their animal natures. "Industry results from our wants," "Spectator" wrote in the *New-Haven Gazette:* "The savages will inform us that their indolence and poverty are the result of their having no other wants but the want of taste and a knowledge of the comforts and conveniences of civil society." But in a higher stage, "taste, refinement & extravagance" produced the "many elegant improvements" which made civilized Americans "so happy" and "so wealthy" and "distinguish[ed] us from savages."[32] "We must be a . . . luxurious people," agreed David Daggett. Americans could only fulfill their natural destiny "by acting in that character in which the God of nature had placed us" and "divesting ourselves of our contracted ideas in politics."[33]

Luxury or elegance were the attributes of a civilized society, the palpable evidence of a progressive movement toward a higher stage of historical development. Writers such as William Vans Murray proceeded to argue that civil liberty was also the product of civilized, commercial society, not the legacy of a more virtuous, bygone age: the real meaning of liberty only became clear with the rise of commercial civilization. "The rights and characteristics, which develope with cultivation," reasoned Murray, could be "enjoyed in that state only of social maturity, from which a sense of them springs." It was a "romantic . . . fiction" to believe that "virtue" was "incompatible with a state of luxurious society." "Luxury, in a correspondent stage of his improvement" was as "natural" to civilized man, Murray concluded, "as that rudeness or simplicity, supposed concomitant with virtue, from which he emerges."[34] The economists' idea of historical progress made luxury safe for republican society by linking it with modern conceptions of liberty and contrasting it to the indolence and sloth that supposedly characterized primitive societies. Instead, taste and refinement spurred industry and improvement: a society of civilized consumers was necessarily a society of industrious producers.

The economists' radical assault on traditional republican values was greeted with considerable skepticism in some quarters. But arguments for private enterprise and accelerated economic development were compelling to many easterners concerned with organizing and exploiting the new nation's vast western hinterland. Prospects of western development in turn helped make the idea of a transcendent national interest more plausible. As long as proponents of constitutional change under the Articles focused on the needs of international traders, a broadly appealing definition of the national interest would remain elusive. But by looking westward and appropriating the rhetoric of development, nationalists could develop a more inclusive vision of a dynamic, interdependent economy. Given full scope, the American "spirit of enterprise" would enrich the entire continent, not just merchants and staple producers in coastal regions.

The emphasis on economic development pointed toward a new conception of the extended republic. An advocate of Potomac River improvements asserted that the new nation was "accommodated by nature in a most extraordinary manner for an easy, general and intimate communication."[35] Americans would be drawn into a closer, more "natural" union as they exploited the "internal riches" of "an immensely rich and extensive continent."[36] "No country under the sun" was "better calculated for commerce."[37] "The empire of the United States," "Lycurgus" explained, was situated in the "most fertile and flourishing region" of the continent, affording "a prospect of wealth and commerce which future ages alone can realize."[38] Enterprising settlers from all parts of the union would move into the inland empire where "the invigorating breath of industry" would "animate . . . all the regenerating powers of nature."[39] The great wealth thus produced would flow back through long-settled regions, promoting both domestic commerce and manufactures and a favorable balance of trade abroad.[40]

Western development promised to mitigate intersectional tensions by promoting the prosperity of the entire union. But commercial expansion would also jeopardize the dominant position of the landed interest and the generally equal distribution of wealth so cherished by republican theorists. According to the traditional view, a free, virtuous citizenry had to enjoy the kind of economic independence that was best secured by landed property. One solution was to deny that the rise of new forms of wealth and the resulting disparities in property holding would have any deleterious consequences "in a genuine republic." "Americanus," for instance, simply rejected the conventional, Harringtonian link between economic and political power. "All good men in private stations, are on an equality, whatever may be the disparity in their fortunes."[41] Constitutional developments in revolutionary America gave such arguments a certain plausibility: the gradual erosion of property tests for voting and office holding promised to extricate private and public realms from their corrupting embrace. Noah Webster took the argument a further, crucial step, suggesting that the nature of property in a free society precluded the oppression of the propertyless. He conceded that unequal landholding in a regime where titles were secured to specific families or classes was incompatible with republicanism. But this was not true of "the very great inequality of property" created by commerce; because this "inequality is *revolving from person to person* and entitles the possessor to no pre-eminence in legislation, it is not dangerous to the liberties of the rest of the state."[42]

The tendency to dissociate political participation and property holding made traditional warnings about the dangers of inequality seem less compelling to revolutionary Americans. Under competitive market conditions and without the artificial support of government power, the pursuit of private interest by individuals or groups would be either rational, and therefore beneficial to the larger community, or self-defeating. Further, as long as there were no obstacles to the free circulation of wealth throughout the community, there would be no fixed, politically dangerous classes of property holders. Finally, the economists argued, the social utility of property freely and productively deployed rendered obsolete the historic anxieties about the self-perpetuating power of the propertied classes.

The vision of a dynamic, interdependent continental economy stood in counterpoint to the parochial suspicions and jealousies engendered by postwar political and economic developments. Proponents of integrated development challenged the widespread perception that the interests of different classes and sections were inevitably opposed, a view that the political struggles of the period amply validated. Merchants in the New York Chamber of Commerce thus rejected the usual narrow appeal to class interest when they proclaimed in 1785 that the "landholder and merchant" had been "seduced into a false idea that their real interests are different."[43] Self-serving as such rhetoric may have been in a period of rising tensions among interest groups, states, and sections, it did suggest a new conception of an all-embracing national interest. The old dichotomy between merchants and the landed interest was beginning to give way to an awareness that an array of domestic producers in myriad economic pursuits contributed to the well-being of the community.

Advocates of national economic development depicted the vast, anticipated expansion of productive activity and wealth as a grand cooperative enterprise. A committee of Boston manufacturers and traders drew out the political implications of this vision: "The States are so extensive in their boundary, various in their climate, and so connected in their national interest, that if a plan could be adopted throughout the confederation for the exchange of the produce and manufactures of each state, we conceive it would serve to cement a general union, and prove a means to promote the interest of the whole."[44] In their view, the union was a continental marketplace, a natural regime of exchange which should not be obstructed by artificial state distinctions. Defects in the organization of national politics and an exaggerated solicitude for state sovereignty thwarted both private interests and the public good. To the extent that states pursued their own interests and thus directed their citizens toward competition and conflict with their counterparts in neighboring states, "the dissolution of all continental connections" was sure to follow. The states, Noah Webster explained, inevitably sought "to enlarge their own bounds, and augment their wealth and respectability at each other's expence." The result was the "jealousy, ill-will and reproaches" characteristic of competing consumers, not the laudable ambition for both private and public wealth and glory that the natural bounties of the continent should have called forth.[45]

Visionary political economists suggested that there was a gap between America's extensive natural endowments and the disappointing performance of the economy under the present political dispensation. One day, a New Jersey writer predicted, Americans would look back "with astonishment at the trivial causes which have impeded their progress."[46] A Marylander added, "No country perhaps abounds with raw materials of every kind, proper for manufactures, more than America; but from various causes, her inhabitants have hitherto neglected to improve the bounties of a benign Providence."[47] According to "Observator," the absence of a coherent national economic policy fractured a natural harmony of interests and prevented the systematic exploitation of nature. The consequence of failing to pursue a "consistent plan" was that "our public, political interests, and with them individual interests (for they will stand or fall together) cannot be promoted, but must be neglected, and in the end inevitably ruined."[48]

Significantly, writers such as "Observator" aligned "nature" with the interests of individuals and of the American people generally against artificial state distinctions. Interest was natural, and those who followed its lead were true patriots. "In a people so enlightened as ours," explained "Cato," "advantages should seem to call forcibly for improvement, and to inspire a generous ambition." Unfortunately, America's natural advantages remained "unoperative, since we refuse to enjoy or direct them to their true and capital purposes." Americans were too influenced by "partial and incomplete notions of civil and political liberty" and thus were unwilling to accord "necessary powers to the national government."[49] In order to sustain the union, a New Yorker wrote on the eve of the Annapolis Convention, the delegates would have to lay "aside all local attachments, and every private sinister view. . . . The natural produce and situation of each state is such that if they can bring them, as it were, to one focus, where they may unite and act together, it must give great energy to the commerce of these states."[50]

Those who favored national constitutional reform counterposed this vision of the continent's natural destiny to the artificial interests of state governments struggling for relative advantage. In Humean fashion, nationalists suggested that private interests were ultimately harmonious. As Tench Coxe put it, "Agriculture appears to be the spring of our commerce and the parent of our manufactures." The circulation of goods created new wealth for enterprising individuals who exploited commercial opportunities at home and abroad. Because these economic pursuits were interrelated, advances in one sector would promote the fortunes of others. The growth of manufactures, for example, "will improve our agriculture . . . accelerate the improvement of our internal navigation, and bring into action the dormant powers of nature and the elements."[51] The pursuit of profit dissolved conventional distinctions among interest groups. In America the crucial distinction was instead between the world of the marketplace—where interests converged—and the savage, barbarian world beyond.

Traditional strictures on the pursuit of private interest gave way in this rhetoric to a more benign view of the social value of self-interested enterprise. The greatest obstacle to the new nation's future prosperity and power was the present imbecilic organization of the union, not private selfishness. Conflicts over commerce and territory among the states could lead to the brutal anarchy of a "state of nature" in the New World. Rather than man mastering nature, according to the economists' visionary projections, nature would master man—surely a reversal of the natural order of things. Enterprise meant industrious activity directed toward *future* rewards. Looking west, then, Americans could conceive of forward progress in time as well as space. Economic development in turn provided the key to both expansion and consolidation: a growing union would be drawn closer together through the quickening pace of market exchange and the spread of internal improvements. Yet everything hinged on strengthening the union, *"the basis of our grandeur and power."*[52]

ENLIGHTENED SELF-INTEREST

The challenge for constitutional reformers was to persuade Americans that the success of their individual and collective enterprises depended on reconstituting the union. Only under a strong national government would "the honest citizen be relieved and protected; industry . . . be encouraged and commerce . . . flourish."[53] The weakness of the Confederation thwarted private interests while subverting the natural harmony and union of the American people. "Because we are not under any form of energetic compact," a Boston writer complained in April 1787, "we are no longer United States." "We live it is true under the appearance of friendship, but we secretly hate and envy, and endeavour to thwart the interest of each other." The nation had been reduced to the tattered remnants of a defensive league, held together more by "a principle of fear" than by a common commitment to republican liberty or a clear perception of common interests. Were "it not for the British colonies and garrisons that surround us," this writer concluded, "we should probably very soon contend in the field for empire."[54]

Reformers advanced the paradoxical argument that a weak union had been sufficient during wartime but woefully inadequate since the peace. The "positive injunction of the law" was not necessary during the war, because the "interests" and "passions" of the people were easily mobilized "in the pursuit of an important object." But the *"acquisition"* and *"preservation"* of American independence were two different things.[55] "Such was the fervour of liberty and such the ready obedience of the people to slight recommendations," a New York essayist told the "Political Freethinkers of America," that Congress had "formed a set of *faint rules* [the Articles of Confederation] which seemed rather to anticipate than to cement a federal combination." In the postwar period, however, as "America sat down in peace among the governors of the earth," the debilities of the union became increasingly obvious.[56] As Thomas Pownall, the former royal governor of Massachusetts, told his American friends in 1783, the American "Sovereign must now come forward amongst the Nations, as an active existing Agent."[57] Otherwise, the great gains of the Revolution would soon be forfeited as the new nation collapsed into disunion, anarchy, and counterrevolution.

Reformers emphasized the discrepancy between a general, popular commitment to national unity and political structures that effectively subverted it. They contrasted the naturalness of a more perfect union with the artificial state interests that now made the formulation and execution of national policy virtually impossible. The states could not satisfy the demands of numerous interest groups clamoring for protection and support. More ominously, incompatible state policies threatened to distort and disrupt the national economy. In short, the nation was not truly represented under the present political arrangements. The Confederation instead presented the "novel" spectacle of a "numerous and encreasing people, and a boundless territory governed by a *committee of ways and means.*"[58]

Nationalist writers suggested that state particularism thwarted the real interests of individual Americans. The pursuit of private interest should serve the national interest, wrote "Lycurgus"—provided "the sentiments of mind bear some proportion to the objects surrounding it." True patriots, he suggested, were both visionary and practical enough to exploit nature's gifts: "The works of nature are certainly much superior in this country to those in any other that has yet been discovered."[59] "Cato" also emphasized the importance of developing the continent's natural advantages for "national happiness and respectability." Unfortunately, too many Americans believed that "our deliverance from Britain" was a sufficient guarantee of the nation's welfare. Their mistake, "Cato" explained, was to set private interest against the public good, thus rendering "liberty" a principle of mutual suspicion rather than collective enterprise. But "private happiness" and the "glory and security" of society were reciprocal.[60] Misguided republicans who preached austerity and self-denial rejected nature's gifts and undermined the foundations of social union. This false opposition of liberty and union obstructed every effort to resuscitate the feeble Congress, dividing and impoverishing the states and jeopardizing their independence.

Reformers sought to discredit the "partial and incomplete" notions of republican liberty that would betray the new nation's dazzling promise. Always assuming the worst about one another and therefore unable to formulate operative national policies, Americans so far had squandered their natural advantages. Only with the institution of an effective national government, "Observator'' concluded, would it be possible to unite the states in ''one consistent plan of measures'' and so ''unite all the streams of water on the continent, and confine them in one channel.''[61] ''Motives of self-interest'' and ''patriotism'' thus converged, another writer agreed, in the campaign for national constitutional reform. A more powerful Congress alone could regulate trade in the national interest and thus ''counteract those illiberal and impolitic systems, whose influence, like that of a malignant comet, has operated so banefully throughout the states.''[62]

In making an appeal to enlightened self-interest the nationalist reformers performed several important functions. First, they suggested that there was a positive, substantial national interest shared by all Americans, not just the small class of merchants, military men, and developers who had taken such a prominent role in earlier efforts to strengthen the central government. The prospective interests of myriad citizens clearly transcended state boundaries, thus enabling nationalist reformers to portray state sovereignty as an artificial barrier to popular enterprise. They called on the patriotism and enlightened self-interest of the American people to resist the dangerous impulses of state particularism and sectionalism. The promise of boundless prosperity could only be fulfilled if a viable national government was instituted.

But visionary rhetoric alone would not create a stronger union. The nationalists' idea of a dynamic, interdependent continental economy stood opposed to the realities of conflicting interests within and among the states. The state governments had won significant support from key interest groups and would resist any assaults on their authority. Meanwhile, the potential role of a reconstituted central government in fostering economic growth was at best speculative. In any case, not all Americans agreed that there *was* a transcendent national interest: ''respectable'' characters across the country were giving serious thought to proposals for creating regional unions that would conform with ''natural'' divisions of interest. To simply assert that interests would be harmonious did not offer any solid assurance that a strong national government would not favor specific groups or sections of the country. And even if Americans were bound by common interests and the political union was in some sense natural, how could republican government be sustained over such a vast territory?

6
Constitutional Convention

Even before the Articles of Confederation were ratified, nationalists such as Alexander Hamilton and James Duane called for a more "solid coercive union."[1] Congress named committees immediately upon ratification in 1781 to strengthen the Articles, especially with respect to requisitions and outstanding debts.[2] In the states, nationalists called on the assemblies to approve plans for "a general convention of all the states" to secure such revisions; some made no secret of their wish to reconstitute the union entirely.[3] By 1787 there was considerable sentiment for increasing congressional power over revenue and commerce. Most merchants and small traders—even in Rhode Island, which was not represented at the Philadelphia Convention—supported the establishment of a much stronger central government. The outbreak of Shays's Rebellion and other agrarian disturbances added urgency to these reform efforts. Skeptical observers predicted that republican government would not survive in the states if the union were not strengthened.[4]

Reformers had moved far beyond the goals of the delegates who met at Annapolis in 1786 to promote a "uniform system in their commercial intercourse and regulations."[5] A more substantial task awaited the framers at Philadelphia: the creation of a new constitutional order that could serve the interests and secure the rights of an enterprising, republican people. The history of the Convention is familiar and will not be recounted in detail here.[6] Our intention instead is to show how the *nationalists* who met at Philadelphia became *federalists* as they sought to translate their vision of national power and prosperity into a politically acceptable constitutional design.

At the very outset, debate over representation revealed deep divisions among nationalists over the role of the states in the new regime. The Convention nearly broke up because of the impasse between large-state advocates of proportional representation and small-state delegates who wanted to preserve the equality of state voting guaranteed by the Articles. For doctrinaire nationalists, the eventual capitulation to the small states in the Connecticut Compromise of July 16 was a serious setback: the state governments, the chief source of the nation's troubles, would control the upper house of the new congress. But most of the framers came to recognize the legitimacy of state claims to constitutional protection—and the undesirability of giving the central government unlimited power. Debate over the organization of the new government thus made the delegates aware of the clashing political interests of the states and therefore increasingly willing to incorporate genuinely federal elements in their design.[7]

This turn toward federalism enabled delegates to deal with the conflicting sectional interests that had, before the Convention met, convinced many skeptics that disunion was inevitable. By mitigating sectionalist impulses, concern with states' rights helped secure national union. On one hand, the debate over representation led delegates from different parts of the country to combine forces, thus retarding the formation of potentially hostile regional blocs. At the same time, delegates came to see that the federal features of the emerging Constitution provided a crucial line of defense against the potential abuse of national power at the expense of specific sectional interests. Most importantly, the compromise on representation that created a "partly federal, and partly national" regime committed the delegates to work towards preserving and strengthening the union.[8] Given this commitment, they could frankly discuss and, to a remarkable extent, accommodate distinctive sectional interests.

The founders' conceptualization of the national economy was shaped by these political exigencies. Discussions on the prospective regulation of commerce by a central authority revealed broadly divergent and apparently contradictory conceptions of local and regional interest. But once the delegates had agreed on the fundamentally important question of how the new government would be organized—and who therefore would have a voice in setting the course of national policy—they could effectively negotiate the precise limits of national power. The result was to circumscribe congressional authority where, as in the case of export duties, it was most likely to have a conspicuously unequal impact on regional economies. Such guarantees, like those securing states' rights, served an important function in making the Constitution acceptable to diverse interests across the continent.

The framers were considerably less clear about how the new national government would deploy its regulatory and revenue powers to foster economic growth. How could they, for instance, determine Congress's role in promoting the internal improvements that seemed so essential to developing the West? Such issues would be left for future resolution. But the vagueness and ambiguity that later generations would find so frustrating were crucial to the Federalist appeal in the ratification debates of 1787–88. Reassured by the new regime's federal structure as well as by specific guarantees of vital local interests, voters could happily imagine any number of alternative versions of future prosperity and intersectional harmony.

EQUAL REPRESENTATION

Small-state support for a strong national government was obscured by the representation controversy. Because proponents of the Virginia Plan considered proportional representation the foundation of a true national regime, advocacy of equal state voting seemed tantamount to full-blown state particularism, leading inevitably toward disunion. But the small-state bloc never disputed the premise that their survival depended on a closer union: Delaware's George Read agreed "that it was [the small states'] interest that we should become one people as much as possible."[9] However, there could be no "union" if the states composing it were dissolved into a transcendent national community. Small-state delegates therefore balked at the consolidationist conclusion that a "Union of the States is a union of the men composing them."[10] They wanted to strengthen the central government without jeopardizing the existing federal compact.

When representation was at issue, small-state delegates became eloquent defenders of the federal compact under the Articles. "An equality of voices" in one of the branches "was conformable to the federal principle," Oliver Ellsworth asserted, "and was necessary to secure the Small States ag[ain]st the large."[11] "Every sovereign state . . . must have an equal vote," proclaimed William Paterson of New Jersey, "or there is an end to liberty."[12] Under a system of proportional representation, Delaware's Gunning Bedford warned, the large states would "crush" the small; Paterson predicted that New Jersey would be "swallowed up," and he, for one, would "rather submit to a monarch, to a despot, than to such a fate."[13] Luther Martin reminded the delegates that independence had left the colonies in a "state of nature" and that they had "entered into the confederation on the footing of equality." He "could never accede to a plan that would introduce an inequality and lay 10 States at the mercy of V[irginia]a Mass[achuset]ts and Penn[sylvani]a."[14] Nor, presumably, would the Delaware delegates, who were bound by legislative instructions obliging them to "retire from the convention" if the equality principle was abandoned.[15]

Despite these threats, however, small-state delegates promoted a limited conception of state sovereignty. Paterson's formula was narrow to the point of circularity: "A confederacy supposes sovereignty in the members composing it," he explained, "& sovereignty supposes equality."[16] The states therefore retained their sovereignty as long as they had an equal vote, regardless of how much the power of the federal government was expanded. Charles Pinckney of South Carolina was not far off the mark when he disgustedly concluded that, given an "equal vote," New Jersey "will dismiss her scruples, and concur in the Nati[ona]l system."[17]

Small-state nationalists sought to preserve equal representation to secure prescribed, defensive ends. Roger Sherman suggested that proportional representation threatened the rights of all the states: each "would remain possessed of certain individual rights" and therefore "ought to be able to protect itself."[18] He later explained that "the equality of votes" was *not* primarily a means to secure small-state interests but rather a crucial guarantee of the federal principle. "The State Gov[ernmen]ts . . . could not be preserved unless they were represented & had a negative in the Gen[era]l Government."[19] Equal representation would enable the state governments to ensure their own existence and, in turn, protect their constituents from unequal treatment.

Madison and his large-state allies insisted that the states had no legitimate role in the proposed "Gen[era]l Gov[ernmen]t" because it would "operate on the people individually."[20] Proportional representation, they claimed, was the only safeguard against the inequalities the small states feared. But the clear message of the convention debates was that opposing plans for organizing the national legislature would affect different interest groups and groups of states unequally. Ironically, Madison could discount the importance of disparities in state size only by raising the specter of sectional conflict: here, he claimed, was "the real difference of interests."[21] Federalists subsequently invoked the notion of popular sovereignty, proclaiming that the relation between the individual citizen and the national government would be direct and unmediated. But convention delegates focused their energies on balancing and aggregating the claims of different interest groups, and it was their remarkable success in doing so that seemed so "miraculous" to defenders of the new order. Madison himself conceded the primacy of factions in the rationale for the extended republic set forth in *Federalist* No. 10.[22]

Small-state delegates argued that their interests in the representation controversy were no less real than those that divided shippers and planters, or slaveowners and nonslaveowners. The assertion that the large states had no "common interest"[23] was belied by their determination to abolish the equality principle. Small-state delegates concluded that their large-state counterparts were adamant for proportional representation because of prospective material advantages. For Martin it was axiomatic that if "no separate interests" distinguished large states from small, "there is no danger of an equality of votes; and if there be danger, the smaller states cannot yield."[24]

Large-state delegates replied that the question was one of principle: "Taking advantage of the moment," the small states had "extorted from the large ones an equality of votes," but "the large States are at liberty now to consider what is right."[25] When, however, Hugh Williamson of North Carolina drew out the practical implications of this alleged inequity, the concrete interests at stake became apparent. He "observed that the small States, if they had a plurality of votes would have an interest in throwing the burdens off their own shoulders on those of the large ones."[26] Presumably such discrimination would take the form of taxation on undeveloped land. But if this was a real danger, would not the small states be justified in fearing equally invidious results if the large states were able to dictate tax policy? Under proportional representation, populous states with large land reserves could make commercial interests in smaller, more developed states shoulder disproportionate burdens.

The state-size issue was the subject of heated debate in early June after John Dickinson introduced the idea of a bicameral legislature incorporating both principles of representation.[27] Small-state delegates boldly challenged the disinterested patriotism of large-state proponents of a strictly proportional scheme. Ostensibly small-state delegates sought a general renegotiation of boundaries and equalization of the states, thus recalling favorite landless-state themes from the western lands controversy. But the real purpose of the small-state offensive was to force large-state delegates to acknowledge that their states had a real interest in preserving extensive jurisdictional claims. Once the large states' motives for constitutional reform were made clear—and their qualified commitment to a strong national government recognized—the small states could plausibly demand the protection that equal voting in one branch would afford.

On June 9, New Jersey's David Brearly suggested "that a map of the U.S. be spread out" and "all the existing boundaries be erased, and that a new partition of the whole be made into 13 equal parts."[28] Paterson raised the alternative possibility of simply doing away with the states altogether: "If a consolidated national government must take place, then state distinctions must cease, or the states must be equalized."[29] If the states were made equal, the contending principles of representation would converge: people and states alike then would be equally represented. But were the large states willing to forego the advantages of size—or even perhaps their corporate existence—to secure proportional representation? Paterson had his doubts: "Will the government of Pennsylvania admit a participation of their common stock of land to the citizens of New-Jersey? I fancy not."[30]

The large-state response was equivocal. Benjamin Franklin of Pennsylvania thought the "proposition of equalizing the States . . . an equitable one." Before the Revolution when colonists' rights differed significantly from colony to colony, the location of a boundary was important to "borderers." But at present when such differences are done away, it is less material. The Interest of a State is made up of the interests of its individual members. If they are not injured, the State is not injured. Small States are more easily well & happily governed than large ones. If therefore in such an equal division, it should be found necessary to diminish Pennsylvania, I should not be averse to the giving a part of it to N[ew] Jersey, and another to Delaware.

Unfortunately, however, such a redistribution of territory was not practicable.[31] James Wilson, Franklin's colleague, also thought that "a new partition" was "desireable, but evidently & totally impracticable."[32]

Both Pennsylvanians implicitly conceded that the small states were at a relative disadvantage in the union; Franklin even endorsed the classic argument that republican states should be small. And neither, at this point, suggested that the proposed alteration of state boundaries violated any important principle. Large-state delegates were unshakably committed to the precept of proportional representation: all American citizens should have an equal voice in the national government. Pennsylvania "would not confederate on any other" plan, Wilson warned.[33] But particularly since they disclaimed any interest in the admitted advantages of superior size and population, large-state delegates could not plausibly argue that their boundaries were also sacrosanct. Instead, "there would probably be considerable difficulties in adjusting such a division" and certainly in readjusting it to future population changes.[34] Nevertheless, although jurisdictional changes might be inconvenient and "impracticable," they could have no effect on the inviolable rights of republican citizens.

The impasse on representation led to a variety of fanciful boundary proposals. After elaborating on the impracticality of a "new partition . . . into 13 equal parts" (citing "dissimelarities" among the states in the "rules of property," and their "manners, habits and prejudices"), Madison urged the small states to secure "their own safety" through "voluntary coalition" with their large neighbors.[35] Madison's outburst may have helped vent his mounting frustration, but it was not a winning argument: after all, the small states opposed proportional representation precisely because they wanted to *avoid* being swallowed up—Madison's putative solution. Luther Martin responded in kind: "Instead of a junction of the small States as a remedy, he thought a division of the large States would be more eligible."[36] During the western lands controversy, of course, such direct assaults on their territorial integrity and interests had driven the large states to contemplate bolting the union.

The convention debates on the state-size issue had a perversely unreal, inside-out character. The delegates' insistence that they would *not* concede on the representation issue but were willing enough to consider boundary changes had no relation to political reality, as they undoubtedly recognized. Whatever liberties they might take with their instructions, certainly the delegates could not alter the boundaries and compromise the corporate integrity of the states they represented. On the other hand, there was no bar to any scheme of representation that could be shown to protect vital state or sectional interests. Although the delegates argued as if representation were a question of principle and boundaries were contingent, they knew that the reverse was in fact more nearly the case.

Small-state intransigence on representation provoked large-state delegates to a sustained, increasingly desperate assault on what Rufus King called the "phantom of *State* sovereignty."[37] This rhetoric was countersuggestive at best. If the states were "artificial beings," little more than "Corporations"[38] and standing toward the union in the same relation as counties to states,[39] then there should have been no impediment to redrawing state boundaries. Madison assured the small states that such "equalization" would be achieved in time.[40] But the promise of reducing all the states to an equal size—or of making them equally impotent— was not the way to reconcile the small states to proportional representation.

The small-state campaign for equalization exposed the limits of large-state nationalism. Representatives of the large states were forced to disclose their interest in preserving the existing distribution of territory as well as their varying commitments to states' rights and individual liberties. Elbridge Gerry, for instance, pulled back from his own contemptuous dismissal of state sovereignty to become a leading opponent of the proposed Constitution.[41] George Mason of Virginia was also convinced that aristocratic consolidationists meant to obliterate the states.[42] Once large-state delegates acknowledged their real determination to promote their own states' corporate rights and interests—a determination disguised by attacks on "state sovereignty"—they could no longer dismiss small-state claims to special protection through equal representation. The resulting Connecticut Compromise was a clear victory for the small-state bloc. Most small-state delegates were persuaded that retention of the state-equality principle in the Senate would prevent the large states from exercising dangerously disproportionate power. The federal compact on which the Confederation was originally based thus would be preserved.

The state-size issue revived briefly in the final days of the Convention when delegates debated the constitutional provision securing state claims and requiring a state to agree to its own division. Dickinson cited the "impropriety of requiring the small States to secure the large ones in their extensive claims of territory"; Martin warned that all the states would be obliged to subjugate separatist movements.[43] Martin's colleague Daniel Carroll invoked the old landless-state argument for a collective title to the Crown lands, urging that the territorial guarantee not prejudice the "claim of the U.S. to vacant lands ceded to them by the Treaty of peace."[44]

Although the new-state clause sparked a brief, angry exchange, the Convention was unwilling to jeopardize the delicate *modus vivendi* between large and small states. The large states' willingness to accord equal representation in the Senate hinged on recognition of their territorial integrity. Provoked by the small states' apparent betrayal of this implicit agreement, Pennsylvania's Wilson denounced this renewed effort to interfere with large-state claims: "Nothing . . . would give greater or juster alarm than the doctrine, that a political society is to be torne asunder without its own consent."[45] Wilson's earlier (theoretical) endorsement of boundary changes was predicated on proportional representation in both branches of the national legislature. But now that the small states were secured against the disproportionate size and power of their large neighbors, they were obligated to uphold the jurisdictional status quo. This understanding was made explicit when the Convention endorsed the new-state clause by an eight-to-three vote, with Maryland, Delaware, and New Jersey dissenting.[46]

In addition to providing a sanction for the voluntary division of old states and creation of new ones, Article IV, Section 3 guaranteed the territorial integrity of the states. Thus the basic features of the old federal compact were sustained: disparities in state size would be mitigated by the scheme of representation. Under the Articles of Confederation, this implicit compact had facilitated a gradual equalization of the states and the resolution of jurisdictional controversies. Federalists promised that this process would continue and even accelerate under the new Constitution.

SECTIONALISM

"Local politics & diversity of interest will undoubtedly find their way into the [Constitutional] Convention," David Humphreys wrote. As a result, he expected "a serious proposal will be made for dividing the Continent into two or three seperate Governments."[47] Madison later insisted that the delegates never discussed the possibility, but it clearly was never far from their minds.[48] An awareness of intractable sectional differences was apparent in Edmund Randolph's early proposal for a triple executive with members "drawn from different portions of the Country." Randolph regarded the alternative, a unitary executive, "as the foetus of monarchy."[49] George Mason, a later opponent of the Constitution, also favored a three-man executive:

> If the Executive is vested in three persons, one chosen from the Northern, one from the Middle, and one from the Southern States, will it not contribute to quiet the minds of the people and convince them that there will be proper attention paid to their respective concerns? Will not three men so chosen bring with them, into office, a more perfect and extensive knowledge of the real interests of this great Union?[50]

Voters must be persuaded, Mason warned, that enlarged national powers would not be exercised at their expense.

Yet such an explicit, constitutional recognition of sectional differences was more likely to arouse than to allay anxieties about the misuse of national power. "If three or more [executives] should be taken from as many districts," Pierce Butler argued, "there would be a constant struggle for local advantages."[51] The institution of the executive mirrored the state of the nation. If there was a unitary, transcendent national interest, Butler suggested, a single executive was most appropriate; but if sectional interests were paramount, disunion probably made more sense than a divided executive. Later in the debates, Gouverneur Morris asked the crucial question: was the alleged distinction between North and South "fictitious or real"? "If fictitious," he concluded, "let it be dismissed & let us proceed with due confidence. If it be real, instead of attempting to blend incompatible things, let us at once take a friendly leave of each other."[52]

The new Constitution could not recognize the preeminence of sectional distinctions without subverting the essential premise of national unity. At the same time, however, the new national government would have to secure vital local and regional interests, most conspicuously in the case of the large slaveholding and slave-importing states. The delegates discovered an answer to these apparently contradictory requirements during their protracted debates over representation in the national legislature: through the complex scheme that incorporated the principle of proportional representation in one house and state equality in the other, divergent interests would be protected against hostile national majorities without being explicitly recognized. Meanwhile, delegates made the crucially important decision to suppress all traces of earlier disunionist proposals. Sectional interests would achieve some sort of accommodation only after the framers agreed to a federal framework that secured the rights of the states.

Advocates of opposing principles of representation were deeply divided, and for several frustrating weeks, no satisfactory compromise seemed possible. But the debate deflected attention away from conflicting sectional interests: both sides were committed to national union, albeit on radically different terms.[53] At the same time, however, they knew that their failure to resolve the controversy over representation would lead to disunion and the formation of separate confederacies. Large-state nationalists were not above threatening the small states with disunion and obliteration.[54] Madison tried to persuade small-state delegates that the Virginia Plan was the safest possible arrangement for their constituents; because of their antagonistic, sectional differences, there was no "real danger" the large states would act in concert. "Look to the votes in congress," he urged in his famous speech of June 29; "most of them stand divided by the geography of the country, not according to the size of the states."[55]

Although the small states remained obdurate, Madison's speech did point the way toward the remarkably forthright intersectional negotiations that dominated the second half of the Convention.[56] Paradoxically, the precondition for such negotiations was an agreement on representation that did not explicitly acknowledge the claims of the "great" sectional interests, but instead juxtaposed the interests of large and small states in the respective houses. Madison insisted that proportional representation was the defining principle of a truly national government. Small-state delegates replied that one section would thereby gain a dominant position in both houses, thus subverting prospects for a continuing union. "Let not too much be attempted," warned Connecticut's Oliver Ellsworth, lest "all may be lost." Any representation scheme that would "deprive" the generally small northeastern states of equal suffrage in at least one house "was at once cutting the body [of America] in two."[57]

Large-state nationalists were forced to accept Ellsworth's premise that the government of the union would have to be "partly federal, and partly national," a formula later embraced by "Publius" in the *Federalist*.[58] If this meant that the political power of the small states would be exaggerated, Madisonian logic suggested that the practical effects would be inconsequential: their interests were as disparate as those of the large states. At the same time, the complicated system of representation established under the Connecticut Compromise provided additional security for sectional interests—as well as for all the states *as states*. Coming from a large, centrally located state with strong interests in national commercial and territorial expansion, the Virginia delegates could discount such safeguards. For them, the interests of the state, region, and nation *apparently* coincided. But opposition to the Virginia Plan exposed the limits of Virginian nationalism. Madison's great achievement at the Virginia ratifying convention was to convince his countrymen that modifications of the Plan were not fatal to their interests.[59]

Virginians might complain that the new Constitution did not adequately recognize or secure their state's preeminent position in the union, but the "partly federal, partly national" system did serve to mitigate intersectional tensions. Once the Convention was committed to the Connecticut Compromise, delegates could begin to talk about sectional interests without directly questioning the future of the union or the presumption of a national interest. Even when they indulged in the most extravagant rhetoric, the desirability of intersectional accommodation was understood. Thus, South Carolinian Pierce Butler could assert that the interests of the southern and eastern (northern) states were "as different as the interests of Russia and Turkey" and also speak in favor of compromise.[60] Indeed, the articulation of distinct interests was essential for fixing the "bargain among the Northern & Southern States" described by Gouverneur Morris: a simple majority in Congress could regulate trade—a concession to northern commerce—but no duties could be laid on exports and there would be no federal interference with the slave trade for another twenty years.[61]

POLITICAL ECONOMY

Nationalists shared a faith in the new nation's vast potential for economic development. They were also skeptical about the ability of the separate states to secure the many interests clamoring for protection and support. But agreement on these general premises was not easily translated into a specific blueprint for a national political economy. The protracted deliberations at Philadelphia showed that even the most committed nationalists could not transcend their local and regional perspectives when substantive political and economic interests were at stake. Differences that were resolved, or at least disguised, in the reformers' conception of a dynamic and expansive national economy had to be confronted directly. Delegates were acutely sensitive to the possible impact of Constitutional proposals on their constituents. The result, ironically but predictably, was that the struggles for relative advantage that had crippled the Confederation were recapitulated at the Convention. Dealing with these problems gave the framers a foretaste of the kinds of opposition they would have to overcome in the ratification controversy. They also learned that the survival of the union depended on guaranteeing specific sectional interests.

Agreement on representation was a necessary foundation for negotiating mutual concessions. The Connecticut Compromise demonstrated that the divergent political interests of the states could be accommodated. Having preserved the union against the challenge of state particularism, the delegates were well rehearsed for bargaining over crucial intersectional compromises in August. The most important centered on the regulation of commerce.

Few delegates questioned the need for some restraints on the economic freedom of the states. Introducing the Virginia Plan on May 29, Edmund Randolph cited the many "advantages" which could only be enjoyed under a strong central government, including "a productive impost—counteraction of the commercial regulations of other nations—[and] pushing of commerce ad libitum."[62] State jealousies under the Confederation prevented enactment of an impost, even though it was "anxiously wished for by the public."[63] New York had blocked the 1783 impost proposal; on June 16, New York delegates Abraham Yates and John Lansing withdrew from the Convention, resisting any innovations that would, in Lansing's words, "sacrifice [the states'] essential rights to a national government."[64] With the New Yorkers gone, only Luther Martin of Maryland continued to argue for state control over commerce.[65] Although the other delegates were divided on the proper objects and objectives for a national revenue from imports, they unanimously supported some sort of impost.

Controversy over *export* taxes most clearly revealed the great diversity of economic interests represented at the Convention. Because "we ought to be governed by national and permanent views," proclaimed Madison, the new national government should have the power to tax exports, "tho' it may not be expedient at present."[66] Export duties, added Gouverneur Morris, were "in many cases, highly politic," and were "a necessary source of revenue."[67] But many delegates were convinced that the state governments had to retain some control over their exports. Without the power to enact embargoes and tonnage duties, the states could not react flexibly to economic adversity.[68] The Maryland delegates, noted James McHenry, "almost shuddered at the fate of [their state's] commerce" should Congress exercise unlimited power in this area. Every effort to expand export production would result in higher taxes, thus accentuating the relative advantage of commercially stronger states with more extensive populations and productive resources.[69] Because of the states' different economic circumstances, asserted Connecticut's Ellsworth, "the taxing of exports would engender incurable jealousies."[70] "It will enable the Gen[era]l Gov[ernmen]t to oppress the States, as much as Ireland is oppressed by Great Britain," warned Gerry of Massachusetts.[71] Planters in staple-exporting states were particularly vulnerable to discriminatory export duties.[72]

Differing perspectives on the proper balance between state and federal power over commerce and the economy generally were shaped by the experiences of the states under the Confederation. With varying degrees of success, state governments had already begun to deal with the issues—the reintegration of the Loyalists, repayment of debts to domestic and foreign creditors, retaliation against commercial discrimination—that constitutional reformers insisted could only be resolved on the national level. Ironically, however, as long as the representation issue dominated the Convention, delegates from the large states, which generally had dealt with these issues more effectively than the small states, pushed most vigorously for the expansion of federal power. Small-state delegates therefore treated nationalist proposals warily, despite their states' obvious weaknesses and vulnerability. They knew that their corporate interests were as much jeopardized by national consolidation on unfavorable terms as by the superior power of their large neighbors in the event of disunion. The history of large-state imposts had shown that small states had interests to protect against their neighbors as well as foreigners.

Resolution of the representation controversy mitigated small-state concerns about the misuse of national power. Yet even as the delegates approached the great compromise, the fundamental rift between northern commercial interests and slaveowning staple exporters of the southern states was exposed to view. On July 13, Gouverneur Morris predicted that concessions to the South on the "representation" of slaves would guarantee that region's domination over the new national government. The rapid expansion of slave-based agriculture to the south and west would lead to a "transfer of power from the maritime to the interior & landed interest," resulting in the "oppression of commerce." If sectional differences were as great as some delegates supposed—Morris "still thought the distinction groundless"—the only hope for the North was to embrace the "vicious principle" of equal representation in the Senate. Then the more numerous middle and eastern states could combine to protect and promote their essential interests.[73]

Morris's sharp juxtaposition of sectional interests constituted an ominous challenge to the nationalists' conception of interlocking, harmonious interests in the new American "empire of liberty." At the same time, of course, he pointed toward the kinds of compromises the delegates would have to negotiate to preserve the union. Ultimately, compromise was possible precisely because interests were not as clearly defined and distinguished as Morris had suggested. Southern nationalists agreed with their northern colleagues on the need for a single impost. From Maryland to Georgia, the southern legislatures had all passed navigation acts in response to British commercial discrimination, and many southern delegates at Philadelphia were committed to creating a national commercial system.[74] Some southerners expected that northerners would continue to carry their agricultural exports; others hoped southern commercial interests would soon rival those of the North.[75]

But the possibility of a mutually beneficial commercial relationship between the two sections was complicated by the issues of slavery and territorial expansion. When southern delegates insisted that their slaves be counted in apportioning representation in the new Congress, northerners such as Morris feared that they soon would be reduced to minority status in the union, particularly given the likelihood that the new western states would be drawn into the southern orbit. For their part, southerners were afraid that the northern states would exploit their temporary advantage in Congress to oppress and impoverish the South. Controversy again focused on export taxes. Northerners believed that export duties could force foreign shippers away from northern ports and so encourage American shipping and commercial interests. Meanwhile, southern staple-exporters were convinced that these duties would make them pay a disproportionate share of the national tax burden and that higher transport costs would undermine their region's prosperity.

The first recommendations on commerce by the Committee of Detail, which met from July 24 to August 6, were favorable to the

South. Drafted by two southerners (Randolph of Virginia and John Rutledge of South Carolina), two New Englanders (Ellsworth of Connecticut and Nathaniel Gorham of Massachusetts), and Wilson of Pennsylvania, the committee report restricted Congress from laying export taxes, required a two-thirds majority for any commercial legislation, and allowed the future importation of slaves.[76] In subsequent weeks, debate focused on export taxes, bringing to the fore a complex of issues—including western expansion, foreign trade, and slavery—that divided North and South.

Southern delegates were quick to emphasize the dangers of allowing a simple majority in Congress to control commerce. Mason of Virginia believed a "northern combination" was determined to block the free export of staples and monopolize the southern carrying trade.[77] The Maryland delegates agreed that if a bare majority of states could determine national commercial policy and delegates from seven states, a quorum, were in attendance, "four [northern] States" could control "the dearest interest of trade."[78] Southerners might be forced to pay export duties in addition to the shipping fees and sales commissions exacted by northern carriers. Mason argued that importations "were the same throughout the States" but that exports were "very different." State discrimination had already demonstrated the "im policy" of taxing staple exports.[79]

Madison and Morris protested the absence of congressional authority over exports in the committee proposals. Granting such power, they insisted, should not be seen as a favor to the North. "Local considerations," said Morris, "ought not to impede the general interest."[80] Judicious export taxes would benefit southerners as well as northerners, small states as well as large. Pennsylvanian Thomas FitzSimons suggested that the survival and success of American manufacturing interests might depend on preventing the export of needed raw materials.[81] Export duties, Morris agreed, were "politic in the view of encouraging American Manufactures."[82]

Not all northerners were enthusiastic about export taxes, however, suggesting that this might be a negotiable issue. Gerry of Massachusetts endorsed the southern view that national authority over exports might be "exercised partially, raising one and depressing another part" of the country.[83] Pennsylvanian George Clymer agreed that export taxes were subject to sectional bias, and not only against the South: "The middle States may apprehend an oppression of their wheat[,] flour, provisions, &c. and with more reason, as these articles were exposed to a competition in foreign markets not incident to Tob[acc]o, rice &c — They may apprehend also combinations ag[ain]st them between the Eastern & Southern States as much as the latter can apprehend them between the Eastern & middle." Clymer concluded that some limitation on export duties was necessary, but his motion to permit them only "for the purpose of revenue" was defeated.[84]

Disagreement among the northern delegates on the need for export taxes may have reassured southerners that the proposed prohibition would stand. But the issue could not be framed simply in terms of relative commercial advantage. The recognition of sectional divisions founded on economic interest inevitably led the delegates to discuss slavery and therefore to confront what Madison and other prescient observers saw as the major impediment to union. The South Carolina delegates, the boldest defenders of slavery at the Convention, dismissed the claims of "Religion & humanity," arguing instead that northerners should recognize their own interests in the expansion of slave-based agriculture. "Interest alone is the governing principle with Nations," pronounced Carolinian Rutledge, and "the true question at present is whether the South[er]n States shall or shall not be parties to the Union. If the Northern States consult their interest, they will not oppose the increase of Slaves which will increase the commodities of which they will become the carriers."[85] Charles Cotesworth Pinckney seconded this sentiment: "The more slaves, the more produce to employ the carrying trade."[86] Pierce Butler suggested that the proposed congressional "power over exports" was "unjust and alarming to the staple States," presumably because it threatened slavery. He "never would agree to the power of taxing exports."[87]

Most northerners were prepared to concede that interest overrode "Religion & humanity." But calculations of interest did not necessarily dictate capitulation to southern slaveowners. "The Eastern States had no motive to Union but a commercial one," Gorham of Massachusetts asserted. "They were able to protect themselves. They were not afraid of external danger, and did not need the aid of the South[er]n States."[88] Given the delegates' heightened awareness of their distinctive sectional concerns, the

Carolinians' candid appeal to interest could just as easily lead to disunion as union.

Madison and Morris had previously emphasized sectional differences in order to counter small-state claims to equal representation. But now Morris took the lead in promoting intersectional compromise. On August 22, he proposed that a new committee "form a bargain among the Northern & Southen States."[89] The resulting compromise, reported by the committee on August 24, guaranteed the interests of slaveholding staple producers by denying Congress the right to prohibit the importation of slaves before 1800; at the same time, however, Congress would have the power to pass, by a simple majority vote, navigation acts that affected shipping and commodities at American ports—a concession to northern commercial interests.[90] The next day General Pinckney's motion to extend the limit on congressional interference in the slave trade to 1808 passed easily; on the 28th, all export duties by the states were banned.[91] Most southern delegates were convinced that the prohibition gave their states sufficient control over their own internal economies to offset the extension of congressional authority over imports. The Convention completed its deliberations on commerce on September 13, when the delegates agreed that the state governments could levy only "incidental duties necessary for the inspection & safekeeping" of exports.[92]

The debate over Congress's commerce powers forced southerners and northerners to define their respective sectional interests and therefore to confront the possibility of disunion. By the same process, however, they identified negotiable areas where mutual concession could preserve the union and so advance their common interests. Southerners saw the need for national commercial regulation and thus were willing to risk policies that might favor the North—at least until the growth of southern population and the addition of new western states shifted the balance of power in Congress. Meanwhile, northerners recognized that staple producers throughout the country required special protection against export duties. They were willing to prohibit Congress from exercising powers that were, in any case, bound to be controversial and divisive. But they insisted that the new government had to have the authority to regulate imports and thus foster American commerce and manufactures.

THE NATIONAL INTEREST

Images of sectional interdependence in an expansive national economy facilitated compromise. Delegates readily agreed that the new government should support enterprise and accordingly referred proposals to a Committee of Detail for advancing "useful knowledge and discoveries" and promoting "agriculture, commerce, trades and manufactures."[93] Delegates anticipated that the expansion of settlement, internal improvements, the spread of commercial agriculture, and the growth of manufactures would secure the new nation's future prosperity and power.

But concrete plans for a dynamic, developing economy did not materialize. The committee charged with considering internal improvements and manufactures never reported, perhaps because the delegates feared that discussion of specific proposals for promoting development would jeopardize intersectional harmony.[94] For instance, different parts of the country would benefit unequally from improved transportation links with frontier settlements; others might gain more from measures fostering manufactures. The idea that the new union might serve these diverse, sometimes conflicting sectional interests was crucial to its appeal. But it was also crucial to avoid express commitments that inevitably would betray a regional bias. As long as the direction of future development was not clearly defined, northerners and southerners alike could continue to identify their own regional interests with the national interest. Meanwhile, the limits of the sections themselves could remain ambiguous. Would the development of the new national domain extend southern influence to the west? Would New York be aligned with the New England states, and did the middle states, as earlier disunionist scenarios suggested, constitute a distinct section?[95]

The delegates at Philadelphia drove hard bargains with one another as they sought to secure specific guarantees for essential local and regional interests. At the same time, however, they avoided detailed consideration of how federal powers would be employed to shape the course of national economic development. This mixture of specific guarantees and vague promises characterized the Convention's deliberations on currency and debt issues. Nationalists agreed that a uniform currency and a well-secured national debt were essential. Many delegates had bitterly opposed the expansion of state power in these areas, arguing that paper money issues, imposts, and navigation acts catered to local interest groups at the expense of the national welfare. By the time of the Convention, an emerging coalition of merchants and public creditors clamored for redemption of securities and notes at face value and institution of a viable national medium of exchange.

Paper currency emissions had been tied to the taxing power as long as Americans could remember.[96] In order to prevent the depreciation of these emissions, governments usually taxed them out of circulation. During the 1780s, the states relied on impost revenues, generally avoiding taxes on land, to service locally held debts and sustain the value of their currencies. With the notable exception of South Carolina, the legislatures enjoyed considerable success in meeting their obligations and thus in gaining the confidence of their constituents. But where debts were high or new revenue needs arose, there was strong resistance from merchants and consumers to raising tariff levels; at the same time, legislators in these states knew that any effort to shift tax burdens onto landholders would be politically disastrous. The solution, some state leaders began to realize, was to extend Congress's authority to collect taxes so that it would be able to consolidate and service outstanding debts.

The Convention made this transfer of power and responsibility possible by providing for a national impost and vesting the new government with the power—which few delegates expected would be used in the near future—to levy direct taxes. But the framers hesitated to give Congress specific authority to issue paper currency, the traditional corollary of the taxing power. After all, nationalists had long insisted that paper money was responsible for the disarray of the American economy: that "accumulation of guilt," as Madison described it in the *Federalist,* destroyed "confidence between man and man," subverted "the industry and morals of the people," and besmirched "the character of Republican Government."[97] Moreover, the question of federal assumption of state debts, which was connected in "the public mind" with repudiating state issues of paper currency, came up only briefly at the Convention. Sensitive to the rigors of chronic specie shortages and tightening credit, too many delegates shared the popular enthusiasm for state currency emissions to make possible a resolution of the debt assumption problem in 1787.[98]

The delegates were also aware that an overly precise delineation of congressional powers would precipitate divisions in their own ranks. In the waning days of the Convention, sporadic attempts to renegotiate agreements on representation, the commerce clause, and other controversial issues showed the fragility of the nationalist consensus.[99] Sensitive to the precariousness of their hard-won compromises, Madison, Morris, and their nationalist allies recognized that they would have to be satisfied with Congress's general authority over commerce, buttressed by specific guarantees of property rights against state legislative interference. Yet the Constitution's compromises—and its silences— proved advantageous to the document's supporters as they sought to convince voters that it would best serve a wide array of interdependent American interests. The economic freedom of enterprising Americans would not be blocked by state tariff barriers; staple producers would be protected against onerous export duties; and revenues from a uniform national impost promised to shield landowners from direct taxation.

After the Convention most of the delegates closed ranks to promote ratification. Delegates who had argued vigorously for their special interests at the Convention now celebrated the "miraculous" compromises that were incorporated in the Constitution. South Carolinian Pierce Butler conceded that "the Constitution we have ventured to recommend to the States has its faults." But as he suggested to a correspondent, "when you consider the Great Extent of Territory, the various Climates & products, the differing manners and . . . the Contending Commercial Interests, You will agree with me that it required a pretty General Spirit of Accomodation in the members of the Convention to bring forward such a system as would be agreed to and approved of by all." In this conciliatory spirit, Butler was prepared to adopt a friendlier posture toward the "northern monopoly." Without the Constitution, "the Eastern States" would continue to be unjustly "deprived . . . of the Carrying Trade." With it, northern and southern interests alike stood to benefit: northern commercial interests would thrive, while southern staple producers would enjoy the "Variety of markets . . . thrown open to them."[100]

The great achievement of the Philadelphia Convention was to establish a framework for national politics that accommodated powerful state-particularist and sectionalist tendencies. Madison and his fellow large-state nationalists were forced to concede the equal representation of the states in the Senate and so recognize the continuing agency of the sovereign states in the new regime. Many of the founders had agreed with Madison that state sovereignty was the original source of America's troubles. But now they began to see that Constitutional guarantees of states' rights could provide a crucial measure of security for sectional interests and thus reverse the tendency toward disunion expressed in earlier proposals for separate confederacies. Pragmatic reformers became aware of the limits on national consolidation set by the numerous conflicting interests represented at Philadelphia and by the delegates' determination to uphold what they deemed their own states' critical interests. They also had to recognize the limits on their own nationalism dictated by distinctive regional interests.[101]

The federal structure created by the great compromise on representation helped make compromises of interest possible. In this sense, contemporary commentators were correct in emphasizing the primacy of the representation controversy. Although, as Madison suggested, conflicts over other issues might have been more important, they only became negotiable once the character of the new national legislature was established.[102] Ellsworth, who had himself broached the possibility of disunion in response to the large-state insistence on proportional representation, became a leading advocate of compromise. The failure to reconcile sectional differences, he told the Convention in late August, would lead "probably into several confederations and not without bloodshed."[103] Guarantees of sectional interests would, in turn, constitute powerful incentives to support the new system.

The genius of states' rights within the framework of a more energetic national union was to secure sectional interests without directly acknowledging their legitimacy and durability. Of course, constitutional guarantees of the interests of slaveowners would later become the leading source of intersectional conflict. In 1787, however, such guarantees seemed crucial to the survival of the union.[104]

7
Republicanism and Federalism

At the Constitutional Convention, Gouverneur Morris spoke for many of his nationalist colleagues when he asserted that "State attachments, and State importance have been the bane of this country."[1] Rufus King was "astonished" that "we should be ready to sacrifice the substantial good [the security of individual rights] to the phantom of *State* sovereignty."[2] Advocates of states' rights and interests were "intoxicated with the idea of their *sovereignty*," commented future Antifederalist Elbridge Gerry, even though "we never were independent States."[3]

Yet if state sovereignty was insubstantial and illusory, the states themselves were durable facts of American political life, and forthright rhetorical assaults on state sovereignty were clearly ill advised. Federalists could hardly expect voters to renounce their states and leave them without adequate constitutional protection against federal encroachments; language that too clearly suggested their subordinate and dependent place in the new scheme seemed to substantiate Antifederalist warnings about the dangers of "consolidation." Advocates of ratification sought to neutralize such concerns by showing that the states retained an integral role in the new federal government and exercised a continuing "sovereignty" where powers were not expressly delegated.[4]

The challenge for reformers was to show that the proposed Constitution "supports and adds a dignity to every government in the United States."[5] The "great end" of the new regime, proclaimed Roger Sherman, was "to protect the several states" against "foreign invasion" and domestic disorder and to facilitate "a beneficial intercourse" among them. Hoping to counter traditional warnings about the dangers of a more powerful and distant national government, Sherman and his fellow Federalists insisted

124

that the Constitution was "well framed to secure the rights and liberties of the people and for preserving the governments of the individual states."[6]

The necessity of compromising the variety of interests represented at Philadelphia gave constitutional reformers a foretaste of political reality. Delegates promoted their constituents' interests shamelessly, threatening to bolt the Convention and, presumably, sacrifice the union if they were not satisfied. As they negotiated terms of union with one another, nationalist-minded reformers thus had to acknowledge the practical necessity—and even the desirability—of preserving the states. Federalists subsequently portrayed these prudential concessions as leading principles of the new order, casting themselves as defenders of the states' essential rights and interests. Thus, during the ratification controversy, they repeatedly claimed that the constitutional provision for equal state representation in the Senate revealed their commitment to the states.[7] Federalists turned the actual process of constitution making on its head: in fact, most delegates had come to Philadelphia intending to create a powerful, fully sovereign national government. Some of them, Antifederalists correctly noted, would happily have dispensed with the states altogether.[8] But the exigencies of the debate over the Constitution drove the Federalists to disavow a thoroughgoing nationalist intent, however much some of them might have preferred a truly consolidated continental republic.

CONCEPTUAL EXCHANGES

In making their case for the Constitution, Federalists faced daunting conceptual and rhetorical challenges from their Antifederalist opponents. As defenders of the status quo, critics of the Constitution were able to invoke widely accepted maxims of the most respected political thinkers of the day in resisting innovations that threatened republican liberty. Antifederalists thus had few incentives or occasions to display the conceptual boldness and originality that so delight intellectual historians and political theorists, and their reputation has suffered accordingly. A more balanced assessment of the Antifederalists' contribution to the ratification debate is long overdue—especially one which appreciates the extent of that contribution.[9] In effect, opponents of ratification sustained the political and rhetorical pressures that had forced nationalists at the Constitutional Convention to concede the agency of the states in the new regime.

Antifederalists were justifiably suspicious of Federalist solicitude for the states: after all, the Federalists also insisted that state sovereignty constituted the leading menace to the survival of republican government in America. But the Antifederalists' rhetoric worked toward compromise, both by forcing their opponents to acknowledge a central role for the states and by expressing "discordant notions" of state interest that revealed how "wretched" the disunited "situation" of the states would be "were the present plan rejected."[10] Antifederalists sought to expose the dangerous general tendencies of the proposed government by identifying specific threats to particular interests. The practical result was to invite their opponents to explain how much the new system would benefit individual states, thus deflecting attention away from its "tendency to annihilate all the state governments indiscriminately."[11]

Many reformers remained convinced that state sovereignty was the bane of American politics, but the process of drafting and defending a national constitution converted them into self-proclaimed proponents of states' rights. Their most formidable task was to define states' rights in a way that could accommodate the radical expansion of federal power. The Federalists' ingenious rhetoric served to rationalize this fundamental shift in their own thinking and to disguise the original intention of at least some of their number to obliterate the states. The Federalists may indeed have won over many skeptical moderates, but they did so by portraying themselves as authentic federalists whose "more perfect union" would best secure the states from a plethora of dire circumstances. As a result, the great compromises worked out in Philadelphia became fundamental principles of the new system—whatever the delegates may have intended.

Federalists insisted that the Constitution alone could secure the states' political salvation. The Articles of Confederation were hopelessly inadequate. According to William Davie, "The encroachments of some states on the rights of the others, and of all on those of the Confederacy, are incontestible proofs of the weakness and imperfection of that system."[12] Because the states were vulnerable in proportion to the weakness of the Confederation, only a more perfect union could guarantee their survival. "We are attempting to build one government out of thirteen," Robert R. Livingston told the New York convention, "preserving, however, the states, as part of the system."[13] Clearly, the states would have to be in some sense taken apart if they were to provide materials for building a single continental government.

Federalists insisted that immediate action was imperative because of the new nation's precarious international position. Conflicting state policies pointed ominously toward the collapse of the union and the emergence of an anarchic "state of nature" among the American republics. The new nation was doomed to betray its enormous promise if it failed to establish an energetic union. Antifederalists were less impressed with the magnitude of commercial and diplomatic problems, warning that the proposed solution—a powerful, consolidated national regime—jeopardized republican liberty and threatened to destroy the states. But both sides agreed that Americans faced a critical choice, whether the crisis was the cause or, as Antifederalists charged, the effect of reform agitation. Federalists and Antifederalists used remarkably similar language to describe the inevitable consequences of disunion or consolidation.[14] Both parties asserted that the people of the states had to act decisively—either by endorsing a stronger union or by foiling the Federalists' consolidationist plot—in order to prevent counterrevolution and preserve American liberty and independence. At the same time, however, each party proclaimed that its own program best served the goals the *other* ostensibly sought to promote. Antifederalists therefore urged that more explicit guarantees of states' rights and interests would strengthen the union, while Federalists insisted that a strong union would secure particular interests and preserve the states.

These rhetorical exchanges and transpositions help account for the Federalists' conspicuous commitment to federal principles. The resulting redefinition of their goals even led some of them to suggest that the movement for constitutional reform had been instigated by the states themselves. Federalists frequently invoked the analogy of individuals emerging from a natural condition. For instance, North Carolinian James White said that "States in Confederacy" were "like individuals in society" who "must part with some of their privileges for the preservation of the rest."[15] In a society of states, added "Plain Truth," each state had to sacrifice its "sovereignty," just as each man emerging from the "state of nature" could not reserve the "natural right of being the judge" in his own case.[16] The federal Constitution would protect the states by preventing them from exercising sovereign powers. "It gently subtracts from the liberties of each" state, "Social Compact" explained, while providing "for the security of all."[17] James Wilson used different language to express the same thought: "More liberty is gained by associating, than is lost by the natural rights which [the new government] absorbs."[18]

In the Federalist formulation, less turned out to be more. As "sovereignties" who acknowledged no superior authority, the states would remain "weak and contemptible."[19] But, the Federalists promised, the states would grow strong and prosperous once they disclaimed sovereign powers and submitted to the rule of law in a more perfect union. Their key premise was that chronic wars would endanger the population and power of the separate states while subverting their republican character. Surrounded by hostile powers and threatened by domestic dissidents, the states stood precariously on the brink of violence. By eliminating these ominous conditions, the Constitution would enable the states to fulfill their republican destiny.

ANTIFEDERALISM

The Antifederalists' insistence that any acceptable federal system would have to secure individual and states' rights set the parameters of the ratification debates. Responding to these concerns, Federalists traced America's many troubles to the rapid deterioration of the union and Congress's notorious "imbecility." Their rhetoric centered less on the excesses of the states under the Confederation than on dire predictions about their probable behavior in the event of disunion.

Challenging the Federalist analysis at every point, Antifederalists asserted that there was no "crisis" in American politics. They concluded that disunion would be preferable to the loss of republican liberty under a consolidated national government. James Winthrop of Massachusetts developed the Antifederalist argument most fully in his "Agrippa" series. Because "Europe is engaged, and we are tranquil," there was no need for precipitate action.[20] After due deliberation, good republicans would realize that "the powers of Congress over the citizens should be small in proportion as the empire is extended."[21] Everyone knew that "no extensive empire can be governed upon republican principles."[22] If the central government was not carefully limited, it would soon exercise despotic authority and destroy the states. Winthrop was convinced that "the authority of Congress to decide disputes between states is sufficient to prevent their recurring to hostility."[23] Meanwhile, mutually beneficial commerce among the states, with their distinctive "situation, wants and produce," would be "a bond of union."[24]

Winthrop implied that the union would perfect itself—unless consolidationists succeeded in imposing a strong government over the states. Under such a despotic regime, Winthrop and his Antifederalist allies explained, the interests of the remote, less favored parts of the empire would be sacrificed. This meant that "the extremes of the empire [including New England] will be drained to fatten an overgrown capital."[25] Under free governments, however, different sections of the continent would meet one another on an equal footing; reciprocal needs would draw the states closer together.

Winthrop was not the only Antifederalist to articulate a broadly optimistic vision of America's future prospects.[26] Contrasting a consolidated union based on force with a voluntary, harmonious union of states, these critics of the Constitution expressed their faith in the transformative powers of republicanism. In republican America, they suggested, commercial exchange and the pursuit of common interests superseded the recourse to threats and coercion that traditionally "governed" relations among states. From this rhetorical high ground, Antifederalists argued that the Federalists' insistence on a more "respectable" nation capable of holding its own against supposedly hostile European powers was tantamount to a disavowal of republicanism itself. The citizens of the separate, independent American republics were being asked to sacrifice their rights and liberties to a distant, irresponsible central government. And whatever constitutional limitations the Federalists promised, Antifederalists were persuaded that the new government would soon take on the characteristics of those despotic regimes against which it was supposed to preserve the continent.

Antifederalists charged that constitutional reformers had little faith in republican government. To promote their own narrow interests, the Federalists intended to make America over in Europe's image. The Federalists' argument that the putative tendency toward disunion would Europeanize American politics was a calumny on the states. "The state governments answer the purposes of preserving the peace," Melancton Smith told his fellow New Yorkers. It was ridiculous to predict that the states would ever go to war with each other, he continued: "The idea of a civil war among the states is abhorrent to the principles and feelings of almost every man of every rank in the union." Anyone who thought differently was only "fit to be shut up in Bedlam."[27]

Republics would never have an interest or incentive to destroy one another. "The citizens of republican borders are only terrible to tyrants," Patrick Henry explained; "instead of being dangerous to one another, they mutually support one another's liberties." Since the true "union" of republics stemmed from their mutual forbearance and support, there was no need to depend on formal political or constitutional arrangements.[28]

Antifederalists also insisted that the division of the continent among sovereign states guaranteed liberty. George Mason opposed the Constitution because he believed "popular governments can only exist in small territories."[29] Invoking the authority of such "celebrated writers" as Montesquieu, Antifederalists unanimously agreed with "Brutus" (probably Melancton Smith) that "a free republic cannot succeed over a country of such immense extent." "In a large extended country," "Brutus" explained, "it is impossible to have a representation, possessing the sentiments, and of integrity, to declare the minds of the people."[30] In the words of Antifederalist dissenters at the Pennsylvania convention, "nothing short of the supremacy of despotic sway could connect and govern these United States under one government."[31]

If the movement for a stronger union endangered liberty and threatened to reestablish monarchical rule in America, it followed that efforts to divide overlarge states advanced the republican cause.[32] Most Antifederalists agreed that nationalists who sought to "melt" the states "into one empire" were enemies of republican liberty. But young Samuel Bryan of Pennsylvania, calling himself "Centinel," went one step further, contrasting the invidious designs of constitutional reformers with the efforts of free-dom-loving separatists who rose up against the "inconveniencies and disadvantages" of "remote," unresponsive, and unrepresen-tative state governments.[33] In Maryland, "A Farmer" (probably John Francis Mercer, a recent arrival from Virginia), developed the most forthright Antifederalist endorsement of separatism. As long as we remain *"in a confederacy,"* he wrote, "our state disputes . . . would subside before injury": the people of the different states would never lose control of their governments. But the genius of republican government, in which the people were "free, govern-ment having no right to them, but they to government," was to protect private interests and nourish "local attachments." This freedom constituted the foundation of social happiness; it in-cluded not only the right to self-government, but the right to "separate and divide as interest or inclination prompted."[34]

Antifederalists such as "A Farmer" discounted the seriousness of interstate conflict under the Confederation. Some even agreed that disunion would not be a catastrophe: the American republics would offer no ready target for foreign invaders, and citizen-soldiers would always be vigilant and valiant in defense of local liberties. In the Virginia convention, James Monroe pointed to the successful resolution of the western lands controversy through the large-state land cessions. "This great source of public calam-ity" had been eliminated *without* benefit of a strong central government. "Nor," he added, "is there an existing controversy between any of the states at present."[35]

The tendency of American politics was toward an increasingly stable balance of power among the states, resulting from the adjustment of state boundaries and the spread of more effective and responsive local governments. Federalists were misled by the apparent discord unleashed by popular partisanship. But because of the "natural moderation of the American character," such disputatiousness never amounted to more than "a warfare of argument and reason." After all, differences of interest and senti-ment over such an extensive continent were natural and inevitable. As long as the United States remained a true confederation of independent republics, these differences would never lead to violence. Because the people were always ready to reject anything approaching despotism, "moderation" must always be the first "law of self-preservation" for the American states.[36]

Antifederalists countered Federalist warnings of approaching anarchy by predicting the outbreak of "a civil war with all its dreadful train of evils" as the states sought to defend the tattered remnants of their sovereignty and independence against consolidation.[37] The resulting "violent dissensions between the state governments and the Congress" would inevitably "terminate in the ruin of the one or the other."[38] Opponents of the Constitution dwelled as much on the horrors of civil discord that would accompany efforts to establish the new order as on the despotic rule consolidation necessarily entailed. Luther Martin thought the Federalists' insidious plan to bypass the state legislatures and gain the endorsement of state ratifying conventions for the new Constitution would "introduce *anarchy* and *confusion*, and . . . light the *torch of discord and civil war* throughout this continent."[39] Consolidationists ultimately would fail, George Mason said, but not before "the People of these united States [were] involved in all the Evils of Civil War."[40] Others feared that credulous voters would be all too willing to endorse the new system; for them, "the seeds of civil discord" were "plentifully sown" in the Constitution itself.[41] The constant struggle for control of the powerful national executive ("an *Elective King*") would "lay the foundation of clamors, broils, and contentions that will end in *blood*."[42]

The common theme in all these predictions was that the campaign to strengthen the union would destabilize American politics. The Americans' love of liberty and their patriotic attachment to their states would provoke resistance to consolidation: by their own strenuous efforts to block ratification, the Antifederalists anticipated a much broader—and much more violent—popular reaction. If dissenters exaggerated the dangers of the new order and the malign intentions of its sponsors, they were only giving fair warning of the depth and scope of the controversy such concentrated power inevitably would promote. Americans would be compelled to reenact the classic struggle between power and liberty that had driven the revolutionaries to declare their independence. But now, with the avatars of power so effectively disguised as republicans, liberty-lovers faced an even more deadly and cunning challenge.

Denying the authenticity of their opponents' crisis, Antifederalists counselled patience. Although most of them acknowledged the need to revitalize Congress, their emphasis on the dangers of consolidation led them to take a relatively benign view of the consequences of disunion. By stressing specific burdens the new regime probably would impose on their states or regions, dissenters implied that no union at all might be preferable. That conclusion flowed logically from the conventional assumption that "mankind are governed by interest."[43] The apparently irreconcilable, "jarring interests" of states so "different in soil, climate, customs, produce, and every thing" argued against their continuing union.[44] Coercion, the reliance on military force to impose national authority, was no substitute for a voluntary union of free republics.

Antifederalists tailored their warnings to their local audiences and thus seemed to offer contradictory arguments against the Constitution. But they all agreed on the basic principle that it should never be in the power of one section to legislate for the others. In the Antifederalist view, the Articles of Confederation, for all their obvious defects, had given the states adequate security against one another and so had enabled them to preserve a union that a strong central government certainly would have long since destroyed. "The southern parts of America have been protected by that weakness so much execrated," Patrick Henry told the Virginia convention.[45] Because the interests of the different parts of the continent were so diverse and their natural connections so tenuous, a *weak* central government, carefully confined to the few common concerns of all the states, was the best guarantor of union. "From the weakness of all," the Maryland "Farmer" added, "you may be governed by the moderation of the combined judgments of the whole, not tyranized ever by the blind passions of a few individuals."[46] Under a Confederation with "limited powers," wrote James Winthrop, a natural harmony and balance would be established among the states. Instead of violent contests for relative advantage, an "enlarged intercourse" among the states would draw them into closer interdependence. As a result, he concluded, "our union shall outlast time itself."[47]

But what sort of "union" did Antifederalists such as Winthrop have in mind? If the Confederation was their model, nationalist reformers charged, opponents of the Constitution were really advocating disunion. Some Antifederalists were so wary of the Federalists' consolidated regime that they appeared willing to concede the point; their "union" was purely voluntary and uncoerced—it had no political existence at all. The Maryland "Farmer" pushed this logic to the extreme, boldly confronting the Federalists' leading justification for a stronger union. Just as he endorsed separatism within the states, he was willing to risk the supposed dangers of disunion. If this meant that American politics would become more like Europe's, he welcomed the change. Europeans had made great progress toward a more enlightened and rational system, precisely because their division "into small, independant States" preserved "a degree of social happiness very different from what exists in other parts of the world." The European state system thus constituted a plausible model for the American union: "Those States who admit the sanction of the laws of nature and nations form as it were a *great federal republic,* and the balance of power, even under an imperfect system, has prevented those great revolutions and shocks which sweeping myriads of mortals at a blow, degrade mankind in the eye of philosophy, to a level with the ants and other insects of the earth." "A Farmer" told the Federalists that they had everything backwards. The proliferation of small, independent states did not reduce the United States to anarchy, with multiplying occasions for war and violence. It was rather the efforts of nationalist reformers to extend and consolidate the authority of the central government that threatened to subvert "the laws of nature and nations."[48]

ANARCHY

Proponents of the new Constitution were decidedly less optimistic about the prospects for a stable balance of power among the American states in the event of disunion. We are "on the eve of war," Edmund Randolph told the Philadelphia Convention.[49] After returning to Virginia, where he belatedly endorsed the Constitution, Randolph expatiated on the dangers of disunion. Union alone could restrain the "dogs of war," he warned:

> I see the dreadful tempest, to which the present calm is a prelude, if disunion takes place. I see the anarchy which must happen if no energetic government be established. . . . If anarchy and confusion follow disunion, an enterprising man

may enter into the American throne. . . . No greater curse can befall her than the dissolution of the political connection between the states.[50]

The association between anarchy and war was close in Federalist rhetoric. Promoters of the Constitution identified the formal condition for a "state of war" among the states as the absence of "political connection" and linked it with the inevitable consequence, tumults and disorder. The idea of war embraced both the latent rivalry of sovereign states in a lawless state of nature and the actual outbreak of violent conflict always immanent in this condition.

The Federalists' Hobbesian assumptions about international relations were familiar to Americans. It was axiomatic, "Cato" told readers of the *New-Haven Gazette* in January 1787, that a state must be sufficiently strong to defend itself. Otherwise "it must expire under the sword of its foes, or sink into submission, both of which are equally the extinction of its felicity."[51] The impending collapse of the union would multiply potential dangers by exposing each state to the "natural" rivalry of other American as well as European states.

Hugh Henry Brackenridge was persuaded that the United States were already suspended between promise and danger. He contrasted the opportunity "of forming a constitution, which shall be the wonder of the universe" with the awful possibility of a war of all against all. Seeking to reassure delegates who thought the framers had exceeded their charge to amend the Articles, Brackenridge told the Pennsylvania convention that the American people were "on the wild and extended field of nature, unrestrained by any former compact." "We are not on federal ground," he concluded; "the former Articles of Confederation have received sentence of death."[52]

Federalists linked the apparently imminent dissolution of the union with the onset of anarchy. "Are not the bands of Union so absolutely relaxed as almost to amount to a dissolution?" asked James Madison.[53] A North Carolinian concurred: "These states are now tottering on the brink of anarchy."[54] With the Articles under "sentence of death," the proposed Constitution represented the only hope for preserving peace and harmony among the states. A Massachusetts writer compared the "*Disunited*

States of America . . . to Thirteen distinct, separate, independent, *unsupported* Columns,'' vulnerable to ''rapid destruction from the ruthless Attacks of *Anarchy,* on the one Hand, and of *Despotism,* on the other.''[55] ''Anarchy'' would probably follow rejection of the Constitution, C. C. Pinckney predicted in the South Carolina debates, thus encouraging ''some daring despot to seize upon the government, and effectually deprive us of our liberties.''[56]

Even now, Pennsylvanian Jasper Yeates asserted, ''the government of laws has been almost superseded by a licentious anarchy.''[57] The ''turbulence of factions'' and ''the flames of internal insurrection'' threatened to burst out ''in every quarter.''[58] Federalists were determined to resist this ''licentiousness, which advances nigh to a contempt of all order and subordination,'' and they saw the preservation of the union as their most important line of defense.[59]

But the most immediate danger was not the collapse of all authority, but rather the *strength,* or war-making capacity, of fully sovereign states. Without some ''confessedly paramount . . . legal authority,'' ''the worst sort of unsubdueable anarc[h]y might be expected to result.''[60] Yet, while the states grew stronger and more dangerous to each other, they would collectively be more vulnerable to external threats. As a result, no stable balance of power among the states was likely to emerge, and the condition of anarchy would prove short-lived. ''If the great union be broken,'' General William Heath told the Massachusetts convention, ''our country, as a nation perishes; and if our country so perishes, it will be as impossible to save a particular state as to preserve one of the fingers of a mortified hand.''[61] In the event of disunion, Federalists warned, even the largest states would be ''weak and contemptible'' and thus ''unable to protect themselves from external or domestic insult.''[62]

Whether or not anarchy among the states gave way to utter licentiousness within them, the result would be the same. America, ''Civis'' concluded, ''will either fall into the hands of an aspiring tyrant, or be divided among European powers.''[63] The British already had ''busy emissaries throughout the states,'' Charles Pinckney warned; ''how long can we flatter ourselves to be free from Indian cruelties and depredations?''[64] Wars among the states, European intervention, and Indian attacks would all lead Americans to embrace order, even at the expense of their liberties. It hardly mattered if the "teeth of the lion" were "again made bare" and the British sought to reconquer their lost colonies,[65] or if some American "Caesar or Cromwell" should "avail himself of our divisions."[66] In any case, were the American states so foolish as to reject the Constitution, "the arm of tyranny" would "impose upon us a system of despotism" and the Revolution would be undone.[67]

REPUBLICAN STATES

Federalists could not deny that the states would have to sacrifice some of their powers in order to avert these awful consequences. One solution was to assert that the sovereign people retained an undivided, undiminished authority that was delegated to government officials for specific purposes. By invoking this idea of "popular sovereignty," defenders of the new scheme could evade the troublesome question of supremacy and subordination in the distribution of powers.[68] Federalists also justified this reallocation of authority by arguing that the exercise of sovereign powers by the states was ultimately incompatible with their republican character. In securing the authority of the national government over all general concerns, most notably over foreign policy, the new Constitution would promote the rule of law over and among the states; the states would only give up the power to do themselves—and one another—harm.

Pelatiah Webster touched on several of the Federalists' most important themes. He argued that a strong national government would best support republican government in the states. He contrasted the likelihood of violent conflict between disunited states with the adjudication of disputes where states acknowledged "a supreme power, *superior to and able to controul* each and all of its parts." Even "a *wrongful decision*" by a recognized tribunal was "preferable to the continuance of such destructive controversies" between "strong contending bodies." Recognizing no authoritative means of rendering justice, states inevitably would resort to force in upholding what they judged to be their rights. Yet, everyone agreed, no man or state was qualified to be judge in his own case: "rights" defined in such partial fashion were indistinguishable from "interests." Reduced to their "natural,'' disunited condition, the American states would not survive long as republics. In the event of disunion, both the ends of state policy (the pursuit of interest masquerading as rights) and the means for implementing it (warfare) would subvert and ultimately destroy republican liberty.

Webster argued that the states could be saved from themselves by being barred from exercising sovereign powers and submitting to the federal government's overseeing authority. "The new Constitution leaves all the Thirteen States, complete republics, as it found them," he wrote; indeed, it "gives an establishment, support, and protection to the internal and separate police of each State, under the superintendency of the federal powers, which it could not possibly enjoy in an independent state."[69]

The Federalists' premise was that the states were interdependent: the union was like a building with each state playing a crucial structural role. If the state pillars were withdrawn, the whole edifice would collapse.[70] The states would not survive the general calamity: "The strongest-nerved state, even the right arm, if separated from the body, must wither."[71] It was clear to Robert R. Livingston, for instance, that New York's very "existence, as a state, depends on a strong and efficient federal government."[72] The states would become progressively weaker and more vulnerable as the bonds of union diminished; by the same logic, James Wilson added, their "respectability and power will increase with that of the general government."[73]

The argument for interdependence was an argument against a broad definition of state sovereignty. Invoking their "realistic" assessment of international politics, Federalists advanced the paradoxical view that the complete independence of the separate states would make them dependent on foreign powers and thus destroy American independence. "Once we were dependent only on Great Britain," wrote Oliver Ellsworth. Because the union was already virtually dissolved, however, "now we are dependent on every petty state in the world."[74] We may be "independent of each other," Thomas Dawes exclaimed in the Massachusetts debates, "but we are slaves to Europe."[75] Only by presenting a united front could the new nation vindicate its rights and promote its interests. Yet if the conduct of foreign policy devolved on the states, the Americans' effective power would decrease even as the occasions for its use—against one another as well as foreigners—multiplied.

By emphasizing the "duty" of the national government "to protect and secure the states," Federalists were able to make a critical rhetorical move.[76] While nationalist reformers typically had inveighed against the states as the root of all evil, Federalists now portrayed them as *victims* of an imperfect union. Edmund Randolph revealed the development of this position in a speech to the Virginia convention. Because of the defective organization of the union under the Articles, he asserted, Congress had not been "able to cherish and protect the states." Indeed, the central government "has been unable to defend itself against the encroachments made upon it *by* the states": "Every one of them [Virginia included] has conspired against it."[77] Randolph thus endorsed the states' claims to protection, while condemning independent efforts to vindicate those claims as dangerous threats to the peace and welfare of the entire union. The states were equally victims and villains in Randolph's account: their character depended ultimately on the viability of the union.

Federalists insisted that only a strong union could guarantee the survival of the states. Outside the union the states were vulnerable to internal and external assaults; even if they successfully resisted division, annexation, or recolonization, their republican governments were imperiled. Without an "effective superintending control," Randolph warned, thirteen distinct states would be unable to "avoid a hatred to each other deep and deadly."[78] Ellsworth explained that the states would then be subject to the same "ambition," "avarice," and "jarring passions" that actuated individuals in a state of nature.[79] Unrestrained by law and unable to look beyond the immediate gratification of selfish interest, the American states would soon degenerate to the moral level of Old World sovereignties—even if their republican forms temporarily survived.

The states had already betrayed republican principles by refusing to acknowledge one another's rights and by selfishly promoting their interests at one another's expense. The apparent premise of interstate relations was that one state's gain was the other's loss. As a result, "the breath of jealousy has blown the cobweb of our confederacy asunder."[80] "Instead of supporting or assisting" the others, complained Hugh Williamson of North Carolina, "we are uniformly taking the advantage of one another."[81] Because of this destructive competition, Noah Webster wrote, the "present situation of our American states is very little better than a state of nature." Under these conditions, he concluded, "our boasted state sovereignties are so far from securing our liberty and property, that they, every moment, expose us to the loss of both."[82]

When states acted "naturally," without restraint of law or respect for the general welfare, they ceased to be republics. Their unwillingness to acknowledge a superior authority would subvert common loyalties, while respect for rights and a rule of law would give way to a vicious struggle for relative advantage. A truly republican state, Federalists suggested, did not pretend to be fully "sovereign." Americans had established state governments on the solid foundation of popular consent, recognizing the necessity of limiting their power in order to guarantee general interests as well as individual rights. Joined in revolutionary union to secure themselves from the dangers of international power politics, the American states had already disavowed the conventional prerogatives of sovereignties.

Federalists suggested that the willingness of the states to submit to the legitimate authority of the general government was the best test of their republican character. Would the American states be as rational as those proverbial, enlightened men who emerged from their natural condition to enter into social contracts? The states would have to sacrifice their natural liberty, wrote "Plain Truth," if they hoped to enjoy the benefits of union: "State sovereignty is as incompatible with the federal Union, as the natural rights of human vengeance is with the peace of society."[83] The progressive deterioration of Congress's power had obscured this vital principle, encouraging states to reclaim the privileges they deemed natural and thus accelerate the union's collapse.

But the sacrifice of states' rights entailed by union, Federalists emphasized, was more apparent than real. After all, states, like individuals in their natural condition, were at best unreliable judges of their own rights and interests. The cool, rational, and impartial deliberations of an effective national government would be a valuable corrective to the passionate excesses of unchecked state power. David Ramsay argued that "the relinquishments of natural rights," whether by individuals joining civil society or by a state joining a federal union, "are not real sacrifices." Each individual or political community "gains more than it loses, for *it only gives up a right of injuring others*, and obtains in return aid and strength to secure itself in the peaceable enjoyment of all remaining rights."[84] By identifying the advantages of civilized society with the renunciation of natural rights "enjoyed" in a condition of lawless anarchy, Federalists such as Ramsay suggested that the American states would fulfill their republican destiny by perfecting their union.

Who would oppose this evidently irresistible logic? The Federalists had no doubt that if efforts to reform the union failed, "it will be owing to the narrow minds, or selfish views of little politicians" in the states.[85] In order to preempt this predictable opposition, the Convention appealed directly to the sovereign people in each state to approve the Constitution. The "demagogues" who gained power so easily in the states had the most to lose if the union were revitalized; they gratified their "ambition" and "avarice" by catering to the whims of the mob and promoting their states' immediate interests, whatever the ultimate cost.[86] Should the union collapse, state leaders would be well situated to seize unlimited power—perhaps under the plausible pretext of military emergency—and extinguish civil liberty.

Attacks on state officeholders followed logically from the redefinition of statehood and state sovereignty in Federalist polemics. Proponents of the new Constitution contrasted the state republics, properly secured in their legitimate rights and interests, with incipient state despotisms, preparing consciously or unconsciously for the inevitable war of all against all. The preservation of republican liberty therefore depended on a stronger union. But if Americans rejected the Constitution and thus chose disunion, the states would come to resemble the dangerously independent sovereignties that perpetuated wars and destroyed liberty in Europe. Demagogues would exploit interstate rivalries and popular discontent until a new regime of tyranny was instituted.

REAL AND APPARENT INTERESTS

Federalists benefited from the discrepancy between the idea of distinct, self-sufficient, state sovereignties that they imputed to their adversaries and the widespread perception that the states were interdependent and their governments exercised only limited powers. The crucial Federalist postulate was that the status quo was inherently unstable: the unmistakeable decline in congressional authority had created a vacuum of power that demagogues in the states had already moved to fill. This same inexorable redistribution of power fragmented interests, weakened the bonds of union, and threatened to inaugurate an anarchic reign of selfishness and party politics. Federalists thus rejected the Antifederalist argument that union naturally grew out of common interests: they were convinced that the true interests of the American people would remain unrecognized and unfulfilled until a strong national government capable of restraining and directing narrow, local interests was instituted.

By depicting Antifederalists as disunionists and aiming their rhetoric at the pernicious effects of unbounded state sovereignty, Federalists could portray themselves as the true conservators of an original federal compact that was jeopardized by the centrifugal tendencies of recent American politics. Wittingly or not, opponents of reform reinforced these tendencies, aiding and abetting the demagogic leaders who stood to benefit most from the collapse of the union. Federalists claimed that the real interests of the continent were disguised and distorted by the ascendancy of state interest. But American voters—once enlightened by Federalist reasoning—would come to see that the success of petty politicians in promoting their states' pretensions to unlimited sovereign power would be disastrous for civil liberty and republican government and ultimately for the states themselves. State governments ceased to be truly republican when they overstepped the boundaries of their legitimate authority: they became artificial, despotic excrescences that thwarted the genuine will and interests of the American people.

Federalists aimed their rhetorical attacks at actual and potential abuses of state power: the possibility of short-run gain in an unstable, highly competitive situation inevitably would corrupt and destroy republican governments. Therefore, it was necessary, Hamilton said, "to attend to the distinction between the real and the apparent interests of the states."[87] Without a viable union, states pursuing their "apparent interests" would not be able to restrain themselves from "privateering upon each other" for commercial or territorial advantage;[88] nothing would hinder large, powerful states from oppressing their small, weak neighbors.[89] The economic dominance of states with large ports would lead to commercial discrimination against other states; states with large land reserves could anticipate lower taxes, while drawing wealth and population from their circumscribed neighbors. The disadvantages of some states—depopulation, depression, and social instability—thus would be translated into advantages for taxpayers and governments in other states.

The distinction between "real" and "apparent" interests was plausible to Americans on several grounds. Republican ideology and the revolutionary commitment to a common cause taught Americans to distrust factious or partisan "self-interest." As a Boston writer claimed, "The true interests of the several parts of the Confederation are the same."[90] Concepts of popular sovereignty also implied a common interest among the people at large and justified a distinction between them and potentially factious governments with their own distinct, apparent interests.[91] Federalists thus could argue that self-interested "state demagogues" and "great men" opposed the new system even though it served the real interests of the states themselves.[92]

Challenges to the legitimacy of state governments had gained momentum with the development of new standards in the writing and interpretation of constitutions that seemed to subject governments as well as citizens to the rule of law.[93] Although the imperial crisis had driven Americans to embrace a Blackstonian notion of legislative sovereignty, representatives were unable and often unwilling to sustain claims to supremacy over the course of the next decade. American republicanism thus came to be as closely identified with constitutional limitations on government as with government by popular consent. But the notion of responsible, limited government under law was endangered by the deterioration of the union: in relation to one another, the American states were irresponsible, acknowledging no lawful limits to their sovereignty. The new state constitutions had abolished sovereignty—the despotic power to command submission—from the states themselves, only to have the discredited doctrine gain new vitality and respectability in the realm of interstate relations. This was the discrepancy that Federalists exploited so brilliantly.

Thus, although constitutional development in the states worked against claims to unlimited power by their governments, Federalists argued that the collapse of the union would reverse this tendency: nothing could then restrain the states from extending their power at one another's expense—and at the expense of their own citizens. Constitutionally limited republican government would not long survive under the lawless, anarchic conditions that disunion would entail. The Federalists argued that all states were reduced to the same hostile and violent level when confronting one another in their natural condition. It was a mistake to believe the "Genius of republics pacific," Hamilton warned: "Jealousy of commerce as well as jealousy of power begets war."[94] It was in their *internal* constitutions, where the rule of law superseded government by force and fear, that republics could properly be denominated "pacific"; Federalists might even concede that the authentic interests of republican citizens in promoting commercial intercourse throughout the world were also pacific. But, by definition, the interests of governments, not citizens, determined the course of international relations.

States spoke the language of domination, power, and relative advantage; their commitments were calculated and contingent, and the only sanction they recognized was force. "A nation stands alone, as an individual in the state of nature," explained "Cato," "and every other [nation] is naturally its hostile rival; for societies have not even the sympathy of men to moderate their enmities."[95] In America, the present power of state governments was limited both by the constitutions under which they acted and by the constraints of the union, a civilized society of republics— albeit a dangerously imperfect one—which preserved peace and harmony. In the event of disunion, however, the states would assume a new, mutually hostile character. John Jay catalogued the resulting horrors to New York voters: "Every State would be a little nation, jealous of its neighbors, and anxious to strengthen itself by foreign alliances, against its former friends. Then farewell to fraternal affection, unsuspecting intercourse; and mutual participation in commerce, navigation and citizenship. Then would arise mutual restrictions and fears, mutual garrisons,—and standing armies."[96] States as sovereignties would distort and disrupt the natural, mutually beneficial intercourse of citizens and states. It was their very artificiality that made sovereign states so frightening and therefore so lethal to fundamental principles of republican government.

The "great desideratum," wrote Madison, was to establish a national government "sufficiently neutral between different parts of the Society to controul one part from invading the rights of another, and at the same time sufficiently controuled itself."[97] This, Federalists proclaimed, was the framers' great achievement. The federal Constitution would preserve the American republics by preventing them from behaving like disconnected, antagonistic sovereignties; at the same time, constitutional limitations on the new central government would protect the states from consolidation. Therefore, Pelatiah Webster concluded, the new system would not "melt down and destroy" the states but would instead "support and confirm them all."[98]

PERPETUAL PEACE

When Federalists emphasized the advantages of the new union for the separate states, they were responding to political realities. Most Americans, Federalists included, were committed to republican self-government in the states, however much they distrusted those who actually exercised authority and even when they challenged existing constitutional arrangements. Nor could many Americans, in view of their own Revolution against British tyranny, lightly dismiss the dangers of a powerful, potentially despotic consolidated regime erected on the ruins of the states.

By definition, there could be no union without states. During the course of the ratification debate, Federalist defenders of the proposed Constitution were forced by their Antifederalist adversaries to acknowledge that the ultimate measure of the new union's "perfection" would be the vigor and vitality of the states—not their obliteration. In doing so, they advanced new claims for the global significance of America's republican revolution: not only had the individual states instituted the most rational and beneficent governments known to modern man, they were also about to adopt a system that would save them from anarchy and disunion and preserve their character as peaceful republics. Thus the Federalists presented the Constitution as a kind of "peace plan" for the American states and as an inspirational example to the Old World.

James Wilson was the most ingenious exponent of the idea that the American union constituted a model world order. "Here is accomplished," exulted Wilson at the Pennsylvania convention, "what the great mind of Henry IV of France had in contemplation" when he developed one of the most famous peace plans. States would now submit to law, not force: "A tribunal is here founded to decide, justly and quietly, any interfering claim." The central government was the "great arbiter," and "the whole force of the Union can be called forth to reduce an aggressor to reason." Wilson thought these new arrangements "an happy exchange for the disjointed contentious state sovereignties!"[99] Marylander Alexander Contee Hanson also claimed that Americans were making the dream of that "great soul . . . HENRY THE FOURTH" into a reality. Seeking to perfect an enduring balance of power, the French king had first "conceived the idea" of a "true and perfect confederate government" for Europe. Now the United States were about to become a "true federal republic, . . . always capable of accession by the peaceable and friendly admission of new single states."[100]

Both Wilson and Hanson noted that Montesquieu—a favorite philosopher of Antifederalists—also endorsed the idea of a federal republic. Such a confederation, wrote Wilson, guaranteed "all the internal advantages of a republic, at the same time that it maintained the external dignity of a Monarchy."[101] This was precisely the combination of national respectability and local liberty called for by Thomas Pownall and other European friends of the American experiment. A strong continental government, capable of collecting and wielding the power of a mighty empire, alone could secure "perpetual peace" and preserve republican government in America.[102]

The Americans would show Europe how interstate relations could be governed by law and reason. They would also be prepared to welcome new states into their union: extending the confederation was their rational, republican alternative to wars of conquest. If the new government would have "energy enough to maintain the Union of the Atlantic states," predicted Madison, it would prove equally capable of binding new western states to the existing union.[103] Thus, Francis Corbin exclaimed, the Americans would extend their union "to all the western world; nay, I may say, ad infinitum." No matter how large the union became, he added, its extent cannot render the new "government oppressive." The states would "retain such powers" as will give them "the advantages of small republics, without the danger commonly attendant on the weakness of such governments."[104]

8
Federalists, Antifederalists, and the Economy

Federalists hoped that the Constitution's guarantees of state and sectional interests would disarm potential critics and thus facilitate the document's speedy ratification. But defenders of the proposed system recognized that they would have to overcome considerable popular skepticism. The obvious strategy was to emphasize the critically dangerous condition of American affairs: a more perfect union was the only alternative to the pervasive conflicts of economic and political interests that impeded recovery from the postwar depression and rendered the United States strategically vulnerable.

In his contributions to the *Federalist* series, Alexander Hamilton asserted that the new central government would frustrate the ambitions of "vindictive and rapacious" European powers to destroy American commerce, while promising relief from the "interfering and unneighbourly regulations of some States."[1] Tench Coxe was convinced that commerce suffered more from the "uncertainty, opposition, and errors of our trade laws" than from the discriminatory "restrictions" of any European power; "If we are to continue one people," the present chaotic situation of interstate commerce "can no longer be supported."[2] The "Utopian idea" that "reason and perfect justice" would govern interstate relations was "long since exploded," concluded William Hillhouse of Connecticut. Peace and prosperity would elude Americans until they adopted a "general plan."[3]

Continuing complaints of widespread distress in the cities seemed to support Federalist assessments and prescriptions. According to "A Citizen" in New York, public creditors were up in arms because they were forced "to dispose of their claims at less than [a] fourth part of their just dues." Debts were reckoned in fixed sums, while state paper money depreciated at ruinous rates and British credit was tight.[4] Other writers reported ''universal complaint'' throughout the states over the ''decay of trade, general bankruptcies, deficiency of money, and the rapaciousness of taxgatherers.'' Yet, although the depressed condition of ''this unhappy country'' was all ''too visible,'' the state governments remained unable or unwilling to act.[5]

Lesser merchants with commercial interests in the West Indies and southern Europe continued to seek remedies from the state legislatures throughout the postwar depression. By the time of the ratification debates, however, many merchants had become convinced that the states were incapable of responding effectively to foreign commercial regulation. Although private indebtedness gradually diminished after 1787, these merchants still complained about depreciated domestic debts and rising interest rates. With their reckless paper money emissions and specie revaluations, some state legislatures had further jeopardized mercantile credit. Many traders thus began to lose faith in the states and joined large wholesalers in supporting ratification.[6]

Federalists succeeded in recruiting a wide array of economic groups by emphasizing their interdependency as well as their common interest in political and economic stability under a strong union. Artisans and manufacturers hoped that commercial recovery would revive their trades and make new enterprises profitable.[7] Shipbuilders, refiners, brewers, iron goods producers, and other entrepreneurs pinned their hopes on federal protection and support.[8]

Federalist polemics combined pessimistic accounts of the sorry state of the American economy with optimistic assessments of the prospects for expanding world trade and western development. Proponents of the Constitution thus appropriated the vision—and gained the support—of the political economists who had been urging their countrymen to exploit the continent's great natural wealth. By focusing on the prospects for economic development, Federalists hoped to counter Antifederalist concerns about the diminution of states' rights or individual liberties that the new system apparently entailed. Under a more perfect and prosperous union, Americans would transcend the debilitating competition for relative advantage that characterized Confederation politics.

UNION AND DEVELOPMENT

The Federalist case for the natural harmony of interdependent interests across the continent inevitably stressed the crucial importance of commerce. Hamilton explained that commerce not only circulated wealth among far-flung producers and consumers but also spurred new enterprises. Commerce was "the most useful as well as the most productive source of national wealth," for "in proportion as commerce has flourished, land has risen in value" and agriculture has become "intimately blended and interwoven" with trade.[9] Domestic prosperity would in turn guarantee favorable commercial and political relations with the world at large. But Americans could not gain favorable terms of trade or diplomatic respect until they abandoned their dissonant, mutually defeating state economic policies. The first, practical step toward securing American commercial interests would be the institution of a national impost.[10]

Advocates of ratification also believed that if Americans adopted "the government offered for our acceptance," they would soon extend their "great and boundless empire" to the west.[11] Prospects for westward expansion enabled political economists to move beyond traditional assumptions about the inevitable cycle of growth and decay.[12] The colonies' dependent condition in the British Empire made economic progress unimaginable. But, wrote David Ramsay, mankind "naturally relishes" economic as well as political "liberty." Independent Americans therefore were poised to capitalize on the magnificent possibilities of a "new and unsettled country."[13]

Development-minded entrepreneurs, manufacturers, and commercial farmers anticipated the Federalist conception of an expanding union of interlocking interests. Spokesmen for these groups had long argued that the success of America's republican experiment depended on exploiting the continent's productive capacity. Nationalists appropriated this vision of integrated economic development in their campaign for constitutional reform. They blamed exaggerated sectional loyalties and discordant state policies for subverting the natural interdependence of interests across the continent. Rumors that western separatists were negotiating with foreign powers underscored the tenuousness of an all-too-imperfect union. Constitutional reform was the necessary precondition for economic progress on a continental scale.

Intersectional cooperation was imperative. In 1786, a South Carolinian explained how a national navigation act would benefit southern planters as well as northern shippers: "The numbers and industry of the northern states would give security, strength, and splendour to the south; and the wealth of the south . . . would then enrich ourselves and reward the laborious inhabitants of the north. . . . [T]he resources of each part would contribute to add to the strength and glory of the whole empire."[14] Growing consciousness of sectional distinctiveness meant that many Americans would be skeptical about such arguments, particularly when they were so obviously designed to promote a program that would serve specific interests. But a clearer and more palatable conception of sectional interdependence emerged when policymakers looked west. The union of East and West hinged on the rapid expansion of commercial agriculture. Improving the "navigation of [the] Potowmack" would facilitate trade, a Virginia developer predicted, and thus constitute "one of the grandest Chains for preserving the federal Union" and guaranteeing that easterners and westerners "shall be one and the same people."[15] The harmony of eastern and western interests was premised on visions of economic development that the natural bounty of the hinterland inspired. The challenge for Federalists was to convince voters in the states that national constitutional reform would spur this development throughout the country and so demonstrate the natural interdependence of American interests.

Federalist arguments drew on the writings of earlier pro-development writers. Commerce, the future Federalist Pelatiah Webster asserted in 1783, was a crucial circulating *"conduit,"* the *"handmaid"* of *"husbandry, fisheries, and manufactures."* Trade is the "servant that tends upon them—the *nurse* that takes away their redundancies, and supplies their wants."[16] The future of trade therefore depended on the expansion of productive enterprise. "The magnificence of the land," newspaper essayist "Lycurgus" exulted, afforded "a prospect of wealth and commerce which future ages alone can realize."[17] In America, another writer explained, "the invigorating breath of industry animates . . . the regenerating powers of nature."[18] Federalists eagerly adopted this notion of "nature" and the nation's "natural" prospects and connected it to westward expansion and rising intersectional trade. On the eve of the Philadelphia Convention, Jedidiah Huntington implored the Connecticut legislature to support the movement to strengthen the union: "The variety of soil and climate within the United States is capable of producing every article which either the convenience or luxury of man requires."[19]

As Federalists elaborated on the great potential of material wealth to meliorate disunionist tendencies and strengthen the union, they also developed a more sophisticated appreciation of how human effort was required to direct and "civilize" this process. If Americans were to benefit from "the wise predisposition of nature," William Vans Murray wrote, they required "the protection of good laws."[20] Tench Coxe epitomized the new political economy in an essay on the "State of Union" published in 1792. Strong government, Coxe insisted, was necessary to foster the natural "marts of trade" that were springing up throughout the interior. A country that exported agricultural surpluses would only thrive if a strong central government preserved order and harmony among diverse interests while negotiating favorable international trade agreements. Only a viable national legislature could attend to the "five or six great local subdivisions of trade, resulting principally from the imperious dictates of *the nature of things*."[21] North Carolina Federalists James Iredell and Hugh Williamson agreed that the central government was better situated than the state governments to promote friendly relations and mutually beneficial exchanges among the continent's natural divisions. "The commercial wars of the States" thwarted accords between exporters and planters or between the commercial states and their agricultural "sisters." The "true objects" of the American people were private property and the general welfare, both of which transcended state boundaries and recognized only the "natural divisions" of geography.[22]

The authors of the *Federalist* insisted that national economic development was contingent on a strong union. The "diversity in the production of different states" was a national blessing, Hamilton pointed out in *Federalist* No. 11: "When the staple of one fails . . . it can call to its aid the staple of another. The variety not less than the value of products for exportation, contribute to the activity of foreign commerce." The new regime would "advance the trade of each [state] by an interchange of their respective productions, not only for the supply of reciprocal wants at home, but for exportation to foreign markets.''[23] This natural reciprocity, he went on to explain in *Federalist* No. 12, could not be sustained without effective central control; a weak union invited anarchy, ''illicit trade,'' and ''frequent evasions of the commercial regulations of each other.'' Uniform economic direction meant that there would be ''but ONE SIDE to guard, the ATLANTIC COAST.''[24] Under the new federal system, Hamilton promised, petty local politics would give way to a general recognition of common interests. If the Constitution was ratified, ''no partial motive, no particular interest, no pride of opinion, no temporary passion or prejudice'' would jeopardize ''the very existence of the nation.''[25]

ANTIFEDERALISTS AND INTEREST

Antifederalist critics of the Constitution discounted what they insisted were exaggerated depictions of the new nation's critical state of affairs and challenged their opponents' promises that ratification would guarantee national prosperity and power. ''Alfred,'' for instance, disputed the Federalist assumption that America was in a ''deplorable, ruined condition.''[26] In 1787, another writer noted, American exports had exceeded imports, thus reversing previous imbalances. He concluded that the new nation's commercial situation ''is not so bad as reported.''[27] Governor George Clinton assured New York legislators in January 1788 that ''the Country is in a great measure recovered from the wastes and injuries of War.''[28]

Antifederalist writers did not question the importance of self-interest and a ''spirit of enterprise'' in their commentary on American political economy. They agreed with their opponents that trade was ''the handmaid of liberty'' in a largely agricultural country and that, in the words of the Antifederalist dissenters at the Pennsylvania ratifying convention, the nation's ''preposterous commerce'' had to be put on a new footing.[29] It was ''the anxious wish of every class of citizens,'' wrote ''Centinel,'' to eradicate state jealousies and regulate trade in the national interest.[30]

But Antifederalists differed fundamentally with their adversaries over how best to perfect the union and promote national prosperity. The central government's regulatory powers, they insisted, should not extend beyond levying modest import duties in order to raise revenues. Antifederalist commentators held forth repeatedly on the pernicious effects of the direct taxes permitted under the Constitution; they also predicted that the constitutional ban on export taxes would not long survive the escalating revenue demands of the new national government.[31] Critics of the proposed system were not reassured by Federalist claims that Congress would only impose direct taxes under the most extraordinary circumstances; after all, Hamilton had been insisting on the advantages of excise taxes for years.[32] "Cato" warned that when new taxes raised the prices of "useful as well as luxurious" commodities, farmers would face "inevitable bankruptcy."[33] Because "gentlemen . . . of great weight and influence" would manipulate fiscal policy to their own advantage, complained "Republican," "honest self-interest" would no longer be rewarded.[34] "Brutus" predicted that taxes would fall "on everything we eat, drink, or wear . . . and come home to every man's house and pocket." Tax-gatherers would "grind the face of the poor" and force merchants to "cease importing or smuggle their goods."[35]

Antifederalists recognized that governments needed revenue in order to fulfill their legitimate obligations at home and abroad. But the tax power, "the main spring in the machine" of government, threatened to "draw into its vortex all other powers." Modest state import duties were acceptable, Yates thought, because "they may be carried no higher than trade will bear or smuggling permit." A distant central authority would be much less sensitive to the deleterious consequences of high taxes. But the gravest danger, Antifederalists argued, was that the national government's taxing power would subvert state sovereignty, that "most precious jewel," and so destroy the people's liberty and property.[36]

Opponents of the Constitution sought to counter Federalist attacks on the states. In fact, they insisted, state economic policies had rarely come into conflict, and the state governments could hardly be blamed for the postwar depression. To the contrary, the states had been remarkably successful in promoting "useful industries" and the expansion of trade in the interior. State experiments with imposts, loan offices, banks, and debt assumption showed that it was possible to establish fair systems of public credit.[37] The success of these experiments, however, depended on the responsibility and responsiveness of state legislators to their constituents. "The true commercial interests of a country not only require just ideas of the general commerce of the world," explained Melancton Smith, but also an intimate knowledge of local agricultural "productions" and of the prospects for local "manufactures." Republican rulers needed to know the "circumstances and ability of the people in general" in order to assess the impact of regulation and taxation "upon the different classes."[38]

Antifederalists thus emphasized the superiority of local control over the economy. "It is vain to tell us that we ought to overlook local interests," James Winthrop wrote in his "Agrippa" series.[39] A Philadelphia writer asserted that "different interests, different manners, and different local prejudices" guaranteed the failure of any attempt to regulate the national economy on just and equitable terms.[40] The "only reliable bond of union," Winthrop reasoned, was in voluntary and mutually beneficial exchanges between the different states with their distinctive "situation, wants and produce." As long as the members of the union confronted one another as true equals, this diversity was itself "sufficient foundation for the most friendly intercourse."[41]

Winthrop's formulation suggested that economic interdependence was incompatible with the political interference in the marketplace that could be anticipated from a strong national government. Few other Antifederalists were prepared to rely so exclusively on market relations to take the place of political obligations, but radical free trade ideas did provide them with a critical perspective on Federalist political economy. "Trade generally finds its own level," explained one Antifederalist writer, "and will naturally and necessarily leave off any undue burdens upon it."[42] Therefore, government regulation would simply encourage illicit traffic and interfere with the natural tendency for supply and demand to come into balance. "When business is unshackled," Winthrop concluded, "it will find out that channel which is most friendly to its course." Let each trader, great or small, enter "into any branch [of trade] that pleases him," for that freedom alone "arouses a spirit of industry and exertion that is friendly to commerce."[43]

The Federalists mistook the interests of large-scale international traders for the national interest. Under their proposed scheme, monopoly interests would emerge to control the economy and stifle development. Privileged and powerful monopolists would gladly sacrifice the "liberty and happiness" of the people to "reap the golden harvest of regulated commerce."[44] Another Anti- federalist writer argued that the economic development of the hinterland would be retarded in a highly regulated economy, dominated by powerful interest groups. There was a "spirit of emulation, of industry, of improvement, [and] of patriotism" in the countryside that would draw rural producers and entrepre- neurs into commerce. But this commercialization could not be promoted "by the interposition of the legislature"; perhaps, indeed, it was "the *want* of an effective government" that was essential to economic progress. Where government "might have meddled," he suggested, it "might have marred."[45]

Opponents of the Constitution also warned that Federalist efforts to control the national economy would impoverish the states. The Federalists were "brokers, usurers, constables, and coiners of circulating coppers" whose goal was to drain resources from the entire continent in order "to fatten [an] overgrown capital."[46] The accumulation of wealth at the seat of the new central government would encourage financiers, speculators, and monopolizers to conspire against the public interest. Because "wealth always creates influence," wrote Winthrop, successful monopolists would soon gain a dominant voice.[47] And because the patriotism and loyalty of these powerful men were so doubt- ful, they were unlikely to show much concern for the rights and interests of their countrymen. "Federal Farmer" thus drew a distinction between smaller-scale, locally oriented traders who were responsive to popular needs and the big merchants who sought to control markets and enrich themselves by fostering gluts and shortages. The latter never hesitated to "avail them- selves" of the "weakness and ardor" of ambitious smaller traders and improvident consumers.[48]

Antifederalists thus championed the "men of middling prop- erty" who were not only the most politically virtuous but also the most enterprising and productive citizens in the American states. They were neither "poor and indifferent to government" nor "in the habit of profuse living."[49] The interests of this great middle class would be sacrificed to those of a few wealthy, would-be aristocrats under the proposed Constitution. Every class, the "Federal Farmer" insisted, should have its "centinels" in the central government in order to secure its essential interests.[50] John

Stevens and other forward-looking Antifederalists further suggested that economic growth depended on responsive local governments.[51] When the political rights and economic interests of "industrious" and "useful" small producers were guaranteed, the American economy would flourish in a system of "reciprocal wants" and satisfactions.[52]

Although most Antifederalists were critical of the "aristocratic" tendencies of the new Constitution, few showed much sympathy for "the little insurgents, men in debt, who want no law, and who want a share of the property of others" who fomented civil unrest in western Massachusetts and in other rural areas across the continent.[53] Nevertheless, while agreeing with their opponents that "excessive importations" bred luxury—the "parent of inequality, the foe to virtue, and the enemy to restraint"—they were less inclined to impugn the character of a "middling" majority.[54] After all, the large importers who flooded American markets with luxury goods were themselves the most conspicuous consumers. The vogue for luxuries illuminated the growing distance between the "high life" of a wealthy and powerful elite and the modest circumstances of most white male Americans.[55] The virtue of these aspiring aristocrats might well be in a state of decline, but the same was not necessarily true for the great majority of productive and patriotic citizens. "The complaints of the decay of *trade* are without foundation," one Antifederalist quipped; "it should rather be said there is a decay of *traders*."[56]

When Antifederalists vindicated the people's "virtue," they did not extol the austerity and self-denial so dear to classical theorists. Wealth, said Pennsylvanian William Findley, was surely a crucial "means of enjoying happiness and independence." But while "wealth in many hands" fostered productive enterprise in the entire community, the "enormous wealth" of the idle and privileged few stifled productivity and jeopardized political and economic freedom.[57] Federalists such as Noah Webster and John Witherspoon tried to convince skeptics that their prescriptions for national economic development would not lead to the creation of an aristocratic political and social order; in a free market, they suggested, luxury was the just reward of enterprise and a degree of inequality was the inevitable concomitant of economic progress.[58] But Antifederalists, arguing for an open economy and identifying economic freedom with local control, successfully exploited apparent contradictions in the Federalist argument. They challenged the premise that a strong central government, with an extensive and intrusive fiscal and regulatory apparatus, would promote enterprise and development. The Federalists claimed to be liberating the American economy from the constraints of faction and conflicting state policies, but their real intention, Antifederalists said, was to establish a national aristocracy on the ruins of the state governments. The Federalists justified their assault on the "real" and naturally complementary interests of the states by invoking a chimerical, merely "apparent" national interest.

MANUFACTURERS

The Federalists had to show that the Constitution would serve the interests of the entire union. To do so, they had to convince influential interest groups that economic development depended on establishing an effective central government.[59] Enlisting the support of an emerging group of manufacturers was particularly crucial to their success. Federalists could counter the charge of aristocratic ambition by linking national constitutional reform to the expansion of productive enterprise.

The surest way for Americans to secure their "natural as well as political independence," Hugh Williamson asserted, was to enhance domestic productivity.[60] By emphasizing the importance of manufactures, Federalists also appealed to vigilant republicans who hoped to protect American virtue from dangerous foreign dependencies and entanglements. "Amicus" warned that excessive reliance on imports encouraged luxury consumption and the spread of vicious "European habits."[61] Investment in productive enterprises that improved the "natural riches of the earth" would reinforce virtuous tendencies toward "industry, frugality, and oeconomy" while "retriev[ing] affairs" from "the evil effects of . . . riot and luxury."[62]

As long as American investors diverted capital from useful manufactures to "paper Speculations," Peter Colt of Hartford believed, the American consumer would be doomed to a "disgracefull dependance on Europe" for his "ordinary Cloathing."[63] The worst excesses of commerce—gluts of grain and other commodities, wild fluctuations in prices, and the "trickery, forgery and usury" of foreign merchants and creditors—could only be suppressed when British agents were driven from the land and Americans produced essential goods for themselves.[64] Ultimately, inhabitants of an infant country would "grow rich" if they were willing to rely on domestic manufactures, however crude and expensive they might be at first.[65] Manufacturing would lay the foundations of the America's future prosperity and power.

Skeptics doubted that government efforts to promote manufactures could have a significant impact in an agricultural, staple-exporting economy. Phineas Bond, British consul for the middle states, believed that home manufactures, notably of textiles, would prosper as a complement to family farming. But the Americans' "strong disposition to husbandry" and "propensity to migrate" to new lands would retard progress toward true "manufactories." Successful manufacturing enterprises would have to await more compact settlement as well as the availability of surplus "capital" and "liberal credit."[66] In the meantime, a few urban enterprises with access to local capital and markets provided the sole basis for "manufactories."[67]

Optimistic Americans challenged the skeptics, however, asserting that the new nation could now surpass its traditionally dependent position in the transatlantic economy. The "arts" of small producers were the best guarantee of a "flourishing and respectable people."[68] The growth of manufactures would spur population growth, Jedidiah Huntington told the Connecticut legislature, thus increasing "our true wealth and independence."[69] William Hillhouse, Jr., believed that "the introduction of arts" and progress in manufacturing did not cause the "ruin of kingdoms"; these were instead "their surest support."[70] This was the "turning point," wrote Simeon Baldwin of New Haven, when "the introduction of manufactures among ourselves" could free Americans from colonial patterns of trade.[71] Northern entrepreneurs broached ambitious schemes to substitute locally produced goods for the imports that still dominated American markets.[72] Southerners such as George Washington thought the depressed state of America's foreign trade afforded an excellent opportunity for more modest rural enterprises. Small-scale establishments that processed agricultural goods and satisfied local demand for textiles, clothing, and leather goods would be "of the most immediate and extensive utility."[73]

Advocates of American manufactures acknowledged that "the present state of America will limit the greatest part of its inhabitants to agriculture."[74] The best prospects for manufactures, Tench Coxe thus concluded, were in the countryside where farmers produced "a considerable surplus for the use of other parts of the union."[75] Peter Colt reported that rural manufacturing "carried on in Families merely for the consumption of those Families" or "for the purpose of barter and sale" was already rapidly expanding and improving, "both as it respects the Quantity & Quality of the Goods." Protective tariffs and other forms of state aid would encourage private investment in these fledgling enterprises and accelerate economic development and population growth.[76]

Visions of internal development enabled political economists to imagine a synthesis of manufacturing, agriculture, and commerce in the future. Land, said William Barton, was "our great staple," and agriculture "our principal manufacture."[77] Coxe called the hinterland, with its natural abundance, "the greatest factory of American raw materials." "Without manufactures," he asserted, "the progress of agriculture would be arrested on the frontier of Pennsylvania"; without a rising agricultural population, manufactures would languish.[78] Coxe's formulation transcended the usual geographical and economic distinctions. Close to the sources of surplus agricultural population, rural manufactures would guarantee full employment and maximum productivity. Coxe predicted that this symbiosis of agriculture and manufacturing would be America's "POLITICAL SALVATION."[79]

Political economists such as Coxe urged legislators everywhere to take strong measures to promote economic growth and secure the new nation's political independence. They campaigned for river improvements and new roads and canals that would harmonize diverse interests and unite scattered settlements; they advocated protectionist legislation that would enable American manufacturers to supply domestic markets.[80] Advocates of manufactures argued that modest tariffs on goods that could be produced in America were not "parochial" but would instead foster "industry" and "frugality" while correcting chronic foreign trade imbalances.[81]

By the time of the Philadelphia Convention, growing numbers of local interest groups had become convinced that the state legislatures were unable and unwilling to promote their interests. In New York, disgruntled manufacturers and smaller merchants complained that large-scale wholesalers exercised disproportionate influence. Legislators, "deluded by an appearance of plenty" and guided by a dangerous "prepossession in favor of foreign commodities," had "mistaken excessive importation for a flourishing trade." As a result, New York had failed to protect or encourage small producers. To the south, manufacturers could expect even less support from state legislatures that were dominated by planters with an interest in keeping import duties low. Proponents of manufactures in every part of the country thus came to agree on the need for a strong national government that could "extend a protecting hand to the interests of commerce *and* the arts."[82]

Many commercial farmers and small producers in the interior who sought the "free unrestricted sale" of their commodities were also drawn into the Federalist coalition by 1788. George Logan and William Barton assured them that discriminatory imposts that discouraged foreign imports were compatible with complete freedom of exchange within the country. The national economy would thrive, Barton promised, when American consumers eschewed the "false refinement" of excessive dependency on luxury imports and the states overcame the "excessive jealousy" that interfered with domestic free trade.[83] Protective duties against foreign imports combined with the elimination of barriers to free trade among the states would increase exports and enhance the prospects for future economic development.[84] Policies that encouraged exports and domestic manufactures, Madison concluded, would secure the "natural harmony of interests" across the continent. The key to the new nation's future prosperity and power was to maximize the economic opportunities of American producers. On the one hand, Madison suggested, this meant minimizing state interference and expanding the scope of private initiative. But economic development also depended on protecting infant industries from destructive foreign competition and on connecting inland producers to markets through internal improvements.[85] Freedom and restriction would work together to create a "system of manufactures" and domestic trade that would in turn create conditions for trade with foreign nations on an equal basis.[86]

THE FEDERALIST MOMENT

Although Federalists and Antifederalists set forth radically different conceptions of the American political economy during the ratification controversy, they shared many assumptions. Spokesmen for both parties sought to reconcile economic freedom with their "realistic" assessments of the need for state or congressional regulation of commerce and promotion of economic development. The fundamental disagreement, of course, was over the advisability of granting extensive new powers to the central government. Federalists enjoyed various political and rhetorical advantages in the resulting exchange: as critics of an "imbecilic" central government—apparently tottering on its last legs—they were able to exploit and foster a pervasive sense of crisis; as proponents of a more perfect federal union, they could promise a prosperous and peaceful future for all Americans. Meanwhile, Antifederalists were forced to defend a status quo that many considered unsatisfactory.

The Federalists seized and helped create a historic opportunity for radical constitutional change. But they did not emerge victorious because they were the party of "modernity" or because their vision actually anticipated the future course of American development. Nor were the Antifederalists the party of reaction, committed to a static, traditional economy or to a classical republican polity. To the contrary, opponents of the Constitution such as William Findley and James Winthrop can be seen as heralds of an emergent democratic liberalism, eager to expand the scope of popular economic freedom. As a group, however, the Antifederalists did not develop a systematic conception of the American political economy, and given the many distinctive local interests they represented and so often invoked, their idea of a great, harmonious middle-class majority was hard to sustain. In fact, many of the "middling" Americans for whom the Antifederalists claimed to speak were already convinced that the state governments could not adequately secure or promote their interests.

Federalists appealed to ambitious and enterprising Americans who felt thwarted by state particularism and national impotence, promising that all "natural interests" would be protected and promoted. Yet, even as the new regime ensured national unity, it would guarantee the states' legitimate interests. Similarly, constitutional compromises over navigation acts, export duties, and slavery allayed intersectional suspicions about the potential misuse of national power while promoting common interests. Federalists sought to convince skeptics not only that a strong central government could be reconciled with a broad range of interests but also that "under a wise government," this "diversity . . . will prove the cement of the union."[87]

By appealing to popular hopes—and fears—about the new nation's future, Federalists identified themselves with a kind of economic freedom that guaranteed orderly economic development for a wide array of expectant and rising interests. In Federalist rhetoric, boundless opportunity was linked with the security of property that a new national government offered. Productivity and patriotism thus converged. A union defined by enlightened self-interest became more concrete to broad segments of the population, even as it transcended the specific local contexts in which "interest" was often defined by Antifederalists. Thus, Federalists, more than their opponents, helped individual Americans see their place in the collective enterprise and imagine a future political economy of unlimited prosperity and peace.[88]

Epilogue:
The Test of Experiment

As the proposed federal Constitution moved toward ratification, Massachusetts Federalist Jonathan Jackson sounded a cautionary note. "We cannot depend upon all our calculations, or reasoning," he warned, "till they are brought to the test of experiment." He quoted from Dean Swift to epitomize the new nation's situation: "In political arithmetic 2 & 2 do not always make 4."[1] Successfully identifying ratification with an expansive vision of national prosperity and power, the Federalists were winning the battle of words. Meanwhile, opponents of the Constitution were forced to assume a defensive posture. Holding forth eloquently on the dangers of concentrated wealth and power in a consolidated national regime, Antifederalists exploited the popular antipathy to aristocracy and privilege that had spurred mobilization in the struggle for independence. But the most trenchant critics of the proposed system moved beyond these familiar themes. They wondered how much the "middling classes" would share in the promised new wealth; some challenged the premise that a strong national government would, in fact, promote national prosperity. These more wary Antifederalists suggested that the new regime would curb economic freedom and stifle initiative in the interests of the privileged and powerful.

Only time would tell if the new political economy would prosper. Although there were already some signs of recovery during the ratification period, the economy as a whole remained unstable and unpredictable. Many of the planters and commercial farmers who benefited from the revival of international prices were disposed to support the movement for constitutional reform. If prices fell, however, this constituency would soon melt away. In any case, the new national government could not possibly satisfy

163

the demands of all the disparate interest groups that supported the Constitution. Manufacturers and artisans and allied commercial interests that sought to foster domestic development through protective tariffs and internal improvements inevitably would clash with the large wholesalers and staple exporters who sought closer ties and freer trade with Britain. Indeed, any discernible course of commercial policy would jeopardize the "natural" harmony of interests touted by the Federalists. By the close of the decade, an apparent tilt toward the transatlantic traders had begun to alienate less favored groups and thus to give some credence to Antifederalist warnings about the designs of would-be "aristocrats" on dominating the national economy.[2]

After 1789, Federalists continued to emphasize the need for security and order to advance the enlightened pursuit of self-interest. But efforts to translate the idea of naturally harmonious interests into concrete policy measures exposed ever-widening rifts within the Federalist ranks and prepared the way for the rise of an opposition party. Treasury Secretary Alexander Hamilton and his supporters believed that financial stability and civic order were indispensable for national economic development. The Hamiltonians claimed that these conditions could only be attained if the new government secured the loyalty and interest of the large importers. Hamilton warned against unrealistic attempts to re-define the new nation's position in the world economy. Americans would remain dependent on British markets and credit, he predicted, whatever measures the new government pursued. As long as this was the case, it would be prudent for policymakers to seek the most favorable terms of trade with Britain and to cultivate the "British interest," that intricate web of Anglo-American agents and traders.[3]

Controversy over national economic policy first centered on import duties. Few Americans in 1789 opposed modest duties for revenue. For the time being, very little income could be expected from public land sales; politically astute policymakers knew that imposition of national land or excise taxes would lead to widespread popular disaffection and resistance to the new regime.[4] But congressmen divided sharply over whether or not to levy discriminatory duties on British imports, and these disagreements deepened as Hamilton spearheaded efforts to assume the states' revolutionary debts, fund the vastly enlarged national debt, and establish a powerful national bank. Hamilton's driving ambition was to guarantee the success of the "experiment" in national government by creating an elaborate financial infrastructure. He meant to succeed where his predecessor Robert Morris, bedeviled by the imbecilities of the Confederation, had failed.[5]

In order to garner the crucial support of commercial interests for his plan, Hamilton knew that the administration would have to pledge economic gains as great in domestic enterprise as they had been in foreign trade. Hamilton therefore endeavored to service the revolutionary debt at high interest, favored the holders of depreciated securities who stood to gain from their conversion into government stocks and bonds, and manipulated bank stock so that interest rates would rise steadily for investors. Hamilton was convinced that key commercial interests would only back his program if the government could ensure substantial returns on investments in the domestic economy. Eventually, he promised, the new financial system would invigorate "every branch of industry and affect the interests of all classes of the community."[6] The onset of the French Revolution and Napoleonic Wars convinced leading merchants and other potential investors of the advantages of Hamilton's plan, for just as international commerce began to decline, the national government created a haven for relatively safe investment and profit.[7]

With the inauguration of the new government, however, significant numbers of Federalists who had embraced the Constitution's framework for continental development became increasingly concerned about the direction of national policy. Hamiltonian finance threatened to replicate the British system by promoting "aristocratic commerce" and establishing a dangerously powerful class of national-debt holders. Critics pointed out that there were no constitutional provisions for banks or the assumption of state debts.[8] Hamilton's program would not serve "all classes of the community," charged Madison. The federal government should help American producers gain access to new markets; as long as foreign trade continued to flow in "its old channels," the new nation would remain economically dependent on Britain. Madison urged Congress to impose discriminatory duties on British imports in order to obtain more favorable terms of trade. The United States would not be able to reap the full benefits of international commerce, Madison insisted, until the national economy was on a firmer footing. Monroe agreed that America should not trade freely with the world until it could do so on equal terms. Hamilton's system would simply perpetuate unfavorable trade and credit balances.[9]

Controversy over fiscal and commercial policy gave rise to an increasingly vociferous anti-Hamiltonian coalition. Opposition to the treasury secretary's funding program signalled a rupture in the Federalist ranks: divergent ideological perspectives and fundamental conflicts of interest were now revealed. Southern planters challenged the patriotism and probity of the "northern speculators" and "monopolists" who, at vastly depreciated prices, had purchased much of the revolutionary debt initially held in the southern states. Madison argued that Hamilton's plan would bestow windfall profits on speculators while denying just recompense to the original holders of government securities—the soldiers and other patriotic citizens whose heroic sacrifices had secured American independence. But Madison's proposals to discriminate against British traders and current security holders were voted down.[10]

The final crucial element in Hamiltonian political economy was set forth in the famous *Report on Manufactures*, presented to Congress in December 1791. Because there was such widespread support for domestic development, the *Report* did not at first raise significant objections. Most thoughtful commentators agreed that American independence would only be guaranteed when the country ceased to rely so heavily on foreign imports. With the new government in a sound financial condition, cautious experiments in fostering American manufactures seemed appropriate. Increased productivity would spur "revenue and consumption," Hamilton wrote, while promoting further investment, new inventions, and the immigration of skilled labor. The growth of manufactures would absorb agricultural surpluses and provide opportunities for unemployed farm children.[11]

Critics began to see ominous implications in Hamilton's *Report*, however, in the light of his ill-fated Society for Establishing Useful Manufactures. It was no secret by 1791 that the Society was designed to serve the "monied interest" and not the interests of nascent manufacturers.[12] Hamilton wanted "active wealth, or, in other words, moneyed capital" to invest in the scrip of the Bank of the United States which, in turn, would fund the Society's projects. Although this system would divert mercantile capital into manufacturing, critics complained that it would privilege a few wealthy investors at the expense of a much more numerous and enterprising class of entrepreneurs. The administration's bias toward commercial interests was already apparent in its commitment to low tariff levels. Skeptical readers of Hamilton's *Report* detected a similar solicitude for northeastern merchants in his advocacy of "pecuniary bounties" for particular products instead of protective duties that would encourage aspiring manufacturers generally.[13] Southerners feared that the excise taxes recommended by Hamilton would fall disproportionately on their staple products.[14]

The Society foundered—and its reputation sank—when speculators diverted its funds from productive enterprise and when merchants used the Bank's liberal loan policies to invest in Britain and Europe rather than in American manufactures.[15] Echoing warnings of Antifederalist opponents of the Constitution, Hamilton's critics suggested that his policies inevitably would create a moneyed aristocracy that would stifle economic growth. "By their large capital," wrote "Clitus," the Society would "bear down . . . all the mechanical branches of the same species in the United States." Once the mechanics were "crushed," "the landed interest" would be the next to fall.[16] Hostile commentators likened the Society's "excessive privileges" to the "political monsters" hatched by the Bank of England, cautioning against a repetition of the feverish stock speculation that had ended in the South Sea Bubble. The Society, these critics concluded, was little better than a "company of gamblers."[17]

Critics such as John Taylor of Caroline continued to evoke the vision of a free domestic economy and commercial reciprocity in world trade that Federalists had used to such advantage in the ratification struggle. Hamilton's policies betrayed that promise, wrote Taylor, by creating "a financial class which threatens to become the aristocratic order of the state."[18] Anti-Hamiltonians admonished against allowing this class to forge closer ties with Britain that would jeopardize American independence and retard American development. As he prepared to step down from his position as secretary of state in 1793, Jefferson reiterated his faith in free trade. But, he warned, the world was not yet "ripe for free commerce in all its extent." It behooved the new nation to "protect our citizens" from foreign predators until American producers could participate in world trade on more equal terms.[19]

Tench Coxe, one of the most vigorous proponents of American development, also began to have misgivings about Hamiltonian political economy. Coxe believed that the steady progress of commercial agriculture and closely related manufacturing enterprises represented America's best hope.[20] But he feared that neither agriculture nor small-scale rural manufacturing would benefit from administration initiatives. Coxe's suspicions were aroused by the kind of people Hamilton recruited for his manufacturing society and the close ties between this "monied interest" and British merchants and creditors.

Objections to Hamiltonian finance reached a crescendo in 1791 and 1792, and as Coxe and other staunch proponents of constitutional reform defected from federalism, the ranks of the opposition swelled. The administration could not prevent a speculative orgy by a multitude of small as well as large-scale investors when the Bank of the United States opened. By March 1792, a full-scale panic brought the new nation's fledgling financial institutions to the brink of collapse.[21] Within another two years, popular hostility to Hamiltonian excise taxes would erupt in the Whiskey Rebellion. The narrow ratification of the controversial Jay Treaty in 1795 added further fuel to oppositionist fires.[22]

Party formation in the 1790s reflected and reshaped tensions between interest groups and sections, especially with respect to the development of the West, internal improvements, and slavery.[23] The emergent Democratic-Republicans appealed to former Antifederalists as well as to a wide variety of groups disenchanted with Hamiltonian finance and Federalist diplomacy. The Democratic-Republicans elaborated many of the same themes opponents of the Constitution had invoked during the ratification debates. They warned that an incipient, artificial aristocracy threatened to corrupt the pure springs of republican virtue and to reduce the new nation to a degrading, dependent, neocolonial condition. But the party of Madison and Jefferson also advanced a more optimistic vision of economic opportunity and development as they sought to appeal to energetic and enterprising citizens across the continent. The Democratic-Republicans promised to renew and redeem the union of interests which, they charged, the Federalists had betrayed.

Notes

INTRODUCTION

1. Letter from M. Turgot to Dr. Price, dtd. Paris, Mar. 22, 1778, in Richard Price, "Observations on the Importance of the American Revolution," 222.

2. James Madison, "Vices of the Political System of the U.S.," Apr. 1787, in Robert Rutland et al., eds., *The Papers of James Madison*, 9:354.

3. See Janet Riesman, "Money, Credit, and Federalist Political Economy"; E. James Ferguson, "Political Economy, Public Liberty, and the Formation of the Constitution"; and Richard D. Brown, "Shays's Rebellion and the Ratification of the Constitution in Massachusetts."

4. For a review of some of these "discourses" see Isaac Kramnick, "The 'Great National Discussion' "; for an analysis of jurisprudential language, see John Philip Reid, *The Concept of Liberty in the Age of the American Revolution*; and on millennial thought, see Ruth Bloch, *Visionary Republic*.

5. On this controversy see the discussion in Peter S. Onuf, "Reflections on the Founding." Other recent review essays include Jack P. Greene, *A Bicentennial Bookshelf*, and Patrick T. Conley, "Posterity Views the Founding."

6. Marc Egnal shows that support for expansionism, "a fervent belief in America's potential for greatness," was widespread among the colonial political elites well before the imperial crisis; Egnal, *A Mighty Empire*, 6 and passim.

7. The term "political economy" was used as early as 1750 and had gained wide currency in America by the 1780s. See the many essays on political economy published in the *American Museum*, beginning in 1787; and the discussion in Drew R. McCoy, *The Elusive Republic*, 5–10.

CHAPTER 1. INTEREST AND IDEOLOGY IN REVOLUTIONARY AMERICA

1. The literature on republicanism is enormous. Works that have particularly influenced our thinking include J. G. A. Pocock, *The Machiavellian Moment*; Isaac Kramnick, *Bolingbroke and His Circle*; and John Murrin, "The Great Inversion, or Court versus Country." On American republicanism see Bernard Bailyn, *The Ideological Origins of the Revolution*; Gary Nash, *The Urban Crucible*, esp. ch. 13; and, for the best general account of republican political

economy, Drew R. McCoy, *The Elusive Republic,* esp. chs. 1–3. For the use of Country ideas by Antifederalists, see James Hutson, "Country, Court, and Constitution."

2. As Lance Banning writes, "The analytical distinctions we detect" are not always "evident to those we study." Banning, "Jeffersonian Ideology Revisited," 12.

3. On the republican idealization of landownership see Alan Macfarlane, *The Origins of English Individualism,* esp. ch. 4.

4. For a classic statement of republican warnings against excessive self-interest, see James Harrington, *The Oceana.* See also Anthony Ashley Cooper, third earl of Shaftesbury, *Characteristicks of Men, Manners, Opinions, Times,* 76, 183, 336.

5. Edward Hatton, *The Merchants Magazine,* 212. See also P. G. M. Dickson, *The Financial Revolution in England,* chs. 1–2; Kramnick, *Bolingbroke and His Circle,* 39–47.

6. Since at least the time of Aristotle, observers typically distinguished between foreign trade, in which "fraudulent" or "unnatural" means might be necessary, and the domestic economy, in which at least a modicum of economic justice was expected. Until the late seventeenth century, opponents of the new commercial interests worried about foreign practices invading the British-American economy. See, e.g., Aristotle, *Politics,* 22–27; Francis Bacon, "Of Seditions and Troubles," in Sidney Warhaft, ed., *Francis Bacon: A Selection of His Works,* 79–86; Charles Wilson, *England's Apprenticeship,* 57–65; and, in America, *A Satyre Upon the Times;* [Lewis Morris], "Dialogue Concerning Trade"; [Robert Hunter], "Androboros"; "A Word in Season," *New-York Weekly Journal,* Sept. 5, 1737, and "Account of the Late Election," ibid., Mar. 19, 1739.

7. "Philosophia," "On Wisdom," *New-York Weekly Journal,* Oct. 5, 1733.

8. "Remarks on a Petition," in William Livingston et al., *The Independent Reflector,* ed. Milton Klein, no. 10, Feb. 1, 1753, 118–27, at 118.

9. Reverend John Miller, *A Description of the Province and City of New York* (New York, 1695), cited in Joseph Dorfman, *The Economic Mind in American Civilization,* 77–78. Also, *New York Mercury,* Feb. 1, 1764, June 1, 1768; Daniel Defoe, *The Complete English Tradesman,* 1:89–90, 356; 2:121, 209, 211, 300, 332, 335; "John Trusty," *New-York Weekly Journal,* Apr. 22, 1734.

10. William Livingston, "A Brief Consideration of New York," Special Collections, Columbia University; also, "Of the Extravagance of our Funerals," in Livingston et al., *Independent Reflector,* no. 29, June 14, 1753, 257–62, at 257.

11. *New York Gazette,* Nov. 14, 1737; Esther Singleton, *Social New York under the Georges,* 2:378–79. By the end of the colonial period, tea was the primary focus of concerns about luxury. See Peter Kalm, *Travels in North America,* 1:361; *Essex Gazette,* Jan. 4, 1774; *Pennsylvania Chronicle,* May 2 and Nov. 28, 1768; *Pennsylvania Gazette,* Nov. 17, 1773; *Newport Mercury,* Jan. 24 and Feb. 7, 1774; *New Hampshire Gazette,* July 22, 1774; *Boston Evening Post,* June 24, 1775.

12. "John Scheme," *New-York Weekly Journal,* Mar. 18, 1734.

13. Robert Livingston, Jr., to William Alexander, Mar. 26, 1753, Alexander Papers, vol. 1, no. 25.

14. "Of Patriotism," in Livingston et al., *Independent Reflector,* no. 23, May 3, 1753, 215–20, at 216.

15. For oppositionists on trade as a helpmate of landed virtue, see, e.g., Joseph Addison, "The Royal Exchange," May 19, 1711, in Angus Ross, ed., *Selections from the Tatler and the Spectator*, 437–40; Richard Steele, "Sir Andrew Freeport Defends Commerce," Sept. 19, 1711, ibid., 447–50; Jonathan Swift, *The History of the Four Last Years of the Queen*. For an example of trade advocates' ambivalent attitudes toward agriculture, see Sir Charles Whitworth, ed., *The Political and Commercial Works of that Celebrated Writer Dr. Charles D'Avenant*, 1:160, 4:240–42. See also Dickson, *The Financial Revolution in England*, ch. 2.

16. Our discussion of economic thought in the early modern era draws on Joyce Appleby, *Economic Thought and Ideology in Seventeenth Century England*. Her excellent study shows that a significant body of contemporary economic literature took issue with the post-Restoration policies commonly referred to as mercantile. We are arguing here not for the existence of a true "mercantile system," but instead that there was a continuing dialogue among various interests and a persistent, important strain of economic behavior that derived from notions of freedom in the marketplace. Other important works include W. A. Speck, "The International and Imperial Context," in Jack P. Greene and J. R. Pole, eds., *Colonial British America*; J. A. W. Gunn, *Politics and the Public Interest in the Seventeenth Century*, chs. 3, 5, 6; Albert O. Hirschman, *The Passions and the Interests*; William Letwin, *Origins of Scientific Economics*; Ralph Lerner, "Commerce and Character"; Wilson, *England's Apprenticeship*, chs. 6, 11; C. B. Macpherson, *The Political Theory of Possessive Individualism*; Charles M. Andrews, *The Colonial Period of American History*, vol. 4.

17. [Dudley North], *Discourses upon Trade*, 13.

18. Carew Reynel, *The True English Benefit*, 8–9.

19. William de Britaine, *The Interest of England in the Present War with Holland*, 3–4. See also the 1674 manuscript of John Locke cited in Macpherson, *Possessive Individualism*, 207; Joshua Gee, *The Trade and Navigation of Great Britain*.

20. James Whiston, *The Mismanagements in Trade Discover'd*, 8.

21. Defoe, *Plan of the English Commerce*, 22.

22. "Public Virtue to be Distinguished by Public Honours," in Livingston et al., *The Independent Reflector*, no. 9, Jan. 25, 1753, 111–17, at 111. Also, Philip Livingston to Jacob Wendell, July 23, 1737, Livingston Manuscripts.

23. William Alexander to Peter Van Brugh Livingston, Mar. 1, 1756, Rutherford Collection, vol. 3, no. 93.

24. Mr. Thomas Cockerell to Mr. Popple, July 2, 1709, in E. B. O'Callaghan, ed., *Documents Relative to the Colonial History of the State of New York*, 5:80–81, at 81. Also, "B.B.," "Modest Inquiry," *New York Gazette*, June, 2, 9, and 16, 1729. For classic statements on the universality of interest see, e.g., Francis Bacon, *The Advancement of Learning*; Thomas Hobbes, *Leviathan*, ch. 13; David Hume, *Essays, Moral, Political, and Literary*, 1:176; Adam Smith, *The Wealth of Nations*, 1:477.

25. Richard Campbell, *The London Tradesman*, 284–86.

26. Addison, "Royal Exchange," in Ross, ed., *Selections from the Tatler and the Spectator*, 437–40, at 439.

27. Malachy Postlethwayt, *The Universal Dictionary of Trade and Commerce*, 2:107-8.

28. Joseph Harris, *An Essay upon Money and Coins*, 28, 101; Thomas Mun, *England's Treasure by Forraign Trade*. See the discussion in Appleby, *Economic Thought and Ideology*, ch. 2.

29. Matthew Decker, *Essay on the Causes of the Decline of the Foreign Trade*, 14.

30. Daniel Defoe asked, "What has trade to do with your political quarrels, and what business have party men with the commerce of the nation?" Defoe, *Some Thoughts on the Subject of Commerce*, 8. On the role of the state see Andrews, *Colonial Period of American History*, vol. 4, ch. 11; Gunn, *Politics and the Public Interest*, ch. 5. See also Gee, *Trade and Navigation of Great Britain*; Richard Gouldsmith, *Some Considerations on Trade and Manufactures*, esp. 1–8; William Wood, *Survey of Trade*, esp. 1:130–36, 152–54.

31. On consumption see Neil McKendrick, "Commercialization and the Economy," in Neil McKendrick et al., *The Birth of a Consumer Society*, 9–194.

32. [North], *Discourses upon Trade*, 27.

33. Nicholas Barbon, *Discourse of Trade*, 72-73.

34. Davenant, *On the Plantation Trade*, in Whitworth, *Works of D'Avenant*, 2:75.

35. Ibid. Also, *An Account of the French Usurpation upon the Trade of England*; and *Considerations on the Present State of the Nation*.

36. On the potential benefits of luxury see John Houghton, *A Collection of Letters for the Improvement of Husbandry and Trade*; Defoe, *The Complete English Tradesman*, 2:226, 231–33; Joseph Massie, "The Natural Rate of Interest," (London, 1750), in Jacob Hollander, ed., *Reprints of Economic Tracts*, 20, 53; and David Hume, "Of Commerce" and "Of the Balance of Trade," in Eugene Rotwein, ed., *David Hume: Writings on Economics*, 3–18, 66–77. See also Kramnick, *Bolingbroke and His Circle*, 201–4; John Sekora, *Luxury: The Concept in Western Thought*, ch. 2.

37. Addison, "Royal Exchange," in Ross, *Selections from the Tatler and the Spectator*, 437–40, at 439.

38. John Trenchard, with Thomas Gordon, *Cato's Letters*, 1:11, 134–35; 2:51-54, 71-74, 272-77; 3:24, 27-28.

39. John Locke, "The Second Treatise," in *Two Treatises of Government*, pars. 22, 123, 127.

40. Hume, "Of Commerce," "Of Interest," "Of the Balance of Trade," in Rotwein, *David Hume*, 3–32, 47–59, 60–77.

41. The Dutch example of free ports and open trade with foreigners was prominent in the diverse writings of Carew Reynel, Dalby Thomas, John Pollexfen, William Petty, Charles Davenant, and, to a lesser degree, Daniel Defoe. See the suggestive comments in Andrews, *Colonial Period*, 4:131–37, 346n. On the shift after 1713 see Charles Wilson, *Profit and Power*, ch. 7; *A Discourse consisting of Motives for the Enlargement of Freedom of Trade*; Sir William Temple, "Observations on the United Provinces," in *The Works of William Temple*, 1:1–36.

42. *New York Mercury*, Jan. 24, 1764.

43. Postlethwayt, *Universal Dictionary*, 2:107–8.

44. Lord Sheffield, *Observations on the Commerce of the American States*, 162.

45. For early proposals to free American trade from duties and prohibitions, see, e.g., O'Callaghan, *Documents Relative to Colonial New York*, 3:46,

51–54; W. Noel Sainsbury and J. W. Fortescue, eds., *Calendar of State Papers*, vol. 10 (1677–80), 41; vol. 9 (1675–76), 871, 898–99.

46. Cadwallader Colden, *The Interest of the City and Country to Lay No Duties*, 1–23; "The Interest of the City and Country," *New York Journal*, Sept. 5, 1757; O'Callaghan, *Documents Relative to Colonial New York*, 3:289; *Journal of the Votes and Proceedings of the Assembly of New York*, 1:548, 551–52, 638, 641, 645.

47. Archibald Kennedy, *Observations on the Importance of the Northern Colonies under Proper Regulation*, 6–9, 16.

48. Gov. Hunter to Board of Trade, Nov. 12, 1715; Cadwallader Colden, on New York's trade, 1723; Gov. Cosby to Board of Trade, Dec. 18, 1732—all in O'Callaghan, *Documents Relative to Colonial New York*, 5:457–63, 685–90, 937–38. On the detrimental effects of mercantile regulations see, e.g., *New York Gazette*, Jan. 21, 28, and Feb. 4, 1735.

49. "John Hampden," *Boston Gazette*, Dec. 9, 1765; also, ibid., Dec. 16 and 23, 1765. On the Seven Years' War see Stanley Pargellis, ed., *Military Affairs in North America*; Fred Anderson, *A People's Army*; Theodore Thayer, "The Army Contractors for the Niagara Campaign," quotation at 32. On the scale of economic opportunities by the time of the war, see Joyce Appleby, "The Social Origins of American Revolutionary Ideology."

50. Robert M. Weir, ed., "Two Letters by Christopher Gadsden," 175.

51. See, e.g., Roger Coke, *A Discourse of Trade*, 24–41; and Decker, *Essay on the Decline of Foreign Trade*, 1–6.

52. "The Commercial Conduct of the Province of New York," (New York, 1767), Special Collections, Columbia University. See also Smith, *Wealth of Nations*, 1:291–93, 2:145.

53. On the connection between smuggling and luxury consumption see Cal Winslow, "Sussex Smugglers," esp. 148–49; James B. Hedges, *The Browns of Providence Plantation*; John W. Tyler, *Smugglers and Patriots*; Victor L. Johnson, "Fair Traders and Smugglers in Philadelphia"; Cathy Matson, "From Free Trade to Liberty," chs. 4, 5. Merchant letters offer considerable evidence; see the papers of Abraham Cuyler, John Ludlow, and Peter R. Livingston in the New-York Historical Society and of Thomas Riche and Thomas Wharton in the Historical Society of Pennsylvania.

54. Hezekiah Niles, *Principles and Acts of the Revolution in America*, 16.

55. Lt. Gov. Colden to Earl of Dartmouth, Nov. 2, 1774, in O'Callaghan, *Documents Relative to Colonial New York*, 8:511; "Virginia Instructions for the Deputies," *New York Gazette*, June 6 and Sept. 26, 1765; *Rivington's New York Gazetteer*, Aug. 25, 1774.

56. Thomas Pownall, *The Administration of the British Colonies*, 1. Also, Malachy Postlethwayt, *Great Britain's Commercial Interest Explained and Improved*, 1:482–83.

57. *The Letters and Papers of Cadwallader Colden*, 6:62–66, 136–40, 161–63, 166–73.

58. O'Callaghan, *Documents Relative to Colonial New York*, 8:217, 219; "Answer . . . by Six Merchants," *New York Gazette and Weekly Mercury*, July 2, 1770; "Philo-Veritas," ibid., July 23, 1770.

59. Marc Egnal, "The Economic Development of the Thirteen Continental Colonies." See the citations in n. 65 below.

60. "Address by John Hancock to the People of Boston," Mar. 5, 1774, in Niles, *Principles and Acts of the Revolution*, 63.

61. Edmund Burke to Richard Champion, Jan. 10, 1775, and to Rockingham, Aug. 23, Sept. 14, 1775, in Charles William, ed., *The Correspondence of Edmund Burke*, 2:2–3, 55–56, 62; William Pitt to General Monckton, Oct. 8, 1759, in G. S. Kimball, ed., *The Correspondence of William Pitt*, 2:320–21; William Cobbett, ed., *Parliamentary History of England*, 18:648.

62. *Public Advertiser* (London), Jan. 15, 1770.

63. Ibid., Jan. 3, Feb. 28, and May 4, 1775.

64. "The Association," Oct. 20, 1774, in Worthington C. Ford, ed., *Journals of the Continental Congress*, 1:75–80.

65. Murrin, "The Great Inversion," 396. On the difficulties of balancing private opportunity and public-spirited sacrifice during nonimportation, see, e.g., Ronald Hoffman, *A Spirit of Dissension*, ch. 2; Edward Papenfuse, Jr., *In Pursuit of Profit*; Edmund S. Morgan, "The Puritan Ethic and the Coming of the American Revolution." For analyses of the economic situation, see Paul G. E. Clemens, *The Atlantic Economy and Maryland's Eastern Shore*, esp. ch. 6; Joseph Ernst and Marc Egnal, "An Economic Interpretation of the American Revolution"; Nash, *Urban Crucible*, ch. 13.

66. Ford, *Journals of Congress*, 3:476–77.

67. Thomas Paine, *The Crisis*, 178; also, 100–101, 120–21, 170–71, 174–75.

68. E. Wayne Carp, *To Starve the Army at Pleasure*, chs. 2–3; Richard D. Brown, *Revolutionary Politics in Massachusetts*, 190; Victor L. Johnson, *The American Commissariat during the Revolutionary War*, 37–47, 51–53; Eric Foner, *Tom Paine and Revolutionary America*, 145–82; Clarence Ver Steeg, *Robert Morris, Revolutionary Financier*, 10–20; Robert A. East, *Business Enterprise in the American Revolutionary War Era*, 30–48, 195–96; Richard Buel, "Time: Friend or Foe of the Revolution?"

69. On "Christian Sparta," see Gordon S. Wood, *The Creation of the American Republic*, 114–18. On nonimportation, see J. E. Crowley, *This Sheba, Self*; Arthur M. Schlesinger, *The Colonial Merchants and the American Revolution*; Matson, "From Free Trade to Liberty," 402–46.

70. McCoy, *The Elusive Republic*, 86–106.

71. See, e.g., Benjamin Rush, "On the Defects of the Confederation," in Dagobert D. Runes, ed., *The Selected Writings of Benjamin Rush*, 28–31; George Washington to James Warren, Mar. 31, 1779, in John C. Fitzpatrick, ed., *The Writings of George Washington*, 14:312; John Adams to Mercy Otis Warren, Jan. 8, 1776, *Warren-Adams Letters*, 2:202; Benjamin Rush to James Searle, Jan. 21, 1778, *Pennsylvania Magazine of History and Biography* 3 (1879), 233. In general, see Carp, *To Starve the Army*, and Charles Royster, *A Revolutionary People at War*, 186–89, 192–94, 200–207.

72. "Notes of Debates," Oct. 4, 20, and 21, 1775, in Ford, *Journals of Congress*, 3:479, 498–99, 501; Richard B. Morris, *Government and Labor in Early America*, 92–135; Wood, *Creation of the American Republic*, 419–40.

73. "A Fair Trader," writing in *Pennsylvania Packet*, Dec. 3, 1778, said that although "private vices" did not create "public benefits," the private enterprises of Americans laid the foundation for future expansion. See also Pelatiah Webster, "An Essay on Free Trade and Finance," in Webster, *Political Essays on the Nature and Operations of Money, Public Finances and Other*

Subjects, 25–28; Marc Egnal, *A Mighty Empire*, passim; East, *Business Enterprise*, ch. 9; and Wood, *Creation of the American Republic*, 606–12.

74. "John Trusty," *New-York Weekly Journal*, Apr. 22, 1734.

75. "A Speech Delivered in Carpenter's Hall," Mar. 16, 1775, in *Pennsylvania Evening Post*, Apr. 13, 1775.

76. "Crispin," *Essex Gazette*, Jan. 14, 1772; "A Plan to perpetuate the union," *Virginia Gazette* (Purdie & Dixon), Apr. 29, 1773.

CHAPTER 2. STATE GOVERNMENTS AND THE ECONOMY, 1776–1785

1. Robert Morris to Silas Deane, 1776, cited by Thomas P. Abernethy, "Commercial Activities of Silas Deane in France," 478–79.

2. David Ramsay, *An Oration on the Advantages of American Independence*, 11.

3. John Jay to Robert R. Livingston, dtd. Paris, Nov. 17, 1782, in Francis Wharton, ed., *The Revolutionary Diplomatic Correspondence of the United States*, 6:11–49, at 31. Jay went on to suggest that if he and his fellow negotiators had been able to dictate the terms of the treaty, "it is not unlikely that it would have contained a prohibition of all laws in restraint of trade, foreign or domestic." See also Edmund Cody Burnett, "Notes on American Negotiations for Commercial Treaties."

4. John Adams to Robert R. Livingston, July 14, 1783, in Wharton, *Revolutionary Diplomatic Correspondence*, 6:540–42.

5. See, e.g., James Monroe to James Madison, May 31, 1786, in Robert A. Rutland et al., eds., *The Papers of James Madison*, 9:84n; Madison to Thomas Jefferson, Apr. 27, 1785, ibid., 8:265–70, at 266; and Monroe to Jefferson, June 16, 1785, in Julian Boyd et al., eds., *The Papers of Thomas Jefferson*, 8:216; J. P. Brissot de Warville, *New Travels in the United States of America*, 1:463, 464. See the discussion in Eric Foner, *Tom Paine and Revolutionary America*, ch. 5.

6. Drew R. McCoy, *The Elusive Republic*, 86–106; Cathy Matson, "From Free Trade to Liberty," chs. 1–2.

7. Proclamation of Gov. Jonathan Trumbull, dtd. Lebanon, Conn., Aug. 25, 1780, in Hugh Hastings, ed., *The Public Papers of George Clinton, First Governor of New York*, 6:175–76.

8. The quotation appears in Robert A. East, *Business Enterprise in the American Revolutionary War Era*, 149–50. See also ibid., part II; Joseph Dorfman, *The Economic Mind in American Civilization*, vol. 1, ch. 11; "Rationalis," *New-Jersey Gazette*, Mar. 11, 1778; *Revolutionary Correspondence*, Rhode Island Historical Society, *Collections*, 6:193–94. The most widely disseminated appeal for free trade in the revolutionary years was Thomas Paine's *Common Sense*. Paine says, "America's plan is commerce, and that, well attended to, will secure us the peace and friendship of all Europe; because it is in the interest of all Europe to have America as a free port." *Common Sense*, 21–22. In general see Curtis P. Nettels, *The Emergence of a National Economy*, ch. 1; and McCoy, *Elusive Republic*, 86–106.

9. *Tanners, Curriers, and Cordwainers of Philadelphia*; Richard B. Morris, *Government and Labor in Early America*, 92–118.

10. For injunctions to temper acquisitiveness with a moral sense or prudence, see John Locke, "Of Property," ch. 5 of "Second Treatise," *Two Treatises of Government;* see also Peter Laslett's introduction. Other discussions appear in James Tully, *A Discourse on Property;* Istvan Hont and Michael Ignatieff, eds., *Wealth and Virtue,* introduction; Eugene Rotwein, ed., *David Hume: Writings on Economics,* introduction; Sheldon Wolin, *Politics and Vision,* 330, 332-33, 344-45; Andrew S. Skinner, "Adam Smith"; and Matson, "From Free Trade to Liberty," ch. 1.

11. Benjamin Rush's Notes of Debates, Feb. 14, 1777, in Paul H. Smith, ed., *Letters of Delegates to Congress,* 6:274-77; report of Gouverneur Morris, June 4, 1778, excerpted in Worthington C. Ford, ed., *Journals of the Continental Congress,* 11:569.

12. See, e.g., Robert R. Livingston to Gouverneur Morris, Apr. 6, 1778, in Robert R. Livingston Papers; John Witherspoon to William C. Houston, Jan. 27, 1778, and William Ellery to Nicholas Cooke, Feb. 15, 1777, in Smith, *Letters of Delegates,* 8:669-72, at 670, 6:282-84, at 282; and Ford, *Journals of Congress,* 12:929, 1048-52 (Sept. 19 and Oct. 26, 1778).

13. Franklin made a proposal for free trade ca. Feb. 26, 1776, in Smith, *Letters of Delegates,* 3:305, and Ford, *Journals of Congress,* 2:200. For John Adams's support of the measure, see Adams to James Warren, Mar. 21, 1776, in Smith, *Letters of Delegates,* 3:421-23. Adams's draft of the Model Treaty is in Ford, *Journals of Congress,* 5:576-78, 768-78 (July 18 and Sept. 10, 1776). See also Richard Henry Lee to Patrick Henry, Apr. 20, 1776, in James C. Ballagh, ed., *Letters of Richard Henry Lee,* 1:177-79; John Adams to Warren, Apr. 16, 1776, in Smith, *Letters of Delegates,* 3:535-37, at 536; and Elbridge Gerry to Warren, Mar. 26, 1776, in Ford, *Journals of Congress,* 4:232n. For the finished draft of Franklin's proposal see ibid., 4:257-59 (Apr. 6, 1776).

14. Joseph Hewes to Samuel Johnston, Mar. 20, 1776, and note on the resolution of Congress to seize and condemn British vessels, Apr. 6, 1776, in which John Adams indicated that the measure did not meet the expectations of Massachusetts, Maryland, and Virginia, in Ford, *Journals of Congress,* 4:222n, 259n; John Penn to Thomas Person, Feb. 14, 1776, in Smith, *Letters of Delegates,* 3:254-56, at 255.

15. Benjamin Franklin to C. W. F. Dumas, Dec. 19, 1775, in Wharton, *Revolutionary Diplomatic Correspondence,* 2:64-67; John Adams to James Warren, Mar. 21, 1776, in Smith, *Letters of Delegates,* 3:421-23.

16. Robert R. Livingston to John Jay, Feb. 2 and Sept. 12, 1782, in Henry P. Johnston, ed., *The Correspondence and Public Papers of John Jay,* 2:173, 336-41; North Carolina Delegates (Hawkins and Williamson) to Governor, Oct. 19, 1783, in Edmund Cody Burnett, ed., *Letters of the Members of the Continental Congress,* 7:343.

17. Richard Henry Lee to Gen. William Whipple, July 1, 1783, in Ballagh, *Letters of Richard Henry Lee,* 2:283-85. Also Samuel Adams to James Warren, Feb. 1, 1777, in Harry A. Cushing, ed., *The Writings of Samuel Adams,* 3:353.

18. Henry Laurens to John Laurens, Jan. 8, 1778, in Smith, *Letters of Delegates,* 8:545-50; Roger Sherman to Richard Henry Lee, Nov. 3, 1777, in Burnett, *Letters of the Members,* 2:540; and John Armstrong to Joseph Reed, Jan. 24, 1780, in Smith, *Letters of Delegates,* 14:364-65, at 365.

19. For support of price controls see, e.g., Richard Henry Lee to Samuel Adams, Nov. 23, 1777, in Smith, *Letters of Delegates*, 8:310–14, at 311. Lee noted that although John Adams opposed controls, he believed that "the American conduct has already shattered and overset the conclusions of the best theorists," thus necessitating them.

20. For congressional support for fixed wages and prices and state taxes, see Ford, *Journals of Congress*, 7:121n, 124–25 (Feb. 14 and 15, 1777); 9:953–58 (Nov. 22, 1777); 9:1043–47, at 1044–45 (Dec. 20, 1777); and 11:569 (June 4, 1778).

21. The quotations are from Alexander Hamilton to James Duane, Sept. 3, 1780, in Harold C. Syrett, ed., *The Papers of Alexander Hamilton*, 1:400–418, at 402, 416–17. For congressional deliberations on the merits of state regulations and popular economic freedom, see Ford, *Journals of Congress*, 11:569 (June 4, 1778).

22. Republican fears of debt among the common people and the ill effects of paper money can be seen over the entire period; see, e.g., the Continental Association agreement, in Ford, *Journals of Congress*, 1:75–81 (Oct. 20, 1774) and its subsequent modifications; and "Primitive Whig," no. 2, dtd. Jan. 16, 1786, *New-Jersey Gazette*, repr. in *Pennsylvania Gazette*, Jan. 25, 1786. These fears were largely centered on *private* debts; for the belief shared by many leading Americans that a public debt would be "the strongest cement" of union, see Clarence Ver Steeg, *Robert Morris, Revolutionary Financier*, 89, 124–28.

23. For criticism of ambitious farmers and small army suppliers see, e.g., George Washington to James Warren, Mar. 31, 1779, in John C. Fitzpatrick, ed., *The Writings of George Washington*, 14:312; John Adams to Mercy Otis Warren, Jan. 8, 1776, *Warren-Adams Letters*, 2:202; and the sources cited in n. 21 above. See the discussions in Foner, *Tom Paine and Revolutionary America*, chs. 3–5, and in ch. 1.

24. On price- and wage-fixing, see Ford, *Journals of Congress*, 7:124, 9:953–57, 1043–47, at 1046 (Feb. 15, Nov. 22, and Dec. 20, 1777); and Albert S. Bolles, *The Financial History of the United States*, 158–73. On embargoes, see Ford, *Journals of Congress*, 11:569, 578, 14:986–87, 15:1137 (June 4 and 5, 1778; Aug. 21 and Oct. 2, 1779).

25. John Adams, as cited by Edmund S. Morgan, "The Puritan Ethic and the Coming of the Revolution," 5. For the state laws, see Morris, *Government and Labor in Early America*, 103–16.

26. On hostility to taxation, see for example the discussion of New York's difficulties in the Hudson River Valley in "The Real Farmer," no. 4, *New York Journal*, Feb. 15, 1779, and items in ibid., July 26, Aug. 2 and 9, 1779.

27. James Wilson, "Considerations on the Bank of North America," 1785, in Robert G. McCloskey, ed., *The Works of James Wilson*, 2:824–40. Wilson believed that the commercial crises of the 1780s were caused not by banks but by overextended credit to consumers. On the liquidity crisis see the following commentaries: Stephen Higginson to John Adams, Aug. 8, 1785, and July 1786, in J. Franklin Jameson, ed., "The Letters of Stephen Higginson," 1:719–20, 740; Samuel House to Jefferson, Aug. 10, 1784, in Boyd et al., *Papers of Thomas Jefferson*, 7:392–94, at 393; and John Sitgreave to John Gray Blount,

Apr. 13, 1785, in Burnett, *Letters of the Members*, 8:92–93. In general see W. A. Low, "Merchant and Planter Relations in Post-Revolutionary Virginia," 314–24; Robert Brunhouse, *The Counter-Revolution in Pennsylvania*, 172–73; E. Wilder Spaulding, *New York in the Critical Period*, 21–24.

28. Jerome Paige, "The Evolution of Mercantile Capitalism and Planter Capitalism," 101–2.

29. James Beekman to John Rolph, Nov. 29, 1785, and to Cooke, Rolph, and Barnardiston, Nov. 2, 1784, in Philip L. White, ed., *The Beekman Mercantile Papers*, 3:1000, 998; Petition of the Merchants and Tradesmen of the Town of Boston to Gov. James Bowdoin, June 4, 1785, in *The Bowdoin and Temple Papers*, 6:50–52; "A meeting of merchants and tradesmen," dtd. Apr. 18, 1785, in *Massachusetts Centinel*, Apr. 20, 1785.

30. Items dtd. Boston, June 18, 1785, in *Pennsylvania Gazette*, June 29, 1785; "Proceedings of the Tradesmen and Manufacturers," dtd. Apr. 26, 1785, in *Massachusetts Centinel*, May 7, 1785.

31. For example, Madison to Monroe, June 21, 1785, in Rutland et al., *Papers of James Madison*, 8:306–8.

32. Item in *New York Packet*, Nov. 21, 1782; "Rough Hewer" [Abraham Yates], *New York Gazetteer*, Oct. 6, 1783; Thomas Cochran, *New York in the Confederation*, 38.

33. See "Rough Hewer" [Yates], *New York Gazetteer*, Oct. 6, 1783; and "Cincinnatus," *Independent Journal and General Advertiser*, May 10, 14, and 21, 1784; Alexander Hamilton to Gov. George Clinton, Jan. 12, Feb. 24, May 14, and June 1, 1783, in Syrett, *Papers of Alexander Hamilton*, 3:240–41, 268–74, 354–55, 367–72; Samuel Flagg Bemis, *The Diplomacy of the American Revolution*, 61, 103.

34. Ford, *Journals of Congress*, 26:23–28, at 26–27 (Jan. 14, 1784).

35. Jeremy Belknap to Ebenezer Hazard, Nov. 30, 1783, in *The Belknap Papers*, 2:277–84, at 282.

36. George Mason to Patrick Henry, May 6, 1783, in Robert A. Rutland, ed., *The Papers of George Mason*, 2:769–73, at 771. Belknap and Mason both favored repayment of debts and lenient treatment of British merchants.

37. Ford, *Journals of Congress*, 19:102, 110, 112–13 (Jan. 31, Feb. 1 and 3, 1781).

38. For remarks on state imposts see Alexander Hamilton, "The Continentalist," nos. 5 and 6, Apr. 19 and July 4, 1782, in Syrett, *Papers of Alexander Hamilton*, 3:75–82, 99–106; and idem, "Remarks on Appropriating the Impost Exclusively to the Army," Feb. 19, 1783, in ibid., 3:262; and items in *New York Packet*, Oct. 24, 1782 and Apr. 21, 1785.

39. Ford, *Journals of Congress*, 24:186–92, 195–201, 257–62 (Mar. 18, 20 and Apr. 18, 1783). For regret about the defeat of the 1783 national impost proposal see, e.g., items in *New York Packet*, July 7, 24, and Aug. 7, 1783. For the opposing view—that the states were the proper vehicle for revenue collection—see Fairfax County Freeholders' Address and Instructions to Assembly Delegates, May 30, 1783, in Rutland, *Papers of George Mason*, 2:779–83, at 781; Fairfax County Petition, June 18, 1783, in ibid., 2:785–87. Authorship of the petitions is disputed; ibid., 2:782–83.

40. Richard Henry Lee to Gen. William Whipple, July 1, 1783, in Ballagh, ed., *Letters of Richard Henry Lee*, 2:283–85.

41. Silas Deane to Simeon Deane, Apr. 1, 1783, in Worthington C. Ford, ed., *Correspondence and Journals of Samuel Blachley Webb*, 3:9–11.

42. Brunhouse, *Counter-Revolution in Pennsylvania*, 132–33, 152, 185–87.

43. E. James Ferguson, *The Power of the Purse*, 209–10, 239–42, 180–81; Ford, *Journals of Congress*, 26:185–97, 297–314 (Apr. 5 and 27, 1784); 29:765–71 (Sept. 27, 1785); 31:461–65 (Aug. 2, 1786); 33:649–58 (Oct. 11, 1787); and 34:433–42 (Aug. 20, 1788).

44. E. James Ferguson, "State Assumption of the Federal Debt during the Confederation."

45. For references to the merchant and farmer coalitions that were satisfied with state policies, see, e.g., items in *New York Packet*, Apr. 14, 1785, Feb. 18 and Mar. 6, 1786; and *New York Daily Advertiser*, Mar. 3, 1786. In general, see Jackson Turner Main, *The Antifederalists*, 47–50; and Nettels, *Emergence of a National Economy*, 96–98.

46. See, e.g., "Cincinnatus," *Independent Journal and General Advertiser*, May 10, 14, and 21, 1784. See also Ferguson, "State Assumption of the Federal Debt," 403–4; and Merrill Jensen, *The New Nation*, 43–53.

47. For optimistic statements about recovery see, e.g., *New York Daily Advertiser*, Jan. 28, Feb. 2 and 5, 1788, reflecting on earlier conditions. Revival came earliest for urban mechanics, artisans, and importers involved in the construction trades, as evidenced in Stewart & Jones Letter Book.

48. Warville, *New Travels in the United States*, 1:464; and Bryan Edwards, *The History, Civil and Commercial, of the British West Indies*, vol. 2, ch. 4. See also Matson, "From Free Trade to Liberty," chs. 4, 5.

49. William Bingham, *Letter from an American Now Resident in London*, 6–7, 9–10, 15. See also Sir Philip Gibbs, *Reflections on the Proclamation*, esp. 14–15; Madison to Jefferson, May 13, 1783, in Rutland et al., *Papers of James Madison*, 7:39–40; John Adams diary entry, Apr. 28, 1783, in Lyman Butterfield, ed., *Diary and Autobiography of John Adams*, 3:113; and John Adams to Robert R. Livingston, July 3 and 14, 1783, in Charles Francis Adams, ed., *The Works of John Adams*, 8:77–81, 97–99. In general, see Matson, "From Free Trade to Liberty," ch. 8.

50. George Bancroft, *History of the Formation of the Constitution of the United States of America*, 1:55–56.

51. Lord Sheffield, *Observations on the Commerce of the American States*, 262–72.

52. Many writers endorsed the West Indies merchants' refutations of Sheffield. See, e.g., "Proclamation" in *Antigua Gazette*, dtd. Oct. 6, 24, repr. in *Pennsylvania Gazette*, Dec. 10, 1783; "Common Sense," dtd. New York, Dec. 9, 1783, in *Pennsylvania Gazette*, Dec. 17, 1783; "Pertinax," *Antigua Gazette*, Sept. 3, 1783, repr. in *Pennsylvania Gazette*, Dec. 17, 1783; and "Many of the People," dtd. Antigua, n.d., in *Pennsylvania Gazette*, Dec. 24, 1783. From 1785 to 1788 this sentiment persisted; see, e.g., items dtd. Kingston, Aug. 3 and July 16, in *Pennsylvania Gazette*, Aug. 31 and Sept. 14, 1785; item dtd. New York, Nov. 4, 1785, in *Virginia Journal*, Nov. 17, 1785; and "On the Situation of the British West India Islands," dtd. Charleston, 1786, in *American Museum* 4 (Sept. 1788), 288–93.

53. "To Henry B. Lightfoot and James Anthill from the freeholders of their district," *Maryland Gazette* (Annapolis), Dec. 18, 1783.

54. Henry B. Dawson, "The Motley Letter," 164–69.

55. Bancroft, *History of the Constitution*, 1:62–67.

56. Predictions of dire consequences proceeding from British acts include John Jay to Gouverneur Morris, July 17, 1783, cited by Bancroft, *History of the Constitution*, 1:65; and John Adams to Robert R. Livingston, July 16 and 18, 1783, in Adams, *Works of John Adams*, 8:99-103, 106-109. See also *The Commercial Conduct of the United States of America Considered by a Citizen of New York*; Tench Coxe, *A Brief Examination of Lord Sheffield's Observations*; and Bingham, *Letter from an American*.

57. On smuggling, see item in *New York Packet*, Apr. 27, 1786; and L. J. Ragatz, *The Fall of the Planter Class in the British Caribbean*, 184-94. Merrill Jensen asserts that smuggling did not increase as a result of the Orders in Council; Jensen, *The New Nation*, 198. On the British carrying American provisions, see *New York Journal*, Feb. 23, 1783; Pierse Long to John Langdon, Jan. 31, 1785, in Burnett, *Letters of the Members*, 8:18; Monroe to Jefferson, Aug. 15, 1785, in ibid., 8:186-88; George Dangerfield, *Chancellor Robert R. Livingston of New York*, 221; and Alfred F. Young, *The Democratic Republicans of New York*, 79.

58. "At a General Town Meeting," dtd. June 6-22, 1785, in *Pennsylvania Gazette*, June 22, 1785; Young, *Democratic Republicans of New York*, 91.

59. Timothy Pitkin, *Statistical View of the Commerce of the United States of America*, 216-17.

60. Madison to Jefferson, Sept. 20, 1783, in Rutland et al., *Papers of James Madison*, 7:352-56; item in *New York Packet*, Apr. 24, 1786; and William B. Weeden, *The Economic and Social History of New England*, 2:818-19.

61. On fisheries and whale oil see Stephen Higginson to unknown, n.d., in Jameson, "Letters of Stephen Higginson," 1:723; Weeden, *Economic and Social History*, 2:828-29. On distilling see Arthur C. Bining, *Pennsylvania Iron Manufacture in the Eighteenth Century*, 159, 177-78; George Cabot to Hamilton [?], Oct. 8, 1791, in Arthur H. Cole, ed., *Industrial and Commercial Correspondence of Alexander Hamilton*, 169.

62. "Common Sense," "To the People of America," dtd. New York, Dec. 9, 1783, in *Pennsylvania Gazette*, Dec. 17, 1783; "Memorial of the Committee of Merchants and Traders of Philadelphia," dtd. April 6, 1785, repr. in *American Museum* 1 (Apr. 1787), 313-14; "A Committee of Boston Merchants," in ibid., 320-21; and discussion of the petitions from merchants in Virginia in William C. Rives, *History of the Life and Times of James Madison*, 2:46-59.

63. John Jay to John Adams, Sept. 6, 1785, in Johnston, *Correspondence of John Jay*, 3:164-67, at 165; John Adams to John Jay, May 4, 5, June 26, and July 19, 1785, in Adams, *Works of John Adams*, 8:239-40, 240-42, 273-76, 279-83; Stephen Higginson to John Adams, Aug. 8, 1785, in Jameson, "Letters of Stephen Higginson," 1:720.

64. Madison to Richard Henry Lee, July 7, 1785, in Rutland et al., *Papers of James Madison*, 8:314-16.

65. E.g., item dtd. Apr. 18, 1785, in *Massachusetts Centinel*, Apr. 20, 1785; item in *Massachusetts Centinel*, Apr. 27, 1785; and "Proceedings of the Tradesmen and Manufacturers," Apr. 26, 1785, in *Massachusetts Centinel*, May 7, 1785.

66. The states were New Jersey, New Hampshire, Massachusetts, Rhode Island, New York, Maryland, North Carolina, Pennsylvania, and Virginia.

See "Abstract of a Law passed . . . by . . . Massachusetts," dtd. June 23, 1785, in *Pennsylvania Gazette,* July 20, 1785; item dtd. New York, July 19, 1785, in *Pennsylvania Gazette,* July 27, 1785; "To the Tradesmen and Manufacturers of Philadelphia," dtd. Boston, Aug. 20, 1785, in *Pennsylvania Gazette,* Sept. 14, 1785; "Draft of a bill for limiting importation to America," *Pennsylvania Gazette,* Nov. 30, 1785; items in *New York Packet,* Mar. 23, 1786; and Minutes of New York Chamber of Commerce, Mar. 3, 1785. In general see Albert Geisecke, *American Commercial Legislation before 1789,* 128–34.

67. Rufus King to John Adams, Dec. 4, 1785, in Burnett, *Letters of the Members,* 8:268. See also Monroe to Jefferson, Aug. 15, 1785, in ibid., 8:186–88, at 187.

68. "Meeting of Boston Merchants and Shopkeepers," *Massachusetts Centinel,* Apr. 16, 1785.

69. Geisecke, *American Commercial Legislation,* 131–35.

70. *Maryland Journal,* Sept. 23, 1785.

71. The first widely circulated interclass agreement was probably "To the United States in Congress Assembled," dtd. Boston, Apr. 22, 1785, by way of New York, May 31, repr. in *Pennsylvania Gazette,* June 8, 1785. See also "Colbert," "To The Inhabitants of Boston," dtd. Boston, Apr. 18, 1785, in *Pennsylvania Gazette,* May 11, 1785; and Gov. James Bowdoin, "A Proclamation For the . . . Suppression of Vice," dtd. Boston, June 8, 1785, in *Pennsylvania Gazette,* July 6, 1785.

72. See letters from Boston tradesmen and manufacturers, promoting manufactures, in *Pennsylvania Gazette,* May 18 and June 28, 1785; and "Arteman," in ibid., Mar. 16, 1785. On fairs and urban markets, see Tench Coxe, *A View of the United States of America,* 26, 51, 228, 254.

73. J. Franklin Jameson, ed., "Letters to the Foreign Office of Great Britain," 1:654; Thomas Earle and Charles T. Congdon, eds., *Annals of the General Society of Mechanics and Tradesmen of the City of New York,* 7–10, 27.

74. Examples abound. See especially items in *New York Packet,* Sept. 1 and Nov. 17, 1785; "An Act to Encourage and Protect the Manufactures of This State," *Pennsylvania Gazette,* Oct. 5, 1785; "At a General Town Meeting," *Pennsylvania Gazette,* June 22, 1785; item dtd. Boston, Aug. 22, 1785, in *Pennsylvania Gazette,* Aug. 31, 1785; item dtd. Apr. 18, 1785, in *Massachusetts Centinel,* Apr. 20, 1785; item in *Massachusetts Centinel,* Apr. 27, 1785; and "Proceedings of the Tradesmen and Manufacturers," dtd. Apr. 26, 1785, in *Massachusetts Centinel,* May 7, 1785.

75. See, e.g., Dawson, "The Motley Letter," 167–68; and John R. Nelson, Jr., "Alexander Hamilton and American Manufacturing."

76. "An Act to Encourage and Protect Manufactures," *Pennsylvania Gazette,* Oct. 5, 1785; Brunhouse, *Counter-Revolution in Pennsylvania,* 172–73.

77. See Hamilton to Duane, Sept. 3, 1780, in Syrett, *Papers of Alexander Hamilton,* 1:400–418, at 402, 416–17, for a prominent nationalist's view of these circumstances. See also, Jensen, *New Nation,* ch. 14; and Cathy Matson, "American Political Economy in the Constitutional Decade."

78. David Hume, "Of the Jealousy of Trade," in Rotwein, *David Hume,* 78. See also Douglass Adair, "That Politics May Be Reduced to a Science."

CHAPTER 3. INTERSTATE CONFLICT AND THE EXPANSION OF THE UNION

1. James Madison to Thomas Jefferson, Aug. 20, 1784, Robert A. Rutland et al., eds., *The Papers of James Madison*, 8:108.

2. *Freeman's Journal*, June 15, 1785.

3. Thomas Pownall and other European sympathizers therefore repeatedly urged the revolutionaries to establish a "respectable" continental government. Pownall, *A Memorial Addressed to the Sovereigns of America*, 129, 137–38; Richard Price, "Observations on the Importance of the American Revolution," 187.

4. Emmerich de Vattel, *The Law of Nations*, 251, 347–49.

5. Price, "Observations on the American Revolution," 187. For good discussions of contemporary theorizing about international relations, see Francis H. Hinsley, *Power and the Pursuit of Peace*, and Daniel George Lang, *Foreign Policy in the Early Republic*.

6. John Witherspoon speech in Congress [July 30, 1776], in Paul H. Smith, ed., *Letters of Delegates to Congress*, 4:584–87, at 587.

7. Peter S. Onuf, *Origins of the Federal Republic*, 8–12, and passim. On the Articles, see Jack N. Rakove, "Articles of Confederation," and Peter S. Onuf, "Articles of Confederation."

8. Edward Rutledge to Robert R. Livingston [Aug. 19, 1776], in Smith, *Letters of Delegates*, 5:25–27, at 27.

9. Abraham Clark to James Caldwell, Aug. 1, 1776, in ibid., 4:596–98, at 597.

10. "It is the best Confederacy that Could be formed," concluded Cornelius Harnett of North Carolina, "especially when we consider the Number of States, their different Interests, Customs &c &c." Harnett to William Wilkinson, Nov. 30, 1777, in ibid., 8:348–49, at 348.

11. Charles Carroll of Carrollton to Benjamin Franklin, Aug. 12, 1777, in ibid., 8:46.

12. John Adams speech, from Jefferson's Notes of Proceedings in Congress, July 12, 1776, in ibid., 4:438–45, at 443.

13. Henry Knox to Stephen Higginson, Jan. 21, 1787, Henry Knox Papers.

14. This theme is more fully developed in Peter S. Onuf, "Maryland: The Small Republic in the New Nation."

15. Witherspoon speech, from Jefferson's Notes, July 12, 1776, in Smith, *Letters of Delegates*, 4:438–45, at 442.

16. William Williams of Connecticut predicted that "the smaller Colonies will be in effect swallow'd up and annihilated" under a scheme of proportional representation. Williams to Jonathan Trumbull, Jr., July 5, 1777, in ibid., 7:302. See also Stephen Hopkins speech, from Jefferson's Notes, July 12, 1776, in ibid., 4:438–45, at 444.

17. Letter from M. Turgot to Dr. Price, dtd. Paris, Mar. 22, 1778, in Richard Price, "Observations on the Importance of the American Revolution," 221n.

18. Resolves of Maryland House, Nov. 30, 1778, in Kate Mason Rowland, ed., *The Life of Charles Carroll of Carrollton*, 2:11–12.

19. Maryland Instructions, Dec. 15, 1778, laid before Congress May 21, 1779, in Worthington C. Ford, ed., *Journals of the Continental Congress*,

14:619–22, at 620–21. See also the Maryland Declaration, Dec. 15, 1778, in William Waller Hening, ed., *The Statutes at Large*, 10:549–52. For a brief review of the western lands controversy, see Peter S. Onuf, *Origins of the Federal Republic*, 75–102.

20. During the ratification controversy, Antifederalist Luther Martin of Maryland made similar predictions about the fate of the small states under the proposed federal Constitution. Martin, "The Genuine Information, Delivered to the Legislature of the State of Maryland, Relative to the Proceedings of the General Convention, Held at Philadelphia, in 1787," *Maryland Gazette* (Annapolis), Dec. 28, 1787–Feb. 8, 1788, in Max Farrand, ed., *Records of the Federal Convention of 1787*, 3:172–232.

21. "Remarks relative to the Controversy between Pennsylvania and Connecticut," no. 7, *Independent Chronicle*, Mar. 17, 1785.

22. "Crazy Jonathan," *Cumberland Gazette*, Sept. 27, 1787. For an excellent discussion of the new idea of "volitional citizenship," see James H. Kettner, *The Development of American Citizenship*, 173–209.

23. "Yankee Doodle," "To the Inhabitants of the State of Connecticut," *Connecticut Courant*, Mar. 6, 1786.

24. The "bare mentioning" of the western lands "rouses Virginia," Maryland delegate John Henry reported in 1778. Henry to the Speaker of the Maryland House, Mar. 17, 1778, in Edmund Cody Burnett, ed., *Letters of the Members of the Continental Congress*, 3:133.

25. Remonstrance of the Virginia General Assembly, Dec. 14, 1779, Hening, *Statutes at Large*, 10:557–59.

26. According to Richard Henry Lee, "Jealousy and envy of [Virginia's] wisdom, vigor, and extent of Territory" accounted for the state's "many enemies" in Congress. Lee to Patrick Henry, May 26, 1777, in James C. Ballagh, ed., *Letters of Richard Henry Lee*, 1:301.

27. Even the usually temperate Madison thought his fellow Virginians "ought in all their provisions for their security, importance & interest to presume that the present Union will but little survive the present war." Madison to Jefferson, Nov. 18, 1781, in Rutland et al., *Papers of James Madison*, 3:308.

28. Theodorick Bland to Jefferson, Nov. 22, 1780, in Burnett, *Letters of the Members*, 5:455–56.

29. Lee to Samuel Adams, Feb. 5, 1781, in Ballagh, *Letters of Richard Henry Lee*, 2:214–15.

30. Bland to Richard Henry Lee, Mar. 5, 1781, in Burnett, *Letters of the Members*, 6:7.

31. "Extract of a Letter from One of the Virginia Delegates," Dec. 10, 1781, in *Freeman's Journal*, Jan. 4, 1786.

32. Arthur Lee to Jefferson, Mar. 13, 1782, in Julian P. Boyd et al., eds., *The Papers of Thomas Jefferson*, 6:164.

33. Motion by Arthur Lee, Apr. 18, 1782, in Ford, *Journals of Congress*, 22:191–92. Three states, Virginia, South Carolina, and Georgia, supported the motion. See Lee to Samuel Adams, Apr. 21, 1782, in Burnett, *Letters of the Members*, 6:331–32; and Madison to Edmund Pendleton, Apr. 23, 1782, in Rutland et al., *Papers of James Madison*, 4:178.

34. Fairfax County Freeholders' Address and Instructions to Assembly Delegates, May 30, 1783, in Robert A. Rutland, ed., *The Papers of George Mason*, 2:779–83.

35. On the peace-plan tradition see Hinsley, *Power and the Pursuit of Peace*. For American attitudes toward world politics see Gerald Stourzh, *Benjamin Franklin and American Foreign Policy*; Felix Gilbert, *To the Farewell Address*; James H. Hutson, *John Adams and the Diplomacy of the Revolution*; Lang, *Foreign Policy in the Early Republic*; and Peter S. Onuf and Nicholas G. Onuf, "American Constitutionalism and the Emergence of a Liberal World Order." For a more extended treatment of the questions raised in this section see Peter S. Onuf, "American Federalism and the Politics of Expansion."

36. For Congress's determination to uphold the territorial monopoly of the original states, see resolutions of June 30, 1777, and May 23, 1780, in Ford, *Journals of Congress*, 8:508–13, 17:452. On constitutional obstacles to admitting new states, see Madison to Edmund Pendleton, Jan. 22, 1782, in Rutland et al., *Papers of James Madison*, 4:38–39; and Ezra L'Hommedieu to Gov. George Clinton, Sept. 8, 1781, in Burnett, *Letters of the Members*, 6:212.

37. *Freeman's Journal*, June 15, 1785; Onuf, *Origins of the Federal Republic*, 34–36.

38. The best general account of Confederation politics is Jack N. Rakove, *The Beginnings of National Politics*.

39. North Carolina delegate Richard Dobbs Spaight—who thought the Virginia cession gave Congress more land than it could "*properly* dispose of for these twenty or thirty years to come"—attributed this agitation to the "envy" of small states that were "so trifling" in size "when compared to the larger ones." Spaight to Gov. Alexander Martin, Apr. 30, 1784, in Burnett, *Letters of the Members*, 7:509–10.

40. Virginia Delegates to Gov. Patrick Henry, Nov. 7, 1785, in ibid., 8:250.

41. Committee report of second Franklin convention, Jonesborough, Dec. 14, 1784, repr. in Samuel Cole Williams, *History of the Lost State of Franklin*, 40. See also "Address to the Western Inhabitants," contained within a letter by Charles Cummings to the Pres. of Congress, Apr. 7, 1785, Papers of the Continental Congress, 48:289; and "Impartialis Secundus," *Falmouth Gazette*, July 9, 1785.

42. Hugh Williamson to Gov. Alexander Martin, Nov. 18, 1782, in Burnett, *Letters of the Members*, 6:545. If Congress did not resolutely resist separatism, Jefferson warned, "our several states will crumble to atoms by the spirit of establishing every little canton into a separate state." Jefferson to Richard Henry Lee, July 12, 1785, in Boyd et al., *Papers of Thomas Jefferson*, 8:287.

43. Memorial repr. in *Freeman's Journal*, Jan. 12, 1785.

44. Judge David Campbell to Gov. Richard Caswell, Nov. 30, 1786, repr. in Williams, *Lost State of Franklin*, 116. For the same argument see "Copy of a letter from a gentleman to his friend in the county of York," *Falmouth Gazette*, Feb. 2, 1786.

45. Rufus King to Elbridge Gerry, June 4, 1786, in Burnett, *Letters of the Members*, 8:380.

46. On antiseparatist arguments see Onuf, *Origins of the Federal Republic*, 36–37, 158–60.

47. "Impartialis Secundus," *Falmouth Gazette*, July 9, 1785.

48. For comments on the Spanish on the Mississippi, see Washington to Henry Knox, Dec. 5, 1784, in John C. Fitzpatrick, ed., *The Writings of George Washington*, 28:4. On the depression of 1785–88, see Curtis P. Nettels, *The Emergence of a National Economy*, ch. 1; Richard B. Morris, *The Forging of the Union*, 130–61; and Cathy Matson, "American Political Economy in the Constitutional Decade." On economic considerations merging with problems of westward settlement, see Peter S. Onuf, *Statehood and Union*, ch. 1; Thomas P. Slaughter, *The Whisky Rebellion*, 36–45; and Drew R. McCoy, *The Elusive Republic*, 48–85.

49. "Extract of a letter from Davidson County, North Carolina," dtd. Oct. 20, 1786, in *Virginia Journal*, Feb. 15, 1787.

50. William Grayson to Beverly Randolph, June 12, 1787, in Burnett, *Letters of the Members*, 8:609–10.

51. "Extract of a letter from Louisville," dtd. Dec. 4, 1786, in *Cumberland Gazette*, July 19, 1787.

52. Grayson to Randolph, cited in n. 50 above. See also James Wilkinson's Memorial, Sept. 23, 1787, in Temple Bodley, ed., *Reprints of Littell's Political Transactions in and concerning Kentucky*, 119–129; and Samuel A. Otis to Theodore Sedgewick, June 6, 1788, in Sedgewick Papers, A.148. See the discussion in Patricia Watlington, *The Partisan Spirit*, 120–21, 139–47.

53. *Pennsylvania Packet*, July 7, 1787.

54. Item in *Kentucky Gazette*, Aug. 2, 1788; Madison to Jefferson, Aug. 23, 1788, in Rutland et al., *Papers of James Madison*, 11:238–39.

55. Nathan Dane to Thomas Dwight, Mar. 12, 1787, in Burnett, *Letters of the Members*, 8:556–57. For an earlier report to this effect, see Capt. John Doughty to Secretary of War, dtd. Ft. McIntosh, Oct 21, 1785, in William Henry Smith, ed., *The St. Clair Papers*, 2.11–12.

56. "Extract of a letter from Halifax," dtd. Oct. 10, 1786, in *Carlisle Gazette*, Nov. 15, 1786; Elbridge Gerry to Rufus King, Nov. 29, 1786, in Charles R. King, ed., *The Life and Correspondence of Rufus King*, 1:197; John Jay to Jefferson, Dec. 14, 1786, in Boyd et al., *Papers of Thomas Jefferson*, 10:596.

57. Henry Knox to Samuel H. Parsons, Nov. 19, 1786, Henry Knox Papers, 19; Henry Lee to Washington, Nov. 11, 1786, in Burnett, *Letters of the Members*, 8:505–6; Lee to Madison, Oct. 19, 1786, in Rutland et al., *Papers of James Madison*, 9:143–45.

58. Edward Carrington to Gov. Edmund Randolph, Dec. 8, 1786, in William R. Palmer, ed., *Calendar of Virginia State Papers*, 4:199. See the discussion in Onuf, *Origins of the Federal Republic*, 181–85.

59. Gov. Alexander Martin's Manifesto, Apr. 25, 1785, in William L. Saunders et al., eds., *The Colonial and State Records of North Carolina*, 17:440–45.

60. "Jonathan of the Valley, from a late Boston paper," *Falmouth Gazette*, Nov. 12, 1785; also York town meeting, Nov. 21, 1785, and North-Yarmouth town meeting, Jan. 2, 1786, in *Falmouth Gazette*, Dec. 14, 1785, and March 9, 1786, respectively.

61. George Washington to Knox, Jan. 10, 1788, in *Documentary History of the Constitution of the United States*, 5:436–37.

62. Letter from Turgot to Price, in Price, "Observations on the American Revolution," 222n.

CHAPTER 4. COMMERCIAL CRISES
AND REGIONAL DEVELOPMENT

1. On "perfect freedom" see James Madison, Report on Debates in Congress, Dec. 24, 1782, and Jan. 1, 1783, in Francis Wharton, ed., *The Revolutionary Diplomatic Correspondence of the United States*, 6:161–62, 189–90. On reciprocity see, e.g., William D. Grampp, "A Re-examination of Jeffersonian Economics." For contemporary commentary on the importance of the West Indies trade, see, e.g., John Adams to Robert R. Livingston, July 14, 1783, and to John Jay, July 19 and Oct. 21, 1785, in Wharton, *Revolutionary Diplomatic Correspondence*, 6:540–42, 216–17, 200; J. P. Brissot de Warville, *New Travels in the United States*, 1:463, 464; Lord Sheffield, *Observations on the Commerce of the American States*; Bryan Edwards, *The History, Civil and Commercial, of the British West Indies*, vol. 2, ch. 4.

2. For the Orders in Council respecting the West Indies, see Henry B. Dawson, "The Motley Letter," 164–69.

3. See, e.g., "Report of the Committee on Dispatches from Foreign Ministries," Sept. 25, 1783, in Edmund Cody Burnett, ed., *Letters of the Members of the Continental Congress*, 7:304–5. Early support for national trade discrimination as a temporary measure to secure future reciprocity may be seen in Charles Pettit, "Letter from a merchant in Philadelphia to his friend in London," dtd. Philadelphia, Jan. 1784, in *American Museum* 8 (Sept. 1790), 27–35. See also "On the Situation of the British West Indies Islands," dtd. Charleston, 1786, in *American Museum* 2 (Sept. 1788), 288–93; and "American," "Essay on the advantages of trade and commerce," in *American Museum* 2 (Oct. 1788), 341–43. Madison echoed these appeals during the first Washington administration; see ch. 8.

4. On Tucker and Hume see Donald Winch, *Classical Political Theory and Colonies*, 5–19. The language of jealousy is especially prominent in Alexander Hamilton's writings; see his "Continentalist" essays, nos. 1 and 2, Apr. 18 and July 4, 1782, in Harold C. Syrett, ed., *The Papers of Alexander Hamilton*, 3:75–82, 99–106; and Jacob E. Cooke, ed., *The Federalist Papers*, nos. 6, 11, 12, 36. For a discussion of economic jealousy see Cathy Matson, "Jealousy, Liberty, and Union." Even in the 1750s, Scottish Enlightenment figures saw that the central weakness of the economic freedom argument was its detachment from a political program; see Istvan Hont and Michael Ignatieff, eds., *Wealth and Virtue*, introduction; Sheldon Wolin, *Politics and Vision*, ch. 8. On the compatibility of a "spirit of commerce" and "political liberty," see Noah Webster, *Sketches of American Policy*, 18, 45; Pelatiah Webster, "An Essay on Free Trade and Finance," dtd. 1781, in *Political Essays on the Nature and Operations of Money, Public Finances and Other Subjects*, 9–10, 27–49; and John F. Roche, *Joseph Reed*, 116–21, 149–62.

5. Adams to Robert R. Livingston, July 14, 1783, in Wharton, *Revolutionary Diplomatic Correspondence*, 6:540–42.

6. Memorial of Philadelphia Merchants, *Virginia Journal*, June 16, 1785.

7. "Common Sense," "To the People of America," dtd. New York, Dec. 2, 1783, in *Virginia Gazette*, Jan. 3, 1784.

8. Memorial of the Committee of Merchants, dtd. Philadelphia, Apr. 6, 1785, in *Virginia Journal*, June 16, 1785.

9. "Brutus," dtd. Sept. 27, 1784, in *Gazette of the State of Georgia*, Sept. 30, 1784.

10. "Candidus," *London Evening Post*, n.d., repr. in *Pennsylvania Gazette*, July 21, 1784.

11. Extract of a letter, dtd. New York, Mar. 14, 1785, in *Independent Chronicle*, Apr. 14, 1785.

12. Thomas Dawes speech, Massachusetts convention, Jan. 21, 1788, in Jonathan Elliot, ed., *The Debates in the Several State Conventions on the Adoption of the Federal Constitution*, 2:58. In Connecticut, Oliver Ellsworth ("A Landholder," no. 2), developed the same point: "Once we were dependent only on Great Britain; now we are dependent on every petty state in the world." Merrill Jensen et al., eds., *The Documentary History of the Ratification of the Constitution*, 3:400–401.

13. "Translation of a letter from Mr. Target, to a particular Friend . . . in Philadelphia," dtd. Paris, Oct. 24, 1783, in *Gazette of the State of Georgia*, Sept. 23, 1784.

14. Abbé Gabriel Bonnet de Mably, *Observations on the Government and Laws of the United States*, Letter 4, dtd. Aug. 20, 1783, 120–21.

15. Item dtd. Philadelphia, Aug. 18, 1787, in *Virginia Gazette and Winchester Advertiser*, Aug. 29, 1787. The best general treatment of early American political economic thought is Drew R. McCoy, *The Elusive Republic*; see also the summary of "Systems of Political Economy" in Forrest McDonald, *Novus Ordo Seclorum*, 97–142.

16. "Observator," no. 3, *New-Haven Gazette*, Oct. 27, 1785. See also item dtd. Aug. 2, 1785, in *Massachusetts Centinel*, Aug. 20, 1785.

17. Item dtd. New York, Nov. 4, 1785, in *Virginia Journal*, Nov. 17, 1785.

18. Thomas Jefferson to G. K. van Hogendorp, Oct. 13, 1785, in Julian P. Boyd et al., eds., *The Papers of Thomas Jefferson*, 8:633. On Jefferson's role as "an early advocate of the commercial exploitation of American agriculture," see Joyce Appleby, "What Is Still American in the Political Philosophy of Thomas Jefferson?" 295.

19. [St. George Tucker], *Reflections on the Policy and Necessity of Encouraging the Commerce*, 14 and passim. On "commercial republicanism" see Ralph Lerner, "Commerce and Character."

20. Tench Coxe, "An address to an assembly of the friends of American manufactures," dtd. Philadelphia, Aug. 9, 1787, in *American Museum* 2 (Sept. 1787), 248–55, at 255. See also Michael Lienesch, *New Order of the Ages*, ch. 4; and Peter S. Onuf, "Liberty, Development, and Union."

21. Pelatiah Webster, "Essay on Free Trade," in *Political Essays*, 9, 24.

22. On the activities of the state legislatures, see Merrill Jensen, *Articles of Confederation*, ch. 2.

23. On the severity of the postwar depression and the intractability of diplomatic problems under the Articles, see Richard B. Morris, *The Forging of the Union*, 130–61, 194–219; and Cathy Matson, "American Political Economy in the Constitutional Decade." Merrill Jensen minimized economic dislocations, attributing the notion of a "critical period" to Federalist propaganda; Jensen, *The New Nation*, 422–28.

24. James Warren to John Adams, Jan. 28 and Sept. 4, 1785, in *Warren-Adams Letters*, 2:248–50 and 262–64, at 264.

25. For example, "Petition of Henry Remsen and Others, Merchants of this City," *Journal of the Votes and Proceedings of the Assembly of New York*, 10th sess., at 89 (Mar. 9, 1787); and resolutions prohibiting the states from passing acts repugnant to treaties, in Worthington C. Ford, ed., *Journals of the Continental Congress*, 32:124–25 (Mar. 21, 1786), and 32:176 (Apr. 13, 1786).

26. Stephen Higginson to John Adams, Dec. 30, 1785, in J. Franklin Jameson, ed., "The Letters of Stephen Higginson," 725–33, at 732.

27. "Cincinnatus," *Independent Journal and General Advertiser*, May 10, 14, and 21, 1784; Ford, *Journals of Congress*, 22:218n, 237–38 (Apr. 30, May 4, 1782).

28. Stephen Higginson to John Adams, Dec. 30, 1785, in Jameson, "Letters of Stephen Higginson," 715–33, at 733. See also Warville, *New Travels in the United States*, 1:128; and "To the United States in Congress assembl'd," dtd. Boston, April 22, 1785, in *Pennsylvania Packet*, June 3, 1785.

29. Anne Bezanson, *Wholesale Prices in Philadelphia*, 81, 127, 160, 179.

30. *Journal of the Assembly of New York*, 8th sess., at 122–24 (Mar. 1, 1785); 9th sess., at 100–101 (Mar. 24, 1786); and 10th sess., at 89 (Mar. 9, 1787); items in *New York Packet*, Feb. 16, 1787; and David Franks, *New-York City Directory, 1786*.

31. Phineas Bond to Duke of Leeds, in J. Franklin Jameson, ed., "Letters to the Foreign Office of Great Britain," 1:611.

32. Stephen Higginson to John Adams, Dec. 30, 1785, in Jameson, "Letters of Stephen Higginson," 715–33, at 732.

33. For New York, see the bankruptcies of Lawrence Marston and many others in New York City, reported in the *Journal of the Assembly of New York*, 8th sess., at 32 (Feb. 11, 1785), and at 181 (Apr. 27, 1785); and 9th sess., at 100–101 (Mar. 24, 1786); and items in *New York Morning Post*, Mar. 10, 1785; and *New York Packet*, Apr. 21, 1785. For Philadelphia, see Thomas M. Doerflinger, *A Vigorous Spirit of Enterprise*, 262.

34. Peter Colt to Jeremiah Wadsworth, Dec. 28, 1783, cited in Margaret Martin, *Merchants and Traders of the Connecticut River Valley*, 40–41.

35. "One of the People," *New-Jersey Gazette*, Sept. 20, 1784. The same point was made by "Farmer," "To the Inhabitants of Maryland," dtd. Feb. 12, 1786, in *Maryland Journal*, Feb. 17, 1786.

36. For New Jersey, see Jensen, *New Nation*, 338–39; and for Delaware, Morris, *Forging of the Union*, 149–50.

37. For Delaware, see Victor S. Clark, *History of Manufactures in the United States*, 1:229–30; and for Rhode Island, H. M. Bishop, "Why Rhode Island Opposed the Federal Constitution."

38. On Connecticut's liberal import policies, see Albert A. Giesecke, *American Commercial Legislation before 1789*, 128. Connecticut consistently supported the movement for congressional imposts and protectionism; its free ports were designed to enable the state to compete with its neighbors. On New Jersey's antipathy to the economic dominance of New York and Pennsylvania and its hopes that congressional action would cure such jealousies, see W. C. Hunter, *The Commercial Policies of New Jersey under the Confederation*, 26–29. New Jersey was not opposed to trade with Great Britain, but was determined to become more competitive with the other American states. In 1791 Tench Coxe gathered information about manufacturing from

businessmen and politicians around the country. Reports to him, including many valuable discussions of conditions in the 1780s, are published in Arthur H. Cole, ed., *Industrial and Commercial Correspondence of Alexander Hamilton;* see esp. Peter Colt to John Chester, July 2, 1791, at 3–7; Benjamin Huntington to Chester, dtd. New London, Conn., Aug. 24, 1791, at 13–14; Jonathan Palmer, Jr., to Chester, dtd. Stonington, Conn., Sept. 15, 1791, at 30; John Mix to Chester, dtd. New Haven, n.d., at 46–50; Silas Condict to Aaron Dunham, dtd. Morristown, N.J., Aug. 25, 1791, at 67–68; Moses Brown to John Dexter, dtd. Providence, July 22, 1791, at 71–79. See also "Proceedings of the General Assembly," Oct. 14, 1786, repr. in *New-Haven Gazette,* Oct. 19, 1786; and Jensen, *New Nation,* 338–39.

39. See, e.g., George Cabot to Hamilton, Sept. 6, 1791, in Cole, *Industrial and Commercial Correspondence of Hamilton,* 61–65; and William Constable to Gouverneur Morris, Dec. 6, 1788, in ibid., 165–68.

40. *Laws of the State of New York,* 1st sess., ch. 10, at 10 (June 1778); 3d sess., ch. 21, at 82 (Sept. 4–Oct, 25, 1779); 4th sess., ch. 2, at 149 (Sept. 1, 1780), and ch. 24, at 173 (Feb. 2–Mar. 31, 1781); 7th sess., ch. 10, at 11 (Mar. 22, 1784); 8th sess., ch. 7, at 180 (Nov. 18, 1784); 10th sess., ch. 81, at 142 (Apr. 11, 1787). On New York's trade policy see Matson, "Jealousy, Liberty, and Union."

41. *Laws of New York,* 8th sess., ch. 7, at 180 (Nov. 18, 1784), and ch. 37, at 88 (Mar. 14, 1785).

42. Item in *Connecticut Courant,* Oct. 16, 1786. See also Hugh Ledlie to General Lamb, Jan. 15, 1788, Lamb Papers.

43. "Proclamation of Governor Trumbull Declaring for Free Trade among the States," Sept. 6, 1780, in Hugh Hastings, ed., *The Public Papers of George Clinton, First Governor of New York,* 6:174; "Proceedings of the General Assembly," Oct. 11, 1786, repr. in *New-Haven Gazette,* Oct. 19, 1786; "State of Connecticut, in the House of Representatives," June 7, 1786, in *New-Haven Gazette,* June 8, 1787; and "State of Connecticut, In Convention," Jan. 7, 1788, in *New-Haven Gazette,* Jan. 17, 1788.

44. Cooke, *The Federalist,* nos. 6 and 7 (Hamilton), at 31, 39, and 40. See also item in *New York Packet,* Nov. 10, 1785.

45. John Jay to unknown, in Henry P. Johnston, ed., *The Correspondence and Public Papers of John Jay,* 4:146–47.

46. [Fisher Ames], *Connecticut Courant,* n.d., repr. in *New York Journal,* Mar. 29, 1787. For other expressions of discontent about trade between Virginia and New York, see George Lux, signed editorial, *Maryland Journal,* Apr. 4, 1788; and "Unitas," *New York Packet,* Mar. 4, 1785.

47. Cooke, *The Federalist,* nos. 7, 22, and 7 (Hamilton), at 40, 137, and 40 (emphasis in original).

48. William B. Weeden, *The Economic and Social History of New England,* 2:783; Jensen, *New Nation,* 298–340.

49. For example, see Jefferson to George Washington, Mar. 15, 1784; to Madison, Feb. 20, 1784; and to G. K. van Hogendorp, Oct. 13, 1785, in Boyd et al., *Papers of Thomas Jefferson,* 7:25–27, 6:547–48, and 8:633.

50. Hugh Williamson to Governor of North Carolina, in Burnett, *Letters of the Members,* 7:593–99, at 596.

51. "Memorial and Petition of Robert Bell," Mar. 6, 1784, in *Pennsylvania Packet,* Mar. 12, 1785.

52. "State of Rhode Island, In General Assembly," *United States Chronicle*, July 21, 1785; and item in *Maryland Journal*, Oct. 17, 1783.

53. Stephen Higginson to John Adams, July 1787, in Jameson, "Letters of Stephen Higginson," 737.

54. For example, George Cabot to Hamilton, Oct. 8, 1791, in Cole, *Industrial and Commercial Correspondence of Hamilton*, 168–70; *Maryland Gazette* (Annapolis), Dec. 25, 1783, June 24, 1784, and Mar. 24, 1785; and brief citations from the documents listed in Herbert C. Bell, David W. Parker, et al., *Guide to British West Indian Archive Materials*, 33, 35, 104, 265, 266, 326, 395.

55. Cabot to Hamilton, Oct. 8, 1791, in Cole, *Industrial and Commercial Correspondence of Hamilton*, 168–70.

56. Timothy Davis, *Thoughts on Taxation in a Letter to a Friend*, 7. See also "Cincinnatus," *Independent Journal and General Advertiser*, May 10, 14, and 21, 1784.

57. "A Plain but real Friend to America," "On American Manufactures," *Maryland Journal*, Oct. 21, 1785.

58. On commercial conditions, see the commentary in John Mercer to Benjamin Harrison, Dec. 10, 1783; Thomas Stone to James Monroe, Dec. 15, 1784; John Habersham to Joseph Clay, June 24, 1785; Pierse Long to John Langdon, Sept. 18, 1785; William Grayson to Madison, Nov. 14, 1785; Nathan Dane to James Bowdoin, Jan. 10, 1786, to Samuel Phillips, Jan. 20, 1786, and to Samuel Adams, Feb. 11, 1786; Henry Lee to Washington, Apr. 21, 1786—all in Burnett, *Letters of the Members*, 7:389–90, 628–31; 8:151–52, 219, 255–56, 282–83, 287–89, 303–6, 343.

59. Rufus King to John Adams, Dec. 4, 1785, in Burnett, *Letters of the Members*, 8:268. See also King to Adams, Nov. 2, 1785, and May 5, 1786, and Elbridge Gerry to King, May 27, 1786, in Charles R. King, ed., *The Life and Correspondence of Rufus King*, 1:113, 171, 101.

60. "Common Sense," *Independent Journal and General Advertiser*, May 10, 14, and 21, 1784; and Jefferson to Madison, July 1, 1784, and to Monroe, June 17, 1785, in Boyd et al., *Papers of Thomas Jefferson*, 7:356 and 8:227–34, at 229.

61. Committee of Merchants and Traders of the City of Philadelphia, June 21, 1785, in *Pennsylvania Packet*, June 24, 1785.

62. Item in *New York Packet*, Nov. 10, 1785. See also ibid., Mar. 7, 1785.

63. "Pro-Bono Republicae," *Pennsylvania Gazette*, May 11, 1785.

64. Item in *Maryland Journal*, Aug. 9, 1785.

65. John Habersham to Joseph Clay, June 24, 1785, and Robert Sherman to Elias Shipman, May 1, 1784, in Burnett, *Letters of the Members*, 8:151–52, 7:516.

66. Minutes of the New York Chamber of Commerce, May 1785; "A Friend to Commerce," *Independent Chronicle*, Sept. 1, 1785, repr. in *Pennsylvania Packet*, Sept. 20, 1785; items in *New York Journal*, May 11, June 15, and July 6, 1786; items in *New York Packet*, May 4, June 9, and Aug. 14, 1786; item dtd. Apr. 1, 1786, in *Pennsylvania Packet*, Sept. 20, 1786; and "The Memorial of the Committee of Merchants and Traders of Philadelphia," Apr. 6, 1785, repr. in *American Museum* 1 (Apr. 1787), 313–14.

67. "Resolutions of the Merchants, Traders and others of the town of Boston," Apr. 22, 1785, in *Pennsylvania Gazette*, June 8, 1785; Samuel Adams to John Adams, July 1785, cited in George Bancroft, *History of the Formation of the Constitution of the United States of America*, 1:444.

68. Committee of Philadelphia Merchants to Merchants and Traders of Boston and New York, May 19, 1785, Broadsides Collection, NYPL.

69. For Congress's first formal requests for authority over commerce, see Ford, *Journals of Congress*, 22:218n, 237–38 (Apr. 30 and May 4, 1782).

70. John Adams to John Jay, May 5, 1785, in Charles Francis Adams, ed., *The Works of John Adams*, 8:240-42, at 241; and congressional requests for more power over foreign imports, in Ford, *Journals of Congress*, 26:269–71 (Apr. 22, 1784); 26:321–22 (Apr. 30, 1784); 28:201–5 (Mar. 28, 1785); 30:124–25 (Mar. 20, 1786); 30:183–84 (Apr. 13, 1786); and 31:907–9 (Oct. 23, 1786).

71. Jefferson to Monroe, June 17, 1785, in Boyd et al., *Papers of Thomas Jefferson*, 8:227–34, at 229.

72. "Harrington" [Benjamin Rush], "To the Freemen of Pennsylvania," *Pennsylvania Gazette*, May 30, 1787, in Jensen et al., *History of Ratification*, 13:116–20, at 119. The editors of this enormously useful series have determined that the "Harrington" essay was reprinted at least thirty times in eleven different states.

73. Richard Henry Lee to Monroe, Jan. 5, 1784, in James C. Ballagh, ed., *Letters of Richard Henry Lee*, 2:286–90, at 289.

74. Monroe to Madison, Sept. 3, 1786, in Burnett, *Letters of the Members*, 8:462; and, for a summary of congressional requests for a national impost, see Ford, *Journals of Congress*, 31:613 (Aug. 31, 1786).

75. William Grayson to Madison, Mar. 22, 1786, in Burnett, *Letters of the Members*, 8:333; ironically, Grayson would later oppose ratification of the Constitution. See also the report of the Grand Committee, recommending congressional jurisdiction over import and export taxes, with some embargo powers left to the states, in Ford, *Journals of Congress*, 31:494–97 (Aug. 4, 1786).

76. Report of the Committee on Commercial Treaties, Mar. 2, 1786, in Ford, *Journals of Congress*, 30:93–94.

77. On growing sectionalism among southern merchants, see, e.g., Benjamin Hawkins to Jefferson, Mar. 8, 1787, in Burnett, *Letters of the Members*, 8:552–53. See also the discussion and references in ch. 5.

78. See the discussions about opinion in these states in Madison to Jefferson, Oct. 3, 1785, in Robert A. Rutland et al., eds., *The Papers of James Madison*, 8:373–76, at 374; and Grayson to Monroe, May 29, 1787, in Max Farrand, ed., *The Records of the Federal Convention of 1787*, 3:30.

79. Madison to Jefferson, Mar. 18, 1786, in Rutland et al., *Papers of James Madison*, 8:500–504, at 502. See also Washington to William Carmichael, June 10, 1785, and to David Humphreys, Sept. 1, 1785, cited in Bancroft, *Formation of the Constitution*, 1:439, 453; and also Madison, Preface to Debates in the Convention of 1787, Mar. 1836, in Farrand, *Records of the Convention*, 3:539–51, at 542, 548.

80. Peter S. Onuf, *Statehood and Union*, 1–20.

81. Cathy Matson, "From Free Trade to Liberty," ch. 7. For the 1781 impost request, see Ford, *Journals of Congress*, 21:102–103, (Jan. 31, 1781); 21:110 (Feb. 1, 1781); and 21:112–13 (Feb. 3, 1781). On the 1783 impost, see ibid., 24:257–62 (Apr. 18, 1783); 24:186–92 (Mar. 18, 1783); and 24:195–201 (Mar. 20, 1783). On the emergence of the nationalists and their association with the national revenue and a "uniform system of commerce," see Hamilton, "The

Continentalist," nos. 1 and 2, Apr. 18 and July 4, 1782, in Syrett, *Papers of Alexander Hamilton*, 3:75–82, 99–106; Hamilton, "Remarks on Appropriating the Impost Exclusively to the Army," Feb. 19, 1783, in ibid., 3:262; items in *New York Packet*, Oct. 24, 1782, and Apr. 21, 1785; and Jensen, *New Nation*, chs. 2–3. Congress tied its requests for western land cessions to the bills for an impost.

82. Matson, "From Free Trade to Liberty," ch. 7.

83. For concise reviews of this history see Jack N. Rakove, "Articles of Confederation," and idem, "From One Agenda to Another."

84. "At a General Town Meeting," June 20, 1785, in *Pennsylvania Gazette*, June 22, 1785. See also Madison's views about interstate cooperation in letters to Monroe, Nov. 27, 1784, and to Jefferson, Apr. 27, 1784, in Rutland et al., *Papers of James Madison*, 8:156–58 and 365–70, at 268–69; and John Lauritz Larson, " 'Bind the Republic Together.' "

85. Thomas P. Abernethy, *Western Lands and the American Revolution*, 295–96.

86. Robert Brunhouse, *The Counter-Revolution in Pennsylvania*, 185–88. On sectional tensions, see Joseph L. Davis, *Sectionalism in American Politics*; Thomas P. Slaughter, *The Whisky Rebellion*, 36–45; and Drew R. McCoy, "James Madison and Visions of American Nationality in the Confederation Period."

CHAPTER 5. UNION OR DISUNION?

1. "Extract of a Letter from Philadelphia," n.d., *Columbian Herald*, July 11, 1785.

2. Item in *Independent Chronicle*, Feb. 15, 1787, in Merrill Jensen et al., eds., *The Documentary History of the Ratification of the Constitution*. The editors have identified nineteen reprintings of this piece in ten states before May 12, 1787; ibid., 13:59n.

3. Alexander Hamilton, "The Continentalist," no. 3, Aug. 9, 1781, in Harold C. Syrett, ed., *The Papers of Alexander Hamilton*, 2:660–61.

4. Richard Champion, *Considerations on the Present Situation of Great Britain and the United States of America*, 238–39.

5. Richard Henry Lee to James Madison, Aug. 11, 1785, in Robert A. Rutland et al., eds., *The Papers of James Madison*, 8:339–41, at 340. See also Theodore Sedgewick to Caleb Strong, Aug. 6, 1786, in Edmund Cody Burnett, ed., *Letters of the Members of the Continental Congress*, 8:415–16.

6. Rufus King to John Adams, Nov. 2, 1785, in Charles R. King, ed., *The Life and Correspondence of Rufus King*, 2:112–13.

7. James Monroe to Madison, Sept. 3, 1786, in Burnett, *Letters of the Members*, 8:462. On sectional tensions in this period, see n. 86, ch. 4; and Peter S. Onuf, *Statehood and Union*, ch. 3.

8. See, e.g., Benjamin Hawkins to Thomas Jefferson, Mar. 8, 1787, in Burnett, *Letters of the Members*, 8:552–53. For a discussion of disunion proposals see editorial note, Jensen et al., *History of Ratification*, 13:54–57.

9. Benjamin Rush to Richard Price, Oct. 27, 1786, in Lyman Butterfield, ed., *The Letters of Benjamin Rush*, 1:408–10.

10. "Lycurgus," dtd. New York, Mar. 30, 1787, in *New York Daily Advertiser,* Apr. 2, 1787, in Jensen et al., *History of Ratification,* 13:58–59.

11. Gordon S. Wood, *The Creation of the American Republic,* 409–13.

12. Rush to Timothy Pickering, Aug. 30, 1787, in Butterfield, *Letters of Benjamin Rush,* 1:439–40. See also Rush speech, Pennsylvania convention, Dec. 3, 1787, in Jensen et al., *History of Ratification,* 2:457–58.

13. Item in *Independent Chronicle,* Feb. 15, 1787, in Jensen et al., *History of Ratification,* 13:57.

14. "Reason," "A Thought for the Delegates to the Convention," *New York Daily Advertiser,* Mar. 24, 1787, in Jensen et al., *History of Ratification,* 13:57–58, repr. nine times in seven states by Apr. 28, 1787.

15. James McClurg to Madison, Aug. 5, 1787, in Rutland et al., *Papers of James Madison,* 10:134–36.

16. On Madison's thinking in this period, see the excellent essays by Lance Banning, including "The Practicable Sphere of a Republic" and "Virginia: Nation, State, and Section."

17. Wood, *Creation of the American Republic,* 530–36.

18. Louise Burnham Dunbar, *A Study of "Monarchical" Tendencies in the United States;* editorial note, Jensen et al., *History of Ratification,* 13:168–72.

19. Item in *American Museum* 1 (Mar. 1787), 202; Jensen et al., *History of Ratification,* 13:76–77.

20. George Washington to John Jay, Aug. 1, 1787, in *Documentary History of the Constitution of the United States,* 5:19–21.

21. David Ramsay to Jefferson, Apr. 7, 1787, in ibid., 5:109.

22. "Extract of a letter from a gentleman in Virginia," *Independent Gazetteer,* June 26, 1787, in Jensen et al., *History of Ratification,* 13:145–47.

23. Madison to Edmund Pendleton, Feb. 24, 1787, in Rutland et al., *Papers of James Madison,* 9:294–96.

24. Peter S. Onuf, *Origins of the Federal Republic,* 7, 16. For a comprehensive and persuasive treatment of this theme, see Jerrilyn Greene Marston, *King and Congress.*

25. James Wilson speech, June 1, 1787 (Rufus King's notes), in Max Farrand, ed., *The Records of the Federal Convention of 1787,* 1:71, our emphasis.

26. Hamilton speech, June 18, 1787, in ibid., 1:288.

27. "Reason," "A Thought for the Delegates," *New York Daily Advertiser,* Mar. 24, 1787, in Jensen et al., *History of Ratification,* 13:57–58.

28. "Lycurgus," *New York Daily Advertiser,* Apr. 2, 1787, in Jensen et al., *History of Ratification,* 13:58–59.

29. See ch. 7 and the discussion in Peter S. Onuf, "State Sovereignty and the Making of the Constitution."

30. [William Barton], *The True Interest of the United States,* 1.

31. Item dtd. Worcester, Mass., Nov. 17, 1785, in *New-Jersey Gazette,* Nov. 28, 1785. See the discussion in J. R. Pole, *The Gift of Government,* 32–40, 146–48.

32. "Spectator," *New-Haven Gazette,* Mar. 3, 1785.

33. David Daggett, "Debate over Sumptuary Laws by M.A. Candidates at Yale," Sept. 13, 1786, in *New-Haven Gazette and Connecticut Magazine,* Oct. 12, 1786. See the discussions in Michael Lienesch, *New Order of the Ages,* 82–115, and Ronald Meek, *Social Science and the Ignoble Savage.*

34. William Vans Murray, "Political Sketches," dtd. Middle Temple, Apr. 1787 (written 1784–85), in *American Museum* 2 (Sept. 1787), 220–48, at 237, 228, 234, 233.

35. "Farmer," "To the Inhabitants of Potowmack River," Aug. 10, 1784, in *Virginia Journal*, Aug. 18, 1784.

36. "Candidus," *London Evening Post*, n.d., repr. in *Pennsylvania Gazette*, July 21, 1784; "Collective Observations" (on the United States), dtd. New York, June 1, 1786, in *Connecticut Courant*, June 5, 1786. For further discussion of the development theme, see Onuf, *Statehood and Union*, 5–20. On the importance of "nature" and "natural rights" arguments for American expansionism, see Albert K. Weinberg, *Manifest Destiny*, esp. ch. 1.

37. Item dtd. New York, July 20, 1786, in *Freeman's Journal*, July 26, 1786.

38. "Lycurgus," no. 1, *New-Haven Gazette and Connecticut Magazine*, Feb. 16, 1786; repr. in *Connecticut Courant*, Feb. 27, 1786, and *Maryland Gazette* (Baltimore), Mar. 24, 1786.

39. Item dtd. New York, July 20, 1786, in *Freeman's Journal*, July 26, 1786.

40. Item dtd. Worcester, Mass., Nov. 17, 1785, in *New-Jersey Gazette*, Nov. 28, 1785.

41. "Americanus" [William Barton?], "On American Manufactures," *Columbian Magazine* 1 (Sept. 1786), 28.

42. Noah Webster, *Sketches of American Policy*, 18, our emphasis. For an earlier argument that the pursuit of commercial interests would tend to redistribute wealth, which in turn would have a salutary effect on political participation, see Sir James Steuart, *Inquiry into the Principles of Political Economy*, 1:215–17, 278–79.

43. New York Chamber of Commerce, "Circular to the States," Sept. 30, 1785, in *New-Jersey Gazette*, Nov. 21, 1785.

44. John Gray et al., "To the Tradesmen and Manufacturers of New-haven," dtd. Boston, Aug. 20, 1785, in *New-Haven Gazette*, Sept. 29, 1785.

45. Webster, *Sketches of American Policy*, 45.

46. Item dtd. Trenton, *New-Jersey Gazette*, July 24, 1786.

47. Item in *Maryland Gazette* (Baltimore), Apr. 17, 1787.

48. "Observator," no. 1, *New-Haven Gazette*, Aug. 25, 1785.

49. "Cato," "To the Public," *New-Haven Gazette and Connecticut Magazine*, Jan. 25, 1787. This "Cato" is not to be confused with the writer often identified as George Clinton, whose essays under the same pseudonym appeared in the *New York Journal* later that year.

50. Item dtd. New York, Aug. 29, 1786, in *New-Jersey Gazette*, Sept. 11, 1786. See also [David Humphreys], "The Happiness of America," *Columbian Magazine* 1 (Oct. 1786), 67.

51. [Tench Coxe], *An Enquiry into the Principles on which a Commercial System for the United States should be Founded*; and idem, "An address to an assembly of the friends of American manufactures," Philadelphia, Aug. 9, 1787, in *American Museum* 2 (Sept. 1787), 255. See also New York [City] Chamber of Commerce, *Gentlemen, the interest of the landholder*, on the importance of "the union of the farmer, the merchant and mechanic"; and [Barton], *True Interest of the United States*, 11.

52. New York Chamber of Commerce, "Circular to the States," Sept. 30, 1785, in *New-Jersey Gazette*, Nov. 21, 1785.

53. "Examiner," no. 1, *Virginia Journal*, Feb. 8, 1787.
54. Item in *Massachusetts Centinel*, Apr. 11, 1787, in Jensen et al., *History of Ratification*, 13:79.
55. Item in *Pennsylvania Herald*, May 9, 1787, in Jensen et al., *History of Ratification*, 13:96–97.
56. "To the Political Freethinkers of America," *New York Daily Advertiser*, May 24, 1787, in Jensen et al., *History of Ratification*, 13:113–15.
57. Thomas Pownall, *A Memorial Addressed to the Sovereigns of America*, 129.
58. "To the Political Freethinkers of America," *New York Daily Advertiser*, May 24, 1787, in Jensen et al., *History of Ratification*, 13:113–15.
59. "Lycurgus," no. 1, *New-Haven Gazette*, Feb. 16, 1786.
60. "Cato," "To the Public," *New-Haven Gazette*, Jan. 25, 1787.
61. "Observator," no. 1, ibid., Aug. 25, 1785.
62. Item in *Pennsylvania Gazette*, June 29, 1785.

CHAPTER 6. CONSTITUTIONAL CONVENTION

1. Alexander Hamilton to James Duane, Sept. 3, 1780, in Harold C. Syrett, ed., *The Papers of Alexander Hamilton*, 1:203–8; James Duane to George Washington, Jan. 29, 1781, in Edmund Cody Burnett, ed., *Letters of the Members of the Continental Congress*, 5:551.
2. For congressional discussions of the debt and its appointments of committees under Robert Morris, see Worthington C. Ford, ed., *Journals of the Continental Congress*, 19:236 (Mar. 6, 1781); 19:290–91 (Mar. 21, 1781); 19:432–33 (Apr. 21, 1781); and 20:723–24 (July 6, 1781). Congressional deliberations over the Bank of North America revealed delegates' concerns about establishing central authority over revolutionary debts; see ibid., 20:545–48 (May 26, 1781).
3. Resolutions of the New York Legislature, July 20 and 22, 1782, in Syrett, *Papers of Alexander Hamilton*, 3:110–13, 117.
4. Several Gentlemen of Rhode Island to the Chairman of the General Convention, May 11, 1787, in Max Farrand, ed., *The Records of the Federal Convention of 1787*, 3:18–19. On responses to agrarian disorders see David P. Szatmary, *Shays' Rebellion*; and Peter S. Onuf, *Origins of the Federal Republic*, 173–85.
5. Address of the Annapolis Convention, Sept. 14, 1786, in Farrand, *Records of the Convention*, 3:686–90, at 687.
6. One of the best brief accounts of the Convention is Lance Banning's "The Constitutional Convention."
7. For opposing views see Jack N. Rakove, "The Great Compromise," and Lance Banning, "The Practicable Sphere of a Republic."
8. Jacob E. Cooke, ed., *The Federalist Papers*, no. 39 (Madison), at 257.
9. George Read speech, June 26, in Farrand, *Records of the Convention*, 1:424 (Madison's notes, et seq., except where otherwise indicated). See also speeches by Madison, June 8 and 19, and Hamilton, June 19, in ibid., 1:168, 1:319, 1:325.
10. Rufus King speech, June 19, in ibid., 1:323.
11. Oliver Ellsworth speech, June 29, in ibid., 1:468.

12. William Paterson speech, June 9, in ibid., 1:183 (Yates's notes).

13. Gunning Bedford speech, June 8, in ibid., 1:167; Paterson speech, June 9, in ibid., 1:179.

14. Luther Martin speech, June 19, in ibid., 1:324.

15. Convention journal, May 25, in ibid., 1:4; Read speech, May 30, in ibid., 1:37.

16. Paterson speech, June 9, in ibid., 1:178.

17. Charles Pinckney speech, June 16, in ibid., 1:255.

18. Roger Sherman speech, June 11, in ibid., 1:196.

19. Sherman speech, July 14, in ibid., 2:5. See also Sherman and Ellsworth to Gov. Samuel Huntington, Sept. 26., 1787, in Merrill Jensen et al., eds., *The Documentary History of the Ratification of the Constitution*, 3:351–53.

20. Madison speech, July 14, in Farrand, *Records of the Convention*, 2:9.

21. We are indebted here to Rosemarie Zagarri, *The Politics of Size*, ch. 3.

22. Cooke, *The Federalist*, no. 10, at 56–65. On popular sovereignty see Gordon S. Wood, *The Creation of the American Republic*, 530–36, and on the founders' "miraculous" achievement see Onuf, *Origins of the Federal Republic*, 207–9.

23. Madison speech, June 28, in Farrand, *Records of the Convention*, 1:447.

24. Martin speech, June 27, in ibid., 1:441 (Yates's notes).

25. Gouverneur Morris speech, July 7, in ibid., 1:552.

26. Hugh Williamson speech, June 28, in ibid., 1:445–46.

27. John Dickinson speech, June 2, in ibid., 1:86–87.

28. David Brearly speech, June 9, in ibid., 1:177.

29. Paterson speech, June 9, in ibid., 1:183 (Yates's notes).

30. Paterson speech, June 16, in ibid., 1:259 (Yates's notes).

31. Benjamin Franklin speech, June 11, in ibid., 1:199.

32. James Wilson speech, June 9, in ibid., 1:180.

33. Ibid.

34. Franklin speech, June 11, in ibid., 1:199.

35. Madison speech, June 19, in ibid., 1:321.

36. Martin speech, June 27, in ibid., 1:438.

37. Rufus King speech, June 30, in ibid., 1:489.

38. Hamilton speeches of June 29 and 19, in ibid., 1:466, 323.

39. Madison speech of June 28, in ibid., 1:449.

40. Ibid. See also Nathaniel Gorham speeches of June 29 and July 6, in ibid., 1:462–63, 540.

41. Elbridge Gerry speech of June 29, in ibid., 1:467. See the discussion in George Athan Billias, *Elbridge Gerry*, 172–78.

42. George Mason speeches at Virginia convention, June 4 and 19, 1788, in Jonathan Elliot, ed., *The Debates in the Several State Conventions on the Adoption of the Federal Constitution*, 3:29–30, 522.

43. Dickinson speech of Aug. 29, in Farrand, *Records of the Convention*, 2:456; Martin speech of Aug. 29, in ibid., 2:455. This complaint was repeated in Martin's, "The Genuine Information, Delivered to the Legislature of the State of Maryland, Relative to the Proceedings of the General Convention, Held at Philadelphia, in 1787," *Maryland Gazette* (Annapolis), Dec. 28, 1787–Feb. 8, 1788, repr. in Farrand, *Records of the Convention*, 3:172–232, at 187.

44. Daniel Carroll speech, Aug. 30, in ibid., 2:465.

45. Wilson speech, Aug. 30, in ibid., 2:462.

46. Convention journal and Madison's notes, Aug. 30., in ibid., 2:458, 464.

47. David Humphreys to George Washington, Apr. 9, 1787, in *Documentary History of the Constitution*, 5:109–10.

48. Madison to Thomas Jefferson, Oct. 24, 1787, in Robert Rutland et al., eds., *The Papers of James Madison*, 10:205–20, at 207.

49. Edmund Randolph speeches, June 2 and 1, in Farrand, *Records of the Convention*, 1:88, 66.

50. Mason speech, June 4, in ibid., 1:113 (Mason's notes).

51. Pierce Butler speech, June 2, in ibid., 1:88–89.

52. Morris speech, July 13, in ibid., 1:604.

53. Zagarri, *Politics of Size*, ch. 3.

54. See Madison speech, June 19, in Farrand, *Records of the Convention*, 1:320–21.

55. Madison speech, June 29, in ibid., 1:476 (Yates's notes); emphasis omitted.

56. For a more elaborate account of the Convention's successive "phases," see Calvin Jillson and Thornton Anderson, "Realignments in the Convention of 1787"; Jillson, "Constitution-Making: Alignment and Realignment in the Federal Convention of 1787"; Jillson and Cecil Eubanks, "The Political Structure of Constitution Making"; and Jillson, "Ideas in Conflict." For a careful reconstruction of the various slavery compromises, see Paul Finkelman, "Slavery and the Constitutional Convention."

57. Ellsworth speech, June 29, in Farrand, *Records of the Convention*, 1:469.

58. Ibid., 1:468; Cooke, *The Federalist*, no. 39 (Madison), at 257.

59. This point is elaborated in Lance Banning, "Virginia: Nation, State, and Section."

60. Butler speech, Aug. 29, in Farrand, *Records of the Convention*, 2:451.

61. Morris speech, Aug. 22, in ibid., 2:374.

62. Randolph speech, May 29, in ibid., 1:19.

63. Wilson speech, June 16, in ibid., 1:254.

64. Lansing speech, June 16, in ibid., 1:258 (Yates's notes).

65. See Martin speech, June 19, in ibid., 4:20–28, at 24–25.

66. Madison speech, Aug. 21, in ibid., 2:361.

67. Morris speech, Aug. 16, in ibid., 2:307.

68. See the New Jersey "propositions," submitted by Paterson, June 15, in ibid., 1:242–45, esp. at 243. For an early attack on the economic implications of the New Jersey Plan, see Hamilton speech, June 18, in ibid., 1:285–86.

69. James McHenry notes of meeting of Maryland delegation at "Mr. Carrolls lodging," Aug. 7, in ibid., 2:210–12, at 211. New Hampshire's John Langdon argued that "non-exporting" states would also pay taxes to the states which exported their products; Langdon speech, Aug. 21, in ibid., 2:359.

70. Ellsworth speech, Aug. 21, in ibid., 2:360.

71. Gerry speech, Aug. 21, in ibid., 2:362.

72. Speeches of Charles Pinckney, July 12, in ibid., 1:592; Mason, Aug. 16, in ibid., 2:305–6; and Williamson, Aug. 16, in ibid., 2:307.

73. Morris speech, July 13, in ibid., 1:604.

74. Madison to Washington, Nov. 8, 1786, Rutland et al., *Papers of James Madison*, 9:166–67; and Merrill Jensen, *The New Nation*, 229–300.

75. Washington to James McHenry, Aug. 22, 1785, in John C. Fitzpatrick, ed., *The Writings of George Washington*, 28:229.

76. Farrand notes that "the idea of a Committee of Detail seems to have been generally accepted previous to this date." Farrand, *Records of the Convention*, 2:95n. For the Committee of Detail's Aug. 6 report, including a draft of all articles of the Constitution (except that relating to the executive), see ibid., 2:177ff. Discussion of Article VII, which covers duties and imposts, began Aug. 16; see ibid., 2:305.

77. Mason speeches of Aug 16 and 21, in ibid., 2:305–6, 362–63. This argument was revived during the first Washington administration; see, e.g., Hugh Williamson in the House of Representatives, Feb. 3, 1792, in ibid., 3:365–66.

78. Meeting of Maryland delegation, Aug. 7, in ibid., 2:210–12, at 211.

79. Mason speech, Aug. 21, in ibid., 2:363; see also speech of Aug. 16, in ibid., 2:305–6.

80. Morris speech, Aug. 21, in ibid., 2:360; see also speech of Aug. 16, in ibid., 2:306–7.

81. Thomas FitzSimons speech, Aug. 21, in ibid., 2:362; see also Morris speech of Aug. 16, in ibid., 2:306–7.

82. Morris speech, Aug. 21, in ibid., 2:360.

83. Gerry speech, Aug. 16, in ibid., 2:307.

84. George Clymer speech, Aug. 21, in ibid., 2:363.

85. John Rutledge speech, Aug. 21, in ibid., 2:364.

86. C. C. Pinckney speech, Aug. 22, in ibid., 2:371.

87. Butler speeches, Aug. 21 and 22, in ibid., 2:360, 374.

88. Gorham speech, Aug. 22, in ibid, 2:375.

89. Morris speech, Aug. 22, in ibid.

90. Proposal of Aug. 24, in ibid., 2:396.

91. Votes of Aug. 25, in ibid., 2:415–17; and vote of Aug. 28, in ibid., 2:442.

92. Madison's notes of Mason motion and vote, Sept. 12 and 13, in ibid., 2:588–89, 607. The states also retained powers over laying temporary embargoes on exports. See the discussion and rejection of Madison's motion on embargoes, Aug. 28, in ibid., 2:440–41.

93. Proposition referred to Committee of Detail, Aug. 18, in ibid., 2:321, 325. See also comments on internal improvements and banks at ibid., 2:335, 343, 463–64, 503–4, 529, and 615–16.

94. For later commentary on Congress's powers over banks and corporate charters, see esp. Madison to Edward Livingston, Apr. 17, 1824, in ibid., 3:463; T. W. Cobb in the U.S. Senate, Feb. 23, 1825, in ibid., 3:464–66; Madison to Reynolds Chapman, in ibid., 3:494–95; and entry for Mar. 11, 1798, in Jefferson's "Anas," repr. in ibid., 3:375–76.

95. On the limits of the sections see Drew R. McCoy, "James Madison and Visions of American Nationality in the Confederation Period." For contemporary speculation on the future of the national domain see Staughton Lynd, "The Compromise of 1787," 210; and Peter S. Onuf, "Liberty, Development, and Union."

96. See the summary of work on this issue in John J. McCusker and Russell B. Menard, *The Economy of British America*, 336–41, 372–73.

97. Cooke, *The Federalist*, no. 44 (Madison), at 300.

98. Rufus King proposal, July 14, in Farrand, *Records of the Convention*, 2:6–7; Rutledge motion, Aug. 18, in ibid., 2:327–28, 355–56; and Morris motion, Aug. 22, in ibid., 2:377. Many delegates opposed paper money in principle, although, in speeches of Aug. 16, Mason, Mercer, and Randolph all noted that it might be "politic" of Congress to issue such currency during emergencies; see ibid., 2:308–10. Luther Martin argued for the general usefulness of paper emissions in his "Genuine Information," repr. in Farrand, *Records of the Convention*, 3:205–6.

99. For instance, Mason and other southern delegates sought to revive the two-thirds requirement for any navigation act previously recommended by the Committee of Detail. They were convinced that the northern majority in the new government would pass navigation acts that would enable northern merchants to charge "exhorbitant freight" rates and "monopolize the purchase of [southern] commodities at their own price." Mason speech, Sept. 15, in ibid., 2:639–40. See also "Landholder" [Ellsworth], no. 6, *Connecticut Courant*, Dec. 10, 1787, in Farrand, *Records of the Convention*, 3:164–65.

100. Pierce Butler to Weedon Butler, May 5, 1788, in ibid., 3:301–4, at 304. See also Rufus King in the Massachusetts convention, Jan. 17, 1788, in ibid., 3:255.

101. Banning suggests that the Convention was a "learning experience" for Madison. Banning, "Practicable Sphere of a Republic," 178.

102. See Madison speech, June 29, in Farrand, *Records of the Convention*, 1:476 (Yates's notes).

103. Ellsworth speech of Aug. 22, in ibid., 2:375.

104. See the discussion in Finkelman, "Slavery and the Constitutional Convention."

CHAPTER 7. REPUBLICANISM AND FEDERALISM

1. Gouverneur Morris speech, July 5, 1787, in Max Farrand, ed., *The Records of the Federal Convention of 1787*, 1:530.

2. Rufus King speech, June 30, 1787, in ibid., 1:489.

3. Elbridge Gerry speech, June 29, 1787, in ibid., 1:467.

4. Peter S. Onuf, *Origins of the Federal Republic*, 198–209.

5. "One of the People," *Pennsylvania Gazette*, Oct. 17, 1787, in Merrill Jensen et al., eds., *The Documentary History of the Ratification of the Constitution*, 2:186–92, at 190.

6. "A Citizen of New Haven" [Roger Sherman], *Connecticut Courant*, Jan. 7, 1788, in Jensen et al., *History of Ratification*, 3:524–27, at 524, 527.

7. See, e.g., Roger Sherman and Oliver Ellsworth to Gov. Samuel Huntington, Sept. 26, 1787, in Jensen et al., *History of Ratification*, 3:351–53; "Aristides" [Alexander Contee Hanson], *Remarks on the Proposed Plan of a Federal Government* (Annapolis, 1788), in Paul Leicester Ford, ed., *Pamphlets on*

the Constitution of the United States, 217-57, at 223-24; and James Madison speech at Virginia convention, in Jonathan Elliot, ed., *The Debates in the Several State Conventions on the Adoption of the Federal Constitution,* 3:97.

8. For a lucid discussion of how the authors of the *Federalist* series were compelled to modify their original positions, see Albert Furtwangler, *The Authority of Publius.* See also Gouverneur Morris, Rufus King, and George Read speeches, July 5, June 30, and June 1, 1787, in Farrand, *Records of the Convention,* 1:530, 489, 202.

9. For a discussion of recent work on the Antifederalists, see Peter S. Onuf, "Reflections on the Founding." Herbert Storing, *What the Anti-Federalists Were For,* provides a sympathetic analysis of Antifederalist thought; the historiography is ably reviewed in James H. Hutson, "Country, Court, and Constitution"; and in Richard E. Ellis, "The Persistence of Antifederalism after 1789."

10. "Federalism," May 8, 1788, in *Maryland Journal,* May 9, 1788.

11. Letters of Luther Martin, no. 3, Mar. 25, 1788, in *Maryland Journal,* Mar. 28, 1788, repr. in Paul Leicester Ford, ed., *Essays on the Constitution of the United States,* 372-77, at 375.

12. William R. Davie speech, North Carolina convention, July 24, 1788, in Elliot, *Debates in the State Conventions,* 4:17-23, at 20.

13. Robert R. Livingston speech, New York convention, July 1, 1788, in Elliot, *Debates in the State Conventions,* 2:385. See also Edward Carrington to Madison, June 13, 1787, in Robert A. Rutland et al., eds., *The Papers of James Madison,* 10:52-53.

14. Onuf, *Origins of the Federal Republic,* 186-209.

15. James White to Gov. Richard Caswell, Nov. 13, 1787, in Edmund Cody Burnett, ed., *Letters of the Members of the Continental Congress,* 8:681-82.

16. "Plain Truth," *Independent Gazetteer,* Nov. 10, 1787, in Jensen et al., *History of Ratification,* 2:218.

17. "Social Compact," *New-Haven Gazette,* Oct. 4, 1787, in Jensen et al., *History of Ratification,* 3:356-57.

18. James Wilson speech, Pennsylvania convention, Nov. 24, 1787, in ibid., 2:335-36.

19. Charles Pinckney speech, South Carolina convention, May 14, 1788, in Elliot, *Debates in the State Conventions,* 4:331.

20. "Agrippa" [James Winthrop], no. 3, *Massachusetts Gazette,* Nov. 30, 1787, in Ford, *Essays on the Constitution,* 59-62, at 62.

21. "Agrippa," no. 9, *Massachusetts Gazette,* Dec. 28, 1787, in Cecelia M. Kenyon, ed., *The Antifederalists,* 134-37, at 136.

22. "Agrippa," no. 4, *Massachusetts Gazette,* Dec. 3, 1787, in ibid., 132-34, at 132-33.

23. "Agrippa," no. 13, *Massachusetts Gazette,* Jan. 14, 1788, in ibid., 138-47, at 146.

24. "Agrippa," no. 8, *Massachusetts Gazette,* Dec. 25, 1787, in Ford, *Essays on the Constitution,* 76-78, at 77; idem, no. 13, *Massachusetts Gazette,* Jan. 14, 1788, in Kenyon, *Antifederalists,* 138-47, at 146.

25. Kenyon, *Antifederalists,* 143. See Onuf, *Origins of the Federal Republic,* 192-93, for further discussion of this point.

26. For a contrasting view see Cecelia Kenyon's influential essay, "Men of Little Faith."

27. "A Plebeian" [Melancton Smith], *An Address to the People of the State of New-York: Showing the necessity of making Amendments to the Constitution* (New York, 1788), in Ford, *Pamphlets on the Constitution,* 87–115, at 95–96, 97. See also Smith speech at New York convention, June 20, 1788, in Elliot, *Debates in the State Conventions,* 2:223–24.

28. Patrick Henry speech at Virginia convention, June 7, 1788, in Elliot, *Debates in the State Conventions,* 3:145.

29. George Mason speech at Virginia convention, June 4, 1788, in ibid., 3:30.

30. "Brutus" [Melancton Smith?], Oct. 18, 1787, in Jensen et al., *History of Ratification,* 13:411–21, at 418.

31. "The Dissent of the Minority," *Pennsylvania Packet,* Dec. 18, 1787, in Jensen et al., *History of Ratification,* 2:617–40, at 626. See also Samuel Chase, Notes of Speeches Delivered to the Maryland Convention, April 1788, in Herbert J. Storing, ed., *The Complete Anti-Federalist,* 5:79–91, at 81.

32. "Old Whig," no. 4, *Independent Gazetteer,* Oct. 27, 1787, in Jensen et al., *History of Ratification,* 13:497–502, at 499; James Monroe speech at Virginia convention, June 10, 1788, in Elliot, *Debates in the State Conventions,* 3:215. For application of these principles to the case of Vermont, see "Cato," no. 3, *New York Journal,* Oct. 25, 1787, in Ford, *Essays on the Constitution,* 255–59, at 258.

33. "Centinel" [Samuel Bryan], no. 1, *Independent Gazetteer,* Oct. 5, 1787, in Jensen et al., *History of Ratification,* 2:158–67, at 164.

34. "A Farmer" [John Francis Mercer], no. 3, *Maryland Gazette* (Baltimore), Mar. 7, 1787, in Storing, *Complete Anti-Federalist,* 5:29–31, at 30–31.

35. Monroe speech at Virginia convention, June 10, 1788, in Elliot, *Debates in the State Conventions,* 3:212.

36. "A Farmer," no. 3, *Maryland Gazette* (Baltimore), in Storing, *Complete Anti-Federalist,* 5:29–32, at 32.

37. Item in *Independent Gazetteer,* Jan. 22, 1788, in Jensen et al., *History of Ratification,* 2:657.

38. "An Officer of the Late Continental Army," *Independent Gazetteer,* Nov. 6, 1787, in Jensen et al., *History of Ratification,* 2:210–16, at 211.

39. Luther Martin, "The Genuine Information, Delivered to the Legislature of Maryland, Relative to the Proceedings of the General Convention, Held at Philadelphia, in 1787," *Maryland Gazette* (Annapolis), Dec. 28, 1787–Feb. 8, 1788, in Farrand, *Records of the Federal Convention,* 3:172–232, at 230.

40. Mason to Gerry, Oct. 20, 1787, in Robert A. Rutland, ed., *The Papers of George Mason,* 3:1005–7, at 1006.

41. Benjamin Harrison to Washington, Oct. 4, 1787, in *Documentary History of the Constitution of the United States,* 4:312–13.

42. Benjamin Gale speech at Connecticut convention, Nov. 12, 1787, in Jensen et al., *History of Ratification,* 3:420–29, at 426.

43. William Grayson speech at Virginia convention, June 11, 1788, in Elliot, *Debates in the State Conventions,* 3:282.

44. Timothy Bloodworth speech at North Carolina convention, July 28, 1788, in ibid., 4:135.

45. Henry speech at Virginia convention, June 9, 1788, in ibid., 3:151–52.
46. "A Farmer" [Mercer], no. 3, *Maryland Gazette* (Baltimore), Mar. 18, 1788, in Storing, *Complete Anti-Federalist*, 5:32–36, at 36 (emphasis omitted).
47. "Agrippa" [Winthrop], no. 14, *Massachusetts Gazette*, Jan. 18, 1788, in Ford, *Essays on the Constitution*, 102–4, at 103.
48. "A Farmer," no. 7, *Maryland Gazette* (Baltimore), Apr. 15, 1788, in Storing, *Complete Anti-Federalist*, 5:64–66, at 65.
49. Edmund Randolph speech, May 29, 1788, in Farrand, *Records of the Convention*, 1:26.
50. Randolph speeches, Virginia convention, June 24 and June 17, 1788, in Elliot, *Debates in the State Conventions*, 3:603, 470–71.
51. "Cato," "To the Public," *New-Haven Gazette*, Jan. 25, 1787 (see n. 49, ch. 5).
52. Hugh Henry Brackenridge speech, Pennsylvania convention, Sept. 28, 1787, in Jensen et al., *History of Ratification*, 2:93.
53. Madison speech, Virginia convention, June 14, 1787, in Elliot, *Debates in the State Conventions*, 3:399.
54. James White to Gov. Richard Caswell, Nov. 13, 1787, in Burnett, *Letters of the Members*, 8:681–82.
55. Item in *Massachusetts Gazette*, n.d., repr. in *Maryland Journal*, Dec. 25, 1787.
56. Gen. C. C. Pinckney speech, South Carolina convention, Jan. 17, 1788, in Elliot, *Debates in the State Conventions*, 4:281–82.
57. Jasper Yeates speech, Pennsylvania convention, Nov. 30, 1787, in ibid., 2:439.
58. Edward C. Papenfuse, "An Undelivered Defense of a Winning Cause," 232; James Wilson speech, Pennsylvania convention, Dec. 11, 1787, in Jensen et al., *History of Ratification*, 2:577. See also "Landholder" [Ellsworth], no. 5, Dec. 3, 1787, in ibid., 3:482.
59. "Letter from New York," *Connecticut Journal*, Oct. 24, 1787, in Jensen et al., *History of Ratification*, 3:386.
60. John Brown Cutting to Jefferson, July 11, 1788, in *Documentary History of the Constitution*, 5:770–79, at 771. The reference is to hostilities between North Carolina and the Franklin separatists.
61. Gen. William Heath speech, Massachusetts convention, Jan. 30, 1788, in Elliot, *Debates in the State Conventions*, 2:121.
62. Charles Pinckney speech, South Carolina convention, May 14, 1788, in Elliot, *Debates in the State Conventions*, 4:331.
63. "Civis," "To the Independent Electors of Maryland," Jan. 26, 1788, in *Maryland Journal*, Feb. 1, 1788.
64. Charles Pinckney's Letter, Jan. 2, 1788, in *State Gazette of South Carolina*, May 5, 1788, repr. in Ford, *Essays on the Constitution*, 411–13, at 411–12.
65. "Landholder" [Ellsworth], no. 10, *Connecticut Courant*, Mar. 3, 1788, in Ford, *Essays on the Constitution*, 189–92, at 192.
66. [Noah Webster], *An Examination into the Leading Principles of the Federal Constitution* (Philadelphia, 1787), in Ford, *Pamphlets on the Constitution*, 25–65, at 63.
67. Richard Law speech, Connecticut convention, Jan. 9, 1788, in Jensen et al., *History of Ratification*, 3:559.

68. The idea of "popular sovereignty" is elaborated in Gordon S. Wood, *The Creation of the American Republic*, 524-36.

69. [Pelatiah Webster], *The Weakness of Brutus Exposed: Or, Some Remarks in Vindication of the Constitution* (Philadelphia, 1787), in Ford, *Pamphlets on the Constitution*, 117-31, at 121, 128.

70. Oliver Wolcott and Richard Law speeches at Connecticut convention, Jan. 9, 1788, in Jensen et al., *History of Ratification*, 3:557, 559. See the discussion in Onuf, *Origins of the Federal Republic*, 201-4.

71. Gen. William Heath speech at Massachusetts convention, Jan. 30, 1788, in Elliot, *Debates in the State Conventions*, 2:121.

72. Livingston speech at New York convention, June 19, 1788, in ibid., 2:211.

73. James Wilson speech at Pennsylvania convention, Dec. 4, 1787, in Jensen et al., *History of Ratification*, 2:469-85, at 477.

74. "Landholder" [Ellsworth], no. 2, *Connecticut Courant*, Nov. 12, 1787, in Jensen et al., *History of Ratification*, 3:400-403, at 401.

75. Thomas Dawes speech at Massachusetts convention, Jan. 21, 1788, in Elliot, *Debates in the State Conventions*, 2:58.

76. Samuel Holden Parsons to William Cushing, Jan. 11, 1788, in Jensen et al., *History of Ratification*, 3:569-73, at 570.

77. Edmund Randolph speech, Virginia convention, June 6, 1788, in Elliot, *Debates in the State Conventions*, 3:82, our emphasis.

78. Randolph, *Letter on the Federal Constitution* (Richmond, 1787), in Ford, *Pamphlets on the Constitution*, 259-76, at 264.

79. Ellsworth speech at Connecticut convention, Jan. 4, 1788, in Jensen et al., *History of Ratification*, 3:541-45, at 542.

80. Item in *Massachusetts Centinel*, Apr. 11, 1787, in Jensen et al., *History of Ratification*, 13:79.

81. Hugh Williamson, "Remarks on the New Plan of Government," *State Gazette of North Carolina* (1788), in Ford, *Essays on the Constitution*, 393-406, at 403.

82. [Noah Webster], *Examination into the leading principles*, in Ford, *Pamphlets on the Constitution*, 25-65, at 55.

83. "Plain Truth," "Reply to An Officer of the Late Continental Army," *Independent Gazetteer*, Nov. 10, 1787, in Jensen et al., *History of Ratification*, 2:216-23, at 218.

84. David Ramsay, *An Address to the Freemen of South Carolina, on the subject of the Federal Constitution* (Charleston, 1788), in Ford, *Pamphlets on the Constitution*, 371-80, at 373, our emphasis.

85. "Extract of a letter from a gentleman in Virginia," *Independent Gazetteer*, June 26, 1787, in Jensen et al., *History of Ratification*, 13:145-47, at 145-46.

86. "Harrington" [Rush], *Pennsylvania Gazette*, May 30, 1787, in Jensen et al., *History of Ratification*, 13:116-20, at 118; Henry Knox to unknown, Sept. 1787, in ibid., 13:279-80; George Nicholas, draft of letter or speech, Feb. 16, 1788, in ibid., 8:369-74, at 373-74.

87. Hamilton speech at New York convention, June 25, 1788, in Elliot, *Debates in the State Conventions*, 2:317-20, at 318.

88. Item in *Middlesex Gazette*, Oct. 22, 1787, in Jensen et al., *History of Ratification*, 3:394-96, at 394.

89. Ellsworth speech, Connecticut convention, Jan. 4, 1788, in ibid., 3:541–45, at 542.

90. Item in *American Herald*, Oct. 1, 1787, in ibid., 13:285–86, at 286.

91. Wood, *Creation of the American Republic*, 363–89 and passim.

92. Henry Knox to unknown, Sept. 1787, in Jensen et al., *History of Ratification*, 13:279–80; George Nicholas draft of address, Feb. 16, 1788, Durrett Collection.

93. Wood, *Creation of the Republic*, 453–63 and passim.

94. Hamilton's notes for a speech, June 18, 1787, in Farrand, *Records of the Federal Convention*, 1:307.

95. "Cato," *New-Haven Gazette*, Jan. 25, 1787.

96. [John Jay], *An Address to the People of the State of New York* (New York, 1788), in Ford, *Pamphlets on the Constitution*, 67–86, at 84.

97. Madison to Jefferson, Oct. 24, 1787, in Rutland et al., *Papers of James Madison*, 10:205–20, at 214.

98. [Pelatiah Webster], *Weakness of Brutus*, in Ford, *Pamphlets on the Constitution*, 117–31, at 129.

99. Wilson speech, Pennsylvania convention, Dec. 11, 1787, in Jensen et al., *History of Ratification*, 2:572–84, at 583.

100. "Aristides" [Hanson], *Remarks on the Proposed Plan*, in Ford, *Pamphlets on the Constitution*, 217–57, at 248. Ezra Stiles referred to the peace plan of Henry IV in *The United States Elevated to Glory and Honor*, 31. The plan itself is reprinted in Edward Everett Hale, ed., *The Great Design of Henry IV*, and its authorship and intent are discussed in Francis H. Hinsley, *Power and the Pursuit of Peace*, 24–27.

101. *The Substance of a Speech Delivered by James Wilson*, Nov. 24, 1787, in Jensen et al., *History of Ratification*, 2:340–50, at 342.

102. Thomas Pownall, *A Memorial Addressed to the Sovereigns of America*, 129. See the discussion in Peter S. Onuf, "Anarchy and the Crisis of the Union."

103. Madison to George Nicholas, May 17, 1788, in Rutland et al., *Papers of James Madison*, 11:44–51, at 45.

104. Francis Corbin speech, Virginia convention, June 7, 1788, in Elliot, *Debates in the State Conventions*, 3:108, 107.

CHAPTER 8. FEDERALISTS,
ANTIFEDERALISTS, AND THE ECONOMY

1. Jacob E. Cooke, ed., *The Federalist Papers*, no. 22 (Hamilton), at 137.

2. [Tench Coxe], *An Enquiry into the Principles on which a Commercial System for the United States should be Founded*, 28–33.

3. William Hillhouse, Jr., *A Dissertation, in Answer to a Late Lecture on the Political States of America*, 6–7, 12; and Hugh Williamson, speech at Edenton, N.C., Feb. 25, 1788, in Merrill Jensen et al., eds., *The Documentary History of the Ratification of the Constitution*, 16:201–9, at 206.

4. "A Citizen," *Hudson Gazette*, Jan. 31, 1788. See also Williamson speech, Feb. 25, 1788, in Jensen et al., *History of Ratification*, 16:201–9, at 205; and Charles Nisbet to the Earl of Buchan, dtd. Carlisle, Pa., Dec. 25, 1787, in ibid., 15:87–90.

5. "A Well Wisher," *New York Journal,* May 5, 1788.

6. See Cathy Matson, "Reluctant Federalists."

7. See Oliver Ellsworth, speech at Connecticut convention, Jan. 7, 1788, in Jensen et al., *History of Ratification,* 3:548–54. In general see Samuel Rezneck, "The Rise and Early Development of Industrial Consciousness in the United States"; and Charles G. Steffen, *The Mechanics of Baltimore,* 83–120.

8. L. Marx Renzulli, *Maryland: The Federalist Years,* 73–77; Paul Goodman, *The Democratic-Republicans of Massachusetts,* 11–14; Robert Brunhouse, *The Counter-Revolution in Pennsylvania,* 195–98; Staughton Lynd, "The Mechanics in New York City Politics," 241–45. For the claim that "all men of property" closed ranks in favor of the Constitution, see Hamilton, "Conjectures about the New Constitution," Sept. 17–30, 1787, in Harold C. Syrett, ed., *The Papers of Alexander Hamilton,* 4:275.

9. Cooke, *The Federalist,* no. 12 (Hamilton), at 73–74. See also John R. Nelson, Jr., "Alexander Hamilton and American Manufacturing"; E. James Ferguson, *The Power of the Purse,* 209–10, 239–42, 180–81; and Gordon S. Wood, "Interests and Disinterestedness in the Making of the Constitution," 103–9.

10. See, e.g., Jonathan Loring Austin, *An Oration,* 16; and item in *Hampshire Gazette* (Northampton, Mass.), Oct. 31, 1787.

11. "Cassius," *New Jersey Journal,* Oct. 31, 1787, in Jensen et al., *History of Ratification,* 13:140–43, at 143.

12. See the discussions in Forrest McDonald, *Novus Ordo Seclorum,* ch. 6; and William Letwin, *The Origins of Scientific Economics.* On America's possible immunity to historical cycles, see Drew R. McCoy, *The Elusive Republic,* ch. 1; and Arthur H. Shaffer, *The Politics of History,* ch. 4.

13. David Ramsay, *The History of the American Revolution,* 1:29, 32, 34.

14. "A writer of South Carolina says . . . ," item dtd. Charlestown, Mass., Feb. 21, 1786, repr. in *Maryland Gazette* (Annapolis), Mar. 17, 1786.

15. Item in *Virginia Journal,* Nov. 25, 1784.

16. Pelatiah Webster, "Sixth Essay on Free Trade and Finance," in Webster, *Political Essays on the Nature and Operations of Money, Public Finances and Other Subjects,* 230–68, at 232–33.

17. "Lycurgus," Feb. 16, 1786, in *Connecticut Courant,* Feb. 27, 1786.

18. Item dtd. New York, July 20, 1786, in *Freeman's Journal,* July 26, 1786.

19. Speech of Jedidiah Huntington, in "Proceedings of the General Assembly," May 12, 1787, in *Connecticut Courant,* May 21, 1787, repr. in Jensen et al., *History of Ratification,* 13:105–11, at 107.

20. William Vans Murray, "Political Sketches, By a Citizen of the United States," *American Museum* 2 (Sept. 1787), 230.

21. Tench Coxe, "Reflections on the State of the Union," dtd. Philadelphia, 1792, in *A View of the United States of America,* 286–379, at 354.

22. "Marcus" [James Iredell], "Answers to Mr. Mason's objections to the New Constitution, recommended by the late Convention," Jan. 1788, in Paul Leicester Ford, ed., *Pamphlets on the Constitution of the United States,* 333–370, at 337; and "Remarks on the New Plan of Government by Hugh Williamson, Printed in the State Gazette of North Carolina, 1788," in Paul Leicester Ford, ed., *Essays on the Constitution of the United States,* 397–406, at 399.

23. Cooke, *The Federalist,* no. 11 (Hamilton), at 71. See Hamilton's argument in nos. 9, 21, and 22 that the states must band together to protect their

commerce from foreign competition, especially during European wars. See also Arthur Young, *Rural Economy*, 3; Thomas F. DeVoe, *The Market Book;* and Winifred B. Rothenberg, "The Market and Massachusetts Farmers," esp. 283-87.

24. Cooke, *The Federalist*, no. 12 (Hamilton), at 76-77.

25. Ibid., no. 85 (Hamilton), at 590. See the discussion in Lance Banning, *Jeffersonian Persuasion,* and Gerald Stourzh, *Alexander Hamilton and the Idea of Representative Government.*

26. "Alfred," *Independent Gazetteer,* Dec. 13, 1787, in Jensen et al., *History of Ratification,* 14:432-35. See also "Centinel," nos. 11 and 12, *Independent Gazetteer,* Jan. 16 and 23, 1788, in Jensen et al., *History of Ratification,* 15:387-91, at 387-88, and 16:446-48, at 447.

27. Item in *Country Journal,* Jan. 22, 1788.

28. Gov. George Clinton to New York Assembly, Jan. 11, 1788, *New York Daily Advertiser,* Jan. 14, 1788. See also item in *Country Journal,* July 11, 1787, and *New York Packet,* Feb. 16, 1787; and Phineas Bond to the Duke of Leeds, Nov. 11, 1789, in J. Franklin Jameson, ed., "Letters to the Foreign Office of Great Britain," 1:652.

29. John Smilie speech at Pennsylvania convention, Dec. 1, 1787, in Jensen et al., *History of Ratification,* 2:459; and William Findley speech at Pennsylvania convention, Dec. 5, 1787, in ibid., 2:502. In general see Joyce Appleby, *Capitalism and a New Social Order,* 39-50; and Alfred Young, "Conservatives, the Constitution, and the 'Spirit of Accommodation.'"

30. "Centinel" [George Bryan?], nos. 3, 4, and 7, *Independent Gazetteer,* Nov. 8, 30, and Dec. 27, 1787. For a slightly different view, see Luther Martin speech at Maryland convention, Nov. 29, 1787, in Jensen et al., *History of Ratification,* 14:285-93, at 291; and item in *Pennsylvania Gazette,* Aug. 1, 1787.

31. For opposition to excises, see, e.g., "Brutus" [Robert Yates], no. 7, *New York Journal,* Jan. 3, 1788; and Luther Martin, "The Genuine Information, Delivered to the Legislature of the State of Maryland, Relative to the Proceedings of the General Convention, Held at Philadelphia, in 1787," *Maryland Gazette* (Annapolis), Dec. 28, 1787-Feb. 8, 1788, in Farrand, *Records of the Convention,* 3:172-232.

32. Hamilton's speech at the New York convention, June 20, 1788, in Jonathan Elliot, ed., *The Debates in the Several State Conventions on the Adoption of the Federal Constitution,* 2:232-34, is one of his firmest statements on the propriety of excises.

33. "Cato" [George Clinton], no. 6, *New York Journal,* Dec. 13, 1787, in Jensen et al., *History of Ratification,* 16:428-32, at 429-30. See also "Federal Farmer," "Letters to the Republican," no. 3, Oct. 10, 1787, in ibid. 14:30-42, at 35-39.

34. "A Republican," *New York Daily Advertiser,* Oct. 19, 1786, and Dec. 27, 1787.

35. "Brutus" [Robert Yates], nos. 1 and 2, *New York Journal,* Oct. 18 and Dec. 13, 1787.

36. [Abraham Yates], *Political Papers,* essay of Oct. 10, 1787, 5-6, 14-15, 18-20, 21.

37. "Philo-Patria," *New York Journal,* Sept. 28, 1787. See also [Abraham Yates], *Political Papers,* essay of Mar. 17, 1785, 8; John Smilie speech at

Pennsylvania convention, Dec. 1, 1787, in Jensen et al., *History of Ratification*, 2:459; and William Findley speech at Pennsylvania convention, Dec. 5, 1787, in ibid., 2:502.

38. Melancton Smith speech at New York convention, June 20, 1788, in Elliot, *Debates in the State Conventions*, 2:233–34.

39. "Agrippa" [James Winthrop], no. 3, *Massachusetts Gazette*, Dec. 25, 1787.

40. "An Address of Thanks," *Freeman's Journal*, Feb. 13, 1788. See also "John de Witt," "To the Free Citizens of the Commonwealth of Massachusetts," nos. 1 and 2, *American Herald*, Oct. 22 and 27, 1787, repr. in Cecelia Kenyon, ed., *The Antifederalists*, at 94, 97, 101.

41. "Agrippa" [Winthrop], nos. 3 and 13, *Massachusetts Gazette*, Dec. 25, 1787, and Jan. 14, 1788.

42. On the origins of this language, see ch. 2. The quotations are from "A Farmer" [George Logan], "Five Letters addressed to the yeomanry of the United States," no. 5, Aug. 21, 1792, in *American Museum* 12 (Sept. 1792), 159–67, at 161. For the association of this argument with small producers and lesser merchants, see item in *New York Journal*, Feb. 16, 1787.

43. "Agrippa" [Winthrop], nos. 7, 12, and 14, *Massachusetts Gazette*, Dec. 18, 1787, Jan. 11 and 18, 1788.

44. "Centinel," no. 6, *Pennsylvania Packet*, Dec. 25, 1787, in Jensen et al., *History of Ratification*, 15:98–101, at 99.

45. Items in *Country Journal*, July 11, 1787, and Jan. 22, 1788.

46. Item in *New York Packet*, Feb. 12, 1788; "Federal Farmer," no. 1, Oct. 8, 1787, in Jensen et al., *History of Ratification*, 14:14–54, at 20–21. For another extreme characterization, see "Tullius," *Gazette of the State of Georgia*, June 19, 1788, in Jensen et al., *History of Ratification*, 3:330–34, at 331.

47. "Agrippa" [Winthrop], nos. 13 and 14, *Massachusetts Gazette*, Jan. 14 and 18, 1788.

48. "Federal Farmer," no. 1, Oct. 8, 1787, in Jensen et al., *History of Ratification*, 14:14–54, at 20–21.

49. Melancton Smith speech at New York convention, June 20, 1788, in Elliot, *Debates in the State Conventions*, 2:233–34.

50. "Federal Farmer," no. 1, Oct. 8, 1787, in Jensen et al., *History of Ratification*, 14:22. For similar conclusions, see "Maryland Farmer," no. 3, *Maryland Gazette* (Baltimore), Mar. 18, 1788.

51. "A Farmer, of New Jersey" [John Stevens], *Observations on Government*, 47–49.

52. Item in *Hudson Gazette*, June 28, 1787. See also "Mediocrity," *Country Journal*, Jan. 17, 1787.

53. [Abraham Yates], *Political Papers*, essay of Mar. 17, 1785, 8. See also essay of Oct. 10, 1787, 5–6, 14–15, 18–20.

54. "A Federal Republican," "A Review of the Constitution, Proposed by the Late Convention Held at Philadelphia," dtd. Philadelphia, Oct. 28, 1787, in Jensen et al., *History of Ratification*, 14:255–79, at 273; and "Cato," no. 5, *New York Journal*, Nov. 22, 1787, in Jensen et al., *History of Ratification*, 14:182–85, at 183.

55. "Cato," no. 5, *New York Journal*, Nov. 22, 1787, in Jensen et al., *History of Ratification*, 14:182–85, at 183–84. See also Samuel Wales, *The Dangers of Our National Prosperity*.

56. Item in *Pennsylvania Gazette,* Aug. 1, 1787.

57. William Findley, quoted in Matthew Carey, ed., *Debates and Proceedings of the General Assembly of Pennsylvania on the Charter of the Bank,* 66, 87–89.

58. Noah Webster, *Sketches of American Policy,* ed. Harry R. Warfel, 28–31; John Witherspoon, *Essay on Money as a Medium of Commerce,* 29–33, 56. See also Pelatiah Webster, "Seventh Essay on Free Trade and Finance," in Webster, *Political Essays,* 447.

59. See Matson, "American Political Economy in the Constitutional Decade."

60. "Sylvius" [Hugh Williamson], "On frugality and industry," *American Museum* 2 (Jan. 1788), 114–21, at 115.

61. "Amicus," "An Essay on the Fatal Tendency of the Prevailing Luxuries," *American Museum* 2 (Mar. 1788), 216–20. For another discussion of the "dissipation and luxury" wrought by "foreign commodities which have . . . deluged our country . . . [and] loaded us with debt," see John Williams speech at New York convention, June 21, 1788, in Elliot, *Debates in the State Conventions,* 2:240.

62. "An honest cheerful citizen," "A Word of Consolation for America," *American Museum* 1 (Mar. 1787), 187–90, at 189. See also "The Fatal Consequences of Luxury," *American Museum* 1 (Feb. 1787), 66–67; and "A Plain but real friend to America," "On American Manufactures," Letter One, *American Museum* 1 (Jan. 1787), 17–19.

63. Peter Colt to John Chester, dtd. Hartford, July 21, 1791, in Arthur H. Cole, ed., *Industrial and Commercial Correspondence of Alexander Hamilton,* 2–7, at 2, 3, 7.

64. Ibid., 7; "Petition of John Broom, Alexander Robertson, and others, Merchants and Manufacturers of New-York," dtd. 1788, NYPL.

65. "Causes of a country's growing rich," *American Museum* 1 (Jan. 1787), 13. See also Samuel Stillman, *An Oration,* 4.

66. Phineas Bond to the Duke of Leeds, Nov. 10, 1789, in Jameson, "Letters to the Foreign Office," 1:630–31, 634, 652.

67. Item in *New York Packet,* Feb. 16, 1787.

68. "Amicus," "Essay on the Fatal Tendency," *American Museum* 2 (Mar. 1788), 218.

69. Jedidiah Huntington speech, "Proceedings of the General Assembly," May 12, 1787, in *Connecticut Courant,* May 21, 1787, repr. in Jensen et al., *History of Ratification,* 13:105–11, at 107.

70. Hillhouse, *Dissertation,* 14.

71. Simeon Baldwin to James Kent, dtd. New Haven, Conn., Mar. 8, 1788, in Jensen et al., *History of Ratification,* 16:349–52, at 351.

72. See the letters collected in Cole, *Industrial and Commercial Correspondence of Hamilton,* and the discussion in Cathy Matson, "Liberty, Jealousy, and Union."

73. Washington to Lafayette, Jan. 29, 1789, and to Jefferson, Jan. 1, 1788, and Feb. 13, 1789, in John C. Fitzpatrick, ed., *The Writings of George Washington,* 30:186–87, 29:275–79, and 30:199–200.

74. "Landholder" [Oliver Ellsworth], no. 13, *Connecticut Courant,* Mar. 24, 1788.

75. Tench Coxe, "Statements . . . in Reply to the Assertions and Predictions of Lord Sheffield " (1791), in Coxe, *View of the United States,* 111–285, at

260. See also "To the Farmers of Duchess County," *Country Journal*, Jan. 24, 31, Feb. 7, 14, 21, 28, and Mar. 7, 1787.

76. Colt to Chester, dtd. Hartford, July 21, 1791, in Cole, *Industrial and Commercial Correspondence of Hamilton*, 2–7, at 2, 3, 7.

77. [William Barton], *The True Interest of the United States*, 11.

78. Tench Coxe, "Sketches of the Subject of American Manufactures " (Aug. 1787), in Coxe, *View of the United States*, 34–56, at 52, 53. See also "An American" [Coxe], "To Richard Henry Lee," *Pennsylvania Herald*, Dec. 29, 1787.

79. Coxe, "Sketches of the Subject of American Manufactures," in Coxe, *View of the United States*, 54.

80. Pelatiah Webster, "Sixth Essay on Free Trade and Finance," in Webster, *Political Essays*, 232–38. See also [Coxe], *Enquiry into the Principles*; and Jedidiah Huntington speech, May 21, 1787, in Jensen et al., *History of Ratification*, 13:105–11, at 107.

81. The states had practiced protectionism, with mixed results, since 1784. See the discussions in ch. 4 and in Matson, "Political Economy in the Constitutional Decade."

82. Petition of the New York Merchants and Manufacturers, repr. in Alfred Chandler, Jr., ed., *The New American State Papers*, 1:34; and "Memorandum to Daniel Stevens from the leather manufacturers at Charleston," Oct. 1791, in Cole, *Industrial and Commercial Correspondence of Hamilton*, 90–91.

83. William Barton, "On the propriety of investing Congress with power to regulate the trade of the United States," *American Museum* 1 (Jan. 1787), 13–17, at 16; idem, "To the Printers of the Museum," *American Museum* 7 (June 1790), 285–92, at 292; and "A Farmer" [George Logan], "Five Letters addressed to the yeomanry of the United States," no. 5, Aug. 21, 1792, in *American Museum* 12 (Sept. 1792), 159–61, at 161.

84. [Coxe], *Enquiry into the Principles*, 2–4.

85. James Madison, "Fashion," Mar. 20, 1792, in Robert Rutland et al., eds., *The Papers of James Madison*, 14:257–59, at 258. See the analysis in McCoy, *The Elusive Republic*, ch. 6. For similar ideas from Jefferson, see William D. Grampp, "A Re-examination of Jeffersonian Economics."

86. Coxe, "Address to the Friends of American Manufactures," dtd. Philadelphia, Oct. 20, 1788, in *American Museum* 4 (Oct. 1788), 341–46, at 342. See also Pelatiah Webster, "Sixth Essay on Free Trade and Finance," in Webster, *Political Essays*, 232–38.

87. "The Politician," dtd. New York, Oct. 21, 1789, in *American Museum* 7 (Mar. 1790), 145.

88. For a good example see "James Wilson's Speech in the State House Yard," dtd. Philadelphia, Oct. 6, 1788, in Jensen et al., *History of Ratification*, 2:167–72, esp. at 171–72.

EPILOGUE: THE TEST OF EXPERIMENT

1. Jonathan Jackson, *Thoughts upon the Political Situation*, 6.
2. Cathy Matson, "Liberty, Jealousy, and Union."
3. Douglas C. North, *The Economic Growth of the United States*, 41–43.

4. See, e.g., items in *American Museum* 3 (Apr. 1788), 347–48, and 4 (Jan. 1790), 19. For the Federalist commitment to keep imposts low, see Jacob Cooke, ed., *The Federalist Papers*, nos. 9, 11, 21, 22; and "Thoughts on navigation and commerce," dtd. New York, Mar. 31, 1790, in *American Museum* 8 (Aug. 1790), 93–94.

5. On Robert Morris, see Janet A. Riesman, "Money, Credit, and Federalist Political Economy," 142–49; and on Alexander Hamilton, see ibid., 154–56. For Hamilton's early ideas, see, e.g., Hamilton to James Duane, Sept. 3, 1780; to Gouverneur Morris, Aug. 30, 1781; and his "Constitution and Outline of a Charter," n.d., in Harold C. Syrett, ed., *The Papers of Alexander Hamilton*, 2:416, 2:604–5, 3:514–20.

6. Hamilton to George Washington, Mar. 27, 1792, in Syrett, *Papers of Alexander Hamilton*, 8:223. See also Hamilton to Washington, July 3, 1787, in ibid., 4:223–25, at 224; and Cooke, *The Federalist*, nos. 1, 6, 11, 12. For doubts about Hamilton's intentions, see James Madison to Thomas Jefferson, Oct. 24, 1787, in Julian P. Boyd et al., eds., *The Papers of Thomas Jefferson*, 12:276–79.

7. See Hamilton's "Report Relative to a Provision for the Support of Public Credit," Jan. 9, 1790; and his "Second Report on the Further Provision Necessary for Establishing Public Credit (Report on a National Bank)," Dec. 13, 1790, in Syrett, *Papers of Alexander Hamilton*, 6:65–110 and 7:236–342.

8. Elbridge Gerry in House of Representatives, Feb. 25, 1790; and Madison in House, Apr. 22, 1790, in Max Farrand, ed., *The Records of the Federal Convention of 1787*, 3:360–61.

9. Madison, "Tonnage Duties," Apr. 21, 1789; "Import Duties," Apr. 25, 1789; "Tonnage Duties," May 4, 1789; and, for a later statement, Madison to Henry Lee, Apr. 15, 1792—all in Robert A. Rutland et al., eds., *The Papers of James Madison*, 12:97–103, 12:109–13, 12:125–30, and 14:287–88. For Madison's attempt in 1789 to secure free trade with a temporary policy of commercial discrimination, see *Annals of the Congress of the United States*, 1st Cong., 1st Sess., 1:116. For Monroe's view, see Monroe to Madison, July 19, 1789, in Rutland et al., *Papers of James Madison*, 12:296–97. On reciprocity in general, see Vernon G. Setser, *The Commercial Reciprocity Policy of the United States*, 102–18.

10. Madison to Jefferson, Feb. 4, 1790, in Boyd et al., *Papers of Thomas Jefferson*, 16:147–50; Madison to Edmund Randolph, Mar. 14, 1790, and to Lee, Apr. 13, 1790, in Rutland et al., *Papers of James Madison*, 13:106 and 13:147–48.

11. Hamilton, "Report on Manufactures," Dec. 1790, in Syrett, *Papers of Alexander Hamilton*, 10:1–340, at 287–90 and 300–301.

12. John R. Nelson, Jr., "Alexander Hamilton and American Manufacturing," 280–90.

13. Hamilton, "Report on Manufactures," in Syrett, *Papers of Alexander Hamilton*, 10:287–90, 300–301. See also Drew R. McCoy, *The Elusive Republic*, 133–34.

14. Hamilton speech at New York convention, June 20, 1788, in Jonathan Elliot, ed., *The Debates in the Several State Conventions on the Adoption of the Federal Constitution*, 2:232–34.

15. Hamilton, "Report on Manufactures," in Syrett, *Papers of Alexander Hamilton*, 10:525; and Joseph S. Davis, *Essays in the Earlier History of American Corporations*, 1:427–53.

16. "Clitus," Nov. 10, 1791, in *General Advertiser*, Nov. 24, 1791.

17. On opposition to the Society and discussion of its "high Federalist" bias, see Davis, *Earlier History of American Corporations*, 1:427–53.

18. John Taylor, *An Enquiry into the Principles and Tendency of Certain Public Measures*, 7, 28–29, 56–57; and idem, *An Examination of the Late Proceedings in Congress*, 1–28.

19. For Jefferson's endorsement of free trade, see his "Report on the Privileges and Restrictions on the Commerce of the United States in Foreign Countries," Dec. 16, 1793, in Paul Leicester Ford, ed., *The Writings of Thomas Jefferson*, 6:470–84, at 479.

20. Tench Coxe, "Sketches of the Subject of American Manufactures," in Coxe, *A View of the United States of America*, 54.

21. Cathy Matson, "Public Vices, Private Benefit."

22. Thomas P. Slaughter, *The Whiskey Rebellion*. For Madison's disappointment with the course of American commercial policy down to Jay's Treaty, see his "Political Observations," Apr. 20, 1795, in Rutland et al., *Papers of James Madison*, 14:511–34.

23. For party divisions on the unresolved issues of the 1780s, see Alfred F. Young, *The Democratic Republicans of New York*, 207–30, and Norman Risjord, *Chesapeake Politics*. Contrast their views with Noble Cunningham, Jr., *The Jeffersonian-Republicans*, who argues that parties arose in response to new issues in the 1790s.

Bibliography

DOCUMENTARY EDITIONS; GUIDES TO SOURCES

Adams, Charles Francis, ed. *The Works of John Adams, Second President of the United States.* 10 vols. Boston: Little, Brown, 1853.

Annals of the Congress of the United States, 1789–1824. 42 vols. Washington, D.C.: Gales & Seaton, 1834–56.

Ballagh, James C., ed. *Letters of Richard Henry Lee.* 2 vols. New York: Macmillan, 1911–14.

The Belknap Papers. Massachusetts Historical Society, *Collections.* 5th ser. 2 vols. Boston, 1877–78.

Bell, Herbert C., David W. Parker, et al. *Guide to British West Indian Archive Materials, in London and in the Islands, for the History of the United States.* Washington, D.C.: Carnegie Institution, 1926.

Bodley, Temple, ed. *Reprints of Littell's Political Transactions in and concerning Kentucky.* Filson Club Publications, no. 31. Louisville, Ky., 1926.

The Bowdoin and Temple Papers. Massachusetts Historical Society, *Collections.* 6th ser., vol. 9, and 7th ser., vol. 6. Boston, 1897–1907.

Boyd, Julian P., et al., eds. *The Papers of Thomas Jefferson.* 22 vols. to date. Princeton, N.J.: Princeton University Press, 1950–.

Burnett, Edmund Cody, ed. *Letters of the Members of the Continental Congress.* 8 vols. Washington, D.C.: Carnegie Institution, 1921–36.

Butterfield, Lyman, ed. *Diary and Autobiography of John Adams.* 4 vols. Cambridge, Mass.: Harvard University Press, 1961.

———, ed. *The Letters of Benjamin Rush.* 2 vols. Princeton, N.J.: Princeton University Press, 1951.

Carey, Matthew, ed. *Debates and Proceedings of the General Assembly of Pennsylvania, on the . . . Charter of the Bank.* Philadelphia, 1786.

Chandler, Alfred, Jr., ed. *The New American State Papers; Manufactures.* 2 vols. Wilmington, Del.: Scholarly Resources Inc., 1972.

Cobbett, William, ed. *Parliamentary History of England.* 36 vols. London: T. C. Hansard, 1806–20.

Cole, Arthur H., ed. *Industrial and Commercial Correspondence of Alexander Hamilton, Anticipating His Report on Manufactures.* New York: A. M. Kelley, 1968; orig. pub. Chicago, 1928.

213

Cushing, Harry A., ed. *The Writings of Samuel Adams*. 4 vols. New York: G. P. Putnam's, 1907.

Documentary History of the Constitution of the United States. 5 vols. Washington, D.C.: Department of State, 1901–5.

Earle, Thomas, and Charles T. Congdon, eds. *Annals of the General Society of Mechanics and Tradesmen of the City of New York, from 1785 to 1880*. New York: The Society, 1882.

Elliot, Jonathan, ed. *The Debates in the Several State Conventions on the Adoption of the Federal Constitution*. 5 vols. Philadelphia: Lippincott, 1876.

Farrand, Max, ed. *The Records of the Federal Convention of 1787*. 4 vols. New Haven, Conn.: Yale University Press, 1911–37.

Fitzpatrick, John C., ed. *The Writings of George Washington*. 39 vols. Washington, D.C.: Government Printing Office, 1931–44.

Ford, Paul Leicester, ed. *Essays on the Constitution of the United States*. Brooklyn, N.Y.: Historical Printing Club, 1892.

———, ed. *Pamphlets on the Constitution of the United States*. Brooklyn, N.Y.: N.p., 1888.

———, ed. *The Writings of Thomas Jefferson*. 5 vols. New York: G. P. Putnam's Sons, 1892–99.

Ford, Worthington C., ed. *Correspondence and Journals of Samuel Blachley Webb*. 3 vols. New York: N.p., 1893.

———, ed. *Journals of the Continental Congress*. 34 vols. Washington, D.C.: Government Printing Office, 1904–37.

Hale, Edward Everett, ed. *The Great Design of Henry IV, from the Memoirs of the Duke of Sully*. Introduction by Edwin D. Mead. Boston: Ginn and Co., 1909.

Hastings, Hugh, ed. *The Public Papers of George Clinton, First Governor of New York*. 10 vols. Albany, N.Y.: Wynkoop, Hallenbeck, & Crawford, 1899–1914.

Hening, William Waller, ed. *The Statutes at Large: Being a Collection of All the Laws of Virginia*. 13 vols. Richmond, Va.: Samuel Pleasants, Jr., 1809–23.

Hunt, Gaillard, ed. *The Writings of James Madison*. 9 vols. New York: G. P. Putnam's, 1900–10.

Jameson, J. Franklin, ed. "Letters to the Foreign Office of Great Britain, 1787–1789 and 1790–1794." In American Historical Association, *Annual Report 1896*. Washington, D.C., 1897, 513–659.

———, ed. "The Letters of Stephen Higginson, 1783–1804." American Historical Association, *Annual Report*. Boston, 1896.

Jenkins, William Sumner, ed. *Records of the States of the United States*. Washington, D.C.: Library of Congress, 1941–49. Microfilm.

Jensen, Merrill, ed. *Tracts of the American Revolution, 1763–1776*. Indianapolis: Bobbs-Merrill, 1966.

Jensen, Merrill, John P. Kaminski, Gaspare P. Saladino, and Richard Leffler, eds. *The Documentary History of the Ratification of the Constitution*. 8 vols. to date (vols. 1–4, 13–16). Madison: State Historical Society of Wisconsin, 1976–.

Johnston, Henry P., ed. *The Correspondence and Public Papers of John Jay*. 4 vols. New York: G. P. Putnam's, 1890–93.

Kenyon, Cecelia M., ed. *The Antifederalists*. Indianapolis: Bobbs-Merrill, 1966.

Kimball, G. S., ed. *The Correspondence of William Pitt.* 2 vols. New York: Macmillan, 1906.

King, Charles R., ed. *The Life and Correspondence of Rufus King.* 6 vols. New York: G. P. Putnam's, 1894-1900.

Laws of the State of New York Comprising the Constitution and Acts of the Legislature Since the Revolution, from the First to the Fifteenth Sessions, Inclusive. 2 vols. New York, 1792.

The Letters and Papers of Cadwallader Colden. New-York Historical Society, *Collections.* 9 vols. (vols. 50-56, 67-68). New York, 1918-37.

McCloskey, Robert G., ed. *The Works of James Wilson.* 2 vols. Cambridge, Mass.: Harvard University Press, 1967.

Niles, Hezekiah, ed. *Principles and Acts of the Revolution in America.* Baltimore: N. O. Niles, 1822.

O'Callaghan, E. B., ed. *Documents Relative to the Colonial History of the State of New York.* 15 vols. Albany, N.Y.: Weed, Parsons, & Co., 1853-87.

Palmer, William R., ed. *Calendar of Virginia State Papers.* 11 vols. Richmond: Commonwealth of Virginia, 1875-93.

Pargellis, Stanley, ed. *Military Affairs in North America, 1748-1765.* New York: D. Appleton-Century, 1936.

Revolutionary Correspondence, 1775-1782. Rhode Island Historical Society, *Collections.* 6th ser. Providence, 1867.

Ross, Angus, ed. *Selections from the Tatler and the Spectator.* London: Penguin, 1982.

Rotwein, Eugene, ed. *David Hume: Writings on Economics.* Madison: University of Wisconsin Press, 1955.

Rowland, Kate Mason, ed. *The Life of Charles Carroll of Carrollton.* 2 vols. New York: G. P. Putnam's, 1898.

Runes, Dagobert D., ed. *The Selected Writings of Benjamin Rush.* New York: Philosophical Library, 1947.

Rutland, Robert A., ed. *The Papers of George Mason.* 3 vols. Chapel Hill: University of North Carolina Press, 1970.

―――, et al., eds. *The Papers of James Madison.* 15 vols. to date. Chicago: University of Chicago Press; Charlottesville: University Press of Virginia, 1962-.

Sainsbury, W. Noel, and J. W. Fortescue, eds. *Calendar of State Papers, Colonial Series, America and the West Indies.* 42 vols. London: Her Majesty's Stationery Office, 1860-1953.

Saunders, William L., et al., eds. *The Colonial and State Records of North Carolina.* 26 vols. Raleigh, Winston, Goldsboro, and Charlotte, N.C.: P. M. Hale et al., 1886-1914.

Smith, Paul H., ed. *Letters of Delegates to Congress, 1774-1789.* 13 vols. to date. Washington, D.C.: Government Printing Office, 1976-.

Smith, William Henry, ed. *The St. Clair Papers: Life and Public Services of Arthur St. Clair.* 2 vols. Cincinnati: R. Clarke & Co., 1882.

Storing, Herbert J., ed. *The Complete Anti-Federalist.* 7 vols. Chicago: University of Chicago Press, 1981.

Syrett, Harold C. and Jacob Cooke, eds., *The Papers of Alexander Hamilton.* 27 vols. New York: Columbia University Press, 1961-87.

Warhaft, Sidney, ed. *Francis Bacon: A Selection of His Works.* Indianapolis: Bobbs-Merrill, 1965.

Warren-Adams Letters: Being Chiefly a Correspondence among John Adams, Samuel Adams, and James Warren. Massachusetts Historical Society, *Collections.* 2 vols. Boston, 1917–25.

Webster, Noah. *Sketches of American Policy.* Ed. Harry R. Warfel. Hartford, Conn., 1785.

Wharton, Francis, ed. *The Revolutionary Diplomatic Correspondence of the United States.* 6 vols. Washington, D.C.: Government Printing Office, 1889.

White, Philip L., ed. *The Beekman Mercantile Papers, 1746–1799.* 3 vols. New York: New-York Historical Society, 1956.

Whitworth, Sir Charles, ed. *The Political and Commercial Works of that Celebrated writer Dr. Charles D'Avenant.* 5 vols. London, 1771.

William, Charles, ed. *The Correspondence of Edmund Burke.* 4 vols. London: F. & J. Rivington, 1844.

CONTEMPORARY BOOKS, PAMPHLETS, AND ESSAYS

An Account of the French Usurpation upon the Trade of England. London, 1679.

Aristotle. *Politics.* Trans. Ernest Barker, with introduction. Oxford: Oxford University Press, 1958.

Austin, Jonathan Loring. *An Oration, Delivered July 4, 1786* [in Boston]. Boston, 1786.

Bacon, Francis. *The Advancement of Learning.* Ed. W. A. Wright. 5th ed. Oxford: Oxford University Press, 1963; orig. pub. London, 1605.

Barbon, Nicholas. *A Discourse of Trade.* London, 1690.

Barlow, Joel. *Advice to the Privileged Orders, in the Several States of Europe.* New York, 1795; orig. pub. London, 1792.

———. *A Letter Addressed to the People of Piedmont.* New York, 1795.

[Barton, William.] *The True Interest of the United States, and Particularly of Pennsylvania.* Philadelphia, 1786.

Bingham, William. *Letter from an American Now Resident in London to a Member of Parliament on the Subject of the Restraining Proclamation.* Philadelphia, 1784.

Britaine, William de. *The Interest of England in the Present War with Holland.* London, 1672.

Campbell, Richard. *The London Tradesman.* London, 1747.

Champion, Richard. *Considerations on the Present Situation of Great Britain and the United States of America.* London, 1784.

Coke, Roger. *A Discourse of Trade.* London, 1670.

Colden, Cadwallader. *The Interest of the City and Country to Lay No Duties.* New York, 1726.

The Commercial Conduct of the United States of America Considered by a Citizen of New York. New York, 1786.

Considerations on the Present State of the Nation. London, 1720.

Cooke, Jacob, ed. *The Federalist Papers.* Middletown, Conn.: Wesleyan University Press, 1961; orig. pub. New York, 1787–88.

Coxe, Tench. *Brief Examination of Lord Sheffield's Observations on the Commerce of the United States.* Philadelphia, 1791.

————. *An Enquiry into the Principles on which a Commercial System for the United States should be Founded.* Philadelphia, 1787.

————. *Observations on the Agriculture, Manufactures, and Commerce of the United States.* New York, 1789.

————. *A View of the United States of America.* Philadelphia, 1794.

Davis, Timothy. *Thoughts on Taxation in a Letter to a Friend.* New York, 1784.

Dawson, Henry B. "The Motley Letter." *Historical Magazine.* 2d ser., 9 (1871), 157–201.

Decker, Matthew. *Essay on the Causes of the Decline of the Foreign Trade.* London, 1744.

Defoe, Daniel. *The Complete English Tradesman.* 2 vols. London, 1727.

————. *A Plan of the English Commerce.* New York: A. M. Kelley, 1967; orig. pub. London, 1728.

————. *Some Thoughts on the Subject of Commerce.* London, 1713.

DeVoe, Thomas F. *The Market Book, Containing a Historical Account of the Public Markets in the Cities of New York, Philadelphia, and Brooklyn.* New York: Hurd & Houghton, 1862.

A Discourse consisting of Motives for the Enlargment of Freedom of Trade. London, 1645.

Edwards, Bryan. *The History, Civil and Commercial, of the British West Indies.* 5 vols. New York: AMS Press, 1966; orig. pub. London, 1819.

Franks, David. *New-York City Directory, 1786.* New York, 1786.

Gee, Joshua. *The Trade and Navigation of Great Britain.* 3d ed. 2 vols. London, 1731.

Gibbs, Sir Philip. *Reflections on the Proclamation of the Second of July 1783.* London, 1783.

Gouldsmith, Richard. *Some Considerations on Trade and Manufactures.* London, 1725.

Harrington, James. *The Oceana.* Ed. John Toland. London, 1747; orig. pub. London, 1656.

Harris, Joseph. *An Essay upon Money and Coins.* London, 1757.

Hatton, Edward. *The Merchants Magazine: or, Tradesman's Treasury.* 9th ed. London, 1734.

Hillhouse, William, Jr. *A Dissertation, in Answer to a late Lecture on the Political States of America.* New Haven, Conn., 1789.

Hobbes, Thomas. *Leviathan.* Harmondsworth, Middlesex: Penguin, 1968; orig. pub. London, 1651.

Hollander, Jacob, ed. *Reprints of Economic Tracts.* Baltimore: N.p., n.d.

Houghton, John. *A Collection of Letters for the Improvement of Husbandry and Trade.* London, 1681.

Hume, David. *Essays, Moral, Political, and Literary.* Ed. T. H. Green and T. H. Grose. 2 vols. London: Longmans, Green, & Co., 1875; orig. pub. London, 1741–42.

[Hunter, Robert.] "Androboros." *Bulletin of the New York Public Library* 68 (1964), 153–90, orig. pub. New York, 1714.

Jackson, Jonathan. *Thoughts upon the Political Situation.* Worcester, Mass., 1788.

Journal of the Votes and Proceedings of the Assembly of New York. 2 vols. New York, 1764–66.

Kalm, Peter. *Travels in North America, 1748–1751.* Ed. Adolph Benson. 2 vols. New York: Dover Publications, 1966.

Kennedy, Archibald. *Observations on the Importance of the Northern Colonies under Proper Regulations.* New York, 1750.

Livingston, William, et al. *The Independent Reflector.* Ed. Milton M. Klein. Cambridge, Mass.: Harvard University Press, 1963.

Locke, John. *Two Treatises of Government.* Ed. Peter Laslett, with introduction. New York: Mentor, 1965; orig. pub. London, 1689.

de Mably, Abbé Gabriel Bonnet. *Observations on the Government and Laws of the United States.* English ed. Amsterdam, 1784.

[Morris, Lewis.] "Dialogue Concerning Trade: A Satirical View of New York in 1726." *New York History* 55 (1974), 199–229; orig. pub. New York, 1727.

Mun, Thomas. *England's Treasure by Forraign Trade.* Oxford: Oxford University Press, 1928; orig. pub. London, 1664.

New York [City] Chamber of Commerce. *Gentlemen, the interest of the landholder . . .* Broadside. New York, 1785.

[North, Dudley.] *Discourses upon Trade.* London, 1691.

———. *The Crisis.* Garden City, N.Y.: Doubleday, 1973; orig. pub. Albany, N.Y., 1792.

Papenfuse, Edward C. "An Undelivered Defense of a Winning Cause: Charles Carroll of Carrollton's 'Remarks on the Proposed Federal Constitution.'" *Maryland Historical Magazine* 71 (1976), 220–51.

Pitkin, Timothy. *Statistical View of the Commerce of the United States of America.* 2d ed. Hartford, Conn., 1817.

Postlethwayt, Malachy. *Great Britain's Commercial Interest Explained and Improved.* 2 vols. London, 1757.

———. *The Universal Dictionary of Trade and Commerce, translated from the French of the celebrated Monsieur Savary.* 2 vols. London, 1766.

Pownall, Thomas. *The Administration of the British Colonies.* 4th ed. London, 1768.

———. *A Memorial Addressed to the Sovereigns of America.* London, 1783.

Price, Richard. "Observations on the Importance of the American Revolution" [2d ed.]. In *Richard Price and the Ethical Foundations of the American Revolution,* ed. Bernard Peach, 177–224. Durham, N.C.: Duke University Press, 1979; orig. pub. London, 1785.

Proclamation of Gov. Jonathan Trumbull. Broadside. Hartford, Conn., Aug. 25, 1780.

Ramsay, David. *The History of the American Revolution.* 2d ed. 2 vols. London, 1793; orig. pub. Philadelphia, 1789.

———. *An Oration on the Advantages of American Independence.* Charleston, 1778.

Reynel, Carew. *The True English Benefit or an Account of the Chief National Improvements.* London, 1674.

A Satyre upon the Times. New York, 1702.

Shaftesbury, third earl of (Anthony Ashley Cooper). *Characteristicks of Men, Manners, Opinions, Times.* 2 vols. Gloucester, Mass.: Peter Smith, 1963; orig. pub. London, 1711.

Sheffield, first earl of (John Baker Holroyd). *Observations on the Commerce of the American States.* London, 1783.

Smith, Adam. *The Wealth of Nations*. Ed. Edwin Canaan. 2 vols. in 1. Chicago: University of Chicago Press, 1976; orig. pub. London, 1776.

Steuart, Sir James. *Inquiry into the Principles of Political Economy*. Ed. A. S. Skinner. 2 vols. Chicago: University of Chicago Press, 1966; orig. pub. London, 1767.

[Stevens, John.] *Observations on Government, Including some Animadversions on Mr. Adams's Defence*. New York, 1787.

Stiles, Ezra. *The United States Elevated to Glory and Honor* (1783 Connecticut election sermon). 2d ed. Worcester, Mass. 1785.

Stillman, Samuel. *An Oration, Delivered July 4, 1789*. Boston, 1789.

Swift, Jonathan. *The History of the Four Last Years of the Queen*. Ed. Herbert Davis. Oxford: Oxford University Press, 1964; orig. pub. London, 1718.

Tanners, Curriers, and Cordwainers of Philadelphia. Broadside. Philadelphia, 1779.

Taylor, John. *An Enquiry into the Principles and Tendency of Certain Public Measures*. Philadelphia, 1794.

————. *An Examination of the Late Proceedings in Congress Respecting the Official Conduct of the Secretary of the Treasury*. Richmond, Va., 1793.

Temple, Sir William. *The Works of Sir William Temple*. 2 vols. London, 1720.

Trenchard, John, with Thomas Gordon. *Cato's Letters*. 3d ed. 4 vols. in 2. New York: Russell & Russell, 1969; facsimile of 1733 London edition; orig. pub. London, 1720–23.

[Tucker, St. George.] *Reflections on the Policy and Necessity of Encouraging the Commerce . . . of the United States*. New York, 1786.

Vattel, Emmerich de. *The Law of Nations, or the Principles of Natural Law Applied to the Conduct . . . of Nations*. Trans. Charles G. Fenwick, 1758 edition. Washington, D.C.: Carnegie Institution, 1916.

Wales, Samuel. *The Dangers of Our National Prosperity*. Hartford, Conn., 1785.

Warville, J. P. Brissot de. *New Travels in the United States of America, Performed in 1788*. 2 vols. New York: A. M. Kelley, 1970; orig. pub. New York, 1792.

Webster, Pelatiah. *Political Essays on the Nature and Operations of Money, Public Finances and Other Subjects*. Philadelphia, 1791.

Weir, Robert M., ed. "Two Letters by Christopher Gadsden." *South Carolina Historical Magazine* 75 (1974), 169–76.

Whiston, James. *The Mismanagements in Trade Discover'd, And Adapt Methods to Preserve and Exceedingly Improve It*. London, 1704.

Witherspoon, John. *Essay on Money as a Medium of Commerce*. Philadelphia, 1786.

Wood, William. *Survey of Trade*. 2 vols. London, 1718.

[Yates, Abraham.] *Political Papers, Addressed to the Advocates for a Congressional Revenue, in the State of New-York*. New York, 1786.

Young, Arthur. *Rural Economy, or Essays on the Practical Parts of Husbandry*. London, 1770.

NEWSPAPERS AND PERIODICALS

American Museum. Philadelphia, Pa. 1786–92.

Boston Evening Post. Boston, Mass. 1775.

Boston Gazette. Boston, Mass. 1765.

Carlisle Gazette. Carlisle, Pa. 1786–87.
Columbian Herald. Boston, Mass. 1785.
Columbian Magazine. Philadelphia, Pa. 1786–87.
Connecticut Courant. Hartford, Conn. 1786–88.
Country Journal. Poughkeepsie, N.Y. 1787–88.
Cumberland Gazette. Portland, Me. 1785–86.
Essex Gazette. Salem, Mass. 1772–74.
Falmouth Gazette. Portland, Mass. 1786–87.
Freeman's Journal. Philadelphia, Pa. 1785–86, 1788.
Gazette of the State of Georgia. Savannah, Ga. 1784.
General Advertiser. Boston, Mass. 1791.
Hampshire Gazette. Northampton, Mass. 1787.
Hudson Gazette. Hudson, N.Y. 1787–88.
Independent Chronicle. Boston, Mass. 1785.
Independent Gazetteer. Philadelphia, Pa. 1786–87.
Independent Journal and General Advertiser. New York, N.Y. 1784.
Kentucky Gazette. Louisville, Ky. 1787–88.
Maryland Gazette. Annapolis, Md. 1783–88.
Maryland Gazette. Baltimore, Md. 1786, 1788.
Maryland Journal. Baltimore, Md. 1783–88.
Massachusetts Centinel. Boston, Mass. 1785–86.
Massachusetts Gazette. Boston, Mass.
New Hampshire Gazette. Portsmouth, N.H. 1774.
New-Haven Gazette and Connecticut Magazine. New Haven, Conn. 1785–88.
New-Jersey Gazette. Trenton, N.J. 1778–86.
Newport Mercury. Newport, R.I. 1774.
New York Daily Advertiser. New York, N.Y. 1786–88.
New York Gazette. New York, N.Y. 1729, 1735, 1737, 1765.
New York Gazette and Weekly Mercury. New York, N.Y. 1770.
New York Gazetteer. Albany, N.Y. 1783.
New York Journal. New York, N.Y. 1783, 1786–88.
New York Mercury. New York, N.Y. 1764, 1768.
New York Morning Post. New York, N.Y. 1785.
New York Packet. New York, N.Y. 1782–88.
New-York Weekly Journal. New York, N.Y. 1733–34, 1739.
Pennsylvania Chronicle. Philadelphia, Pa. 1768.
Pennsylvania Evening Post. Philadelphia, Pa. 1775.
Pennsylvania Gazette. Philadelphia, Pa. 1773, 1783–88.
Pennsylvania Herald. Philadelphia, Pa.
Pennsylvania Packet. Philadelphia, Pa. 1778, 1785–88.
Public Advertiser. London, England. 1770, 1775.
Rivington's New York Gazetteer. New York, N.Y. 1774.
State Gazette of South Carolina. Charleston, S.C. 1786.
Times. London, England. 1785–86.
United States Chronicle, Political, Commercial and Historical. Providence, R.I. 1785.
Virginia Gazette. Richmond, Va. 1784–85.
Virginia Gazette (Hayes). Richmond, Va. 1783.
Virginia Gazette (Purdie & Dixon). Williamsburg, Va. 1773.

Virginia Gazette and Winchester Advertiser. Winchester, Va. 1787.
Virginia Journal. Alexandria, Va. 1784–87.

MANUSCRIPT COLLECTIONS

Alexander Papers. New-York Historical Society, New York.
Broadsides Collection. New York Public Library.
Papers of the Continental Congress. National Archives, Washington, D.C.
Abraham Cuyler Papers. New-York Historical Society, New York.
Durrett Collection. University of Chicago, Chicago.
Henry Knox Papers. Massachusetts Historical Society, Boston.
Lamb Papers. New-York Historical Society, New York.
Livingston Manuscripts. Museum of the City of New York, New York.
Peter R. Livingston Papers. New-York Historical Society, New York.
Robert R. Livingston Papers. New-York Historical Society, New York.
Ludlow Papers. New-York Historical Society, New York.
Minutes of New York Chamber of Commerce. New York Public Library, New
    York.
Thomas Riche Papers. Historical Society of Pennsylvania, Philadelphia.
Rutherford Collection. New-York Historical Society, New York.
Sedgwick Papers. Massachusetts Historical Society, Boston.
Special Collections. Columbia University Library, New York.
Stewart & Jones Letter Book. New-York Historical Society, New York.
Thomas Wharton Papers. Historical Society of Pennsylvania, Philadelphia.

SECONDARY SOURCES

Abernethy, Thomas P. "Commercial Activities of Silas Deane in France."
    American Historical Review 39 (1934), 477–85.
———. *Western Lands and the American Revolution.* New York: Russell &
    Russell, 1959; orig. pub. New York, 1937.
Adair, Douglass. "That Politics May Be Reduced to a Science: David Hume,
    James Madison, and the Tenth *Federalist.*" *Huntington Library Quarterly* 20
    (1957), 343–60.
Anderson, Fred. *A People's Army: Massachusetts Soldiers and Society in the Seven
    Years' War.* Chapel Hill: University of North Carolina Press, 1984.
Andrews, Charles M. *The Colonial Period of American History.* 4 vols. New
    Haven, Conn.: Yale University Press, 1928.
Appleby, Joyce. *Capitalism and a New Social Order.* New York: New York
    University Press, 1984.
———. *Economic Thought and Ideology in Seventeenth Century England.* Prince-
    ton, N.J.: Princeton University Press, 1978.
———. "Republicanism in Old and New Contexts." *William and Mary
    Quarterly,* 3d ser., 43 (1986), 20–34.
———. "The Social Origins of American Revolutionary Ideology." *Journal of
    American History* 64 (1978), 935–58.

––––––. "What Is Still American in the Political Philosophy of Thomas Jefferson?" *William and Mary Quarterly*, 3d ser., 39 (1982), 287–309.

Bailyn, Bernard. *The Ideological Origins of the American Revolution*. Cambridge, Mass.: Harvard University Press, 1967.

Ball, Terence, and J. G. A. Pocock, eds. *Conceptual Change and the Constitution*. Lawrence: University Press of Kansas, 1988.

Bancroft, George. *History of the Formation of the Constitution of the United States of America*. 2 vols. New York: D. Appleton & Co., 1896.

Banning, Lance. "The Constitutional Convention." In *Framing and Ratification of the Constitution*, ed. Leonard Levy and Dennis J. Mahoney, 112–31. New York: Macmillan, 1986.

––––––. "Jeffersonian Ideology Revisited: Liberal and Classical Ideas in the New American Republic." *William and Mary Quarterly*, 3d ser., 43 (1986), 3–19.

––––––. *The Jeffersonian Persuasion: Evolution of a Party Ideology*. Ithaca, N.Y.: Cornell University Press, 1978.

––––––. "The Practicable Sphere of a Republic: James Madison, the Constitutional Convention, and the Emergence of Revolutionary Federalism." In *Beyond Confederation: Origins of the Constitution and American National Identity*, ed. Richard Beeman, Stephen Botein, and Edward C. Carter II, 162–87. Chapel Hill: University of North Carolina Press, 1987.

––––––. "Virginia: Nation, State, and Section." In *Ratifying the Constitution*, ed. Michael Gillespie and Michael Lienesch. Lawrence: University Press of Kansas, 1989.

Beeman, Richard, Stephen Botein, and Edward C. Carter II, eds. *Beyond Confederation: Origins of the Constitution and American National Identity*. Chapel Hill: University of North Carolina Press, 1987.

Belz, Herman, Ronald Hoffman, and Peter J. Albert, eds. *To Form a More Perfect Union: The Critical Ideas of the Constitution*. Charlottesville: University Press of Virginia, forthcoming.

Bemis, Samuel Flagg. *The Diplomacy of the American Revolution*. Bloomington: Indiana University Press, 1957; orig. pub. New York, 1935.

Bezanson, Anne. *Wholesale Prices in Philadelphia, 1784–1861*. Philadelphia: University of Pennsylvania Press, 1936.

Billias, George Athan. *Elbridge Gerry: Founding Father and Republican Statesman*. New York: McGraw-Hill, 1976.

Bining, Arthur C. *Pennsylvania Iron Manufacture in the Eighteenth Century*. Harrisburg: Pennsylvania Historical Commission, 1938.

Bishop, H. M. "Why Rhode Island Opposed the Federal Constitution." *Rhode Island History* 8 (1949), 1–10, 33–44.

Bloch, Ruth H. *Visionary Republic: Millennial Themes in American Thought, 1756–1800*. New York: Cambridge University Press, 1985.

Bolles, Albert S. *The Financial History of the United States from 1774 to 1789*. 2d ed. New York: Appleton & Co., 1884.

Brown, Richard D. *Revolutionary Politics in Massachusetts: The Boston Committee of Correspondence and the Towns, 1772–1774*. Cambridge, Mass.: Harvard University Press, 1970.

––––––. "Shays's Rebellion and the Ratification of the Constitution in Massachusetts." In *Beyond Confederation: Origins of the Constitution and*

American National Identity, ed. Richard Beeman, Stephen Botein, and Edward C. Carter II, 113–27. Chapel Hill: University of North Carolina Press, 1987.

Brunhouse, Robert. *The Counter-Revolution in Pennsylvania, 1776–1790*. Philadelphia: Pennsylvania Historical Commission, 1942.

Buel, Richard. "Time: Friend or Foe of the Revolution?" In *Reconsiderations on the Revolutionary War*, ed. Don Higginbotham, 124–43. Westport, Conn.: Greenwood Press, 1978.

Burnett, Edmund Cody. "Notes on American Negotiations for Commercial Treaties, 1776–1786." *American Historical Review* 26 (1911), 579–87.

Carp, E. Wayne. *To Starve the Army at Pleasure: Continental Army Administration and American Political Culture, 1775–1783*. Chapel Hill: University of North Carolina Press, 1984.

Clark, Victor S. *History of Manufactures in the United States, 1607–1860*. 3 vols. Washington, D.C.: Library of Congress, 1916.

Clemens, Paul G. E. *The Atlantic Economy and Maryland's Eastern Shore: From Tobacco to Grain*. Ithaca, N.Y.: Cornell University Press, 1980.

Cochran, Thomas. *New York in the Confederation: An Economic Study*. Philadelphia: University of Pennsylvania Press, 1932.

Conley, Patrick T. "Posterity Views the Founding: General Published Works Pertaining to the Constitution; A Bibliographic Essay." In *The Constitution and the States: The Role of the Original Thirteen in the Framing and Adoption of the Federal Constitution*, ed. Patrick T. Conley and John P. Kaminski, 295–329. Madison, Wis.: Madison House, 1988.

Crowley, J. E. *This Sheba, Self: The Conceptualization of Economic Life in Eighteenth-Century America*. Baltimore: Johns Hopkins University Press, 1974.

Cunningham, Noble, Jr. *The Jeffersonian-Republicans: The Formation of Party Organization, 1789–1801*. Chapel Hill: University of North Carolina Press, 1957.

Dangerfield, George. *Chancellor Robert R. Livingston of New York, 1746–1813*. New York: Harcourt, Brace, 1960.

Davis, Joseph L. *Sectionalism in American Politics, 1774–1787*. Madison: University of Wisconsin Press, 1977.

Davis, Joseph S. *Essays in the Earlier History of American Corporations*. 2 vols. Cambridge, Mass.: Harvard University Press, 1917.

Dickson, P. G. M. *The Financial Revolution in England: A Study in the Development of Public Credit*. London: Macmillan, 1967.

Doerflinger, Thomas M. *A Vigorous Spirit of Enterprise: Merchants and Economic Development in Revolutionary Philadelphia*. Chapel Hill: University of North Carolina Press, 1986.

Dorfman, Joseph. *The Economic Mind in American Civilization, 1606–1933*. 3 vols. New York: Viking Press, 1946–59.

Dunbar, Louise Burnham. *A Study of "Monarchical" Tendencies in the United States from 1776 to 1801*. Urbana: University of Illinois Press, 1922.

East, Robert A. *Business Enterprise in the American Revolutionary War Era*. Gloucester, Mass.: Peter Smith, 1964; orig. pub. London and New York, 1938.

Egnal, Marc. "The Economic Development of the Thirteen Continental Colonies, 1720 to 1775." *William and Mary Quarterly*, 3d ser., 32 (1975), 191–222.

————. *A Mighty Empire: The Origins of the American Revolution.* Ithaca, N.Y.: Cornell University Press, 1988.

Ellis, Richard E. "The Persistence of Antifederalism after 1789." In *Beyond Confederation: Origins of the Constitution and American National Identity,* ed. Richard Beeman, Stephen Botein, and Edward C. Carter II, 295–314. Chapel Hill: University of North Carolina Press, 1987.

Epstein, David F. *The Political Theory of the Federalist.* Chicago: University of Chicago Press, 1984.

Ernst, Joseph, and Marc Egnal. "An Economic Interpretation of the American Revolution." *William and Mary Quarterly,* 3d ser., 29 (1972), 3–36.

Ferguson, E. James. "Political Economy, Public Liberty, and the Formation of the Constitution." *William and Mary Quarterly,* 3d ser., 40 (1983), 389–412.

————. *The Power of the Purse: A History of American Public Finance, 1776–1790.* Chapel Hill: University of North Carolina Press, 1961.

————. "State Assumption of the Federal Debt during the Confederation." *Mississippi Valley Historical Review* 38 (1951), 403–24.

Finkelman, Paul. "Slavery and the Constitutional Convention: Making a Covenant with Death." In *Beyond Confederation: Origins of the Constitution and American National Identity,* ed. Richard Beeman, Stephen Botein, and Edward C. Carter II, 188–225. Chapel Hill: University of North Carolina Press, 1987.

Foner, Eric. *Tom Paine and Revolutionary America.* New York: Oxford University Press, 1976.

Fraser, Leon. *English Opinion of the American Constitution and Government (1783–1798).* New York: Columbia University Press, 1915.

Furtwangler, Albert. *The Authority of Publius.* Ithaca, N.Y.: Cornell University Press, 1984.

Giesecke, Albert. *American Commercial Legislation before 1789.* Philadelphia: University of Pennsylvania Press, 1910.

Gilbert, Felix. *To the Farewell Address: Ideas of Early American Foreign Policy.* Princeton, N.J.: Princeton University Press, 1961.

Gillespie, Michael, and Michael Lienesch, eds. *Ratifying the Constitution.* Lawrence: University Press of Kansas, 1989.

Goodman, Paul. *The Democratic-Republicans of Massachusetts: Politics in a Young Republic.* Cambridge, Mass.: Harvard University Press, 1964.

Grampp, William D. "A Re-examination of Jeffersonian Economics." *Southern Economic Journal* 12 (1946), 263–82.

Greene, Jack P. *A Bicentennial Bookshelf: Historians Analyze the Constitutional Era.* Philadelphia: Friends of Independence National Historical Park, 1986.

Greene, Jack P., and J. R. Pole, eds. *Colonial British America: Essays in the New History of the Early Modern Era.* Baltimore: Johns Hopkins University Press, 1984.

Gunn, J. A. W. *Politics and the Public Interest in the Seventeenth Century.* London: Routledge & Kegan Paul, 1969.

Hedges, James B. *The Browns of Providence Plantation: The Colonial Years.* Cambridge, Mass.: Harvard University Press, 1952.

Hinsley, Francis H. *Power and the Pursuit of Peace: Theory and Practice in the History of Relations between States.* Cambridge: Cambridge University Press, 1963.

Hirschman, Albert O. *The Passions and the Interests: Political Arguments for Capitalism before Its Triumph.* Princeton, N.J.: Princeton University Press, 1977.

Hoffman, Ronald. *A Spirit of Dissension: Economics, Politics, and the Revolution in Maryland.* Baltimore: Johns Hopkins University Press, 1973.

Hont, Istvan, and Michael Ignatieff, eds. *Wealth and Virtue: The Shaping of Political Economy in the Scottish Enlightenment.* Cambridge: Cambridge University Press, 1983.

Hunter, W. C. *The Commercial Policies of New Jersey under the Confederation.* Princeton, N.J.: Princeton University Press, 1922.

Hutson, James H. "Country, Court, and Constitution: Antifederalism and the Historians." *William and Mary Quarterly,* 3d ser., 38 (1981), 337–68.

———. *John Adams and the Diplomacy of the American Revolution.* Lexington: University of Kentucky Press, 1980.

Jensen, Merrill, *Articles of Confederation: An Interpretation of the Social Constitutional History of the American Revolution, 1774–1781.* Madison: University of Wisconsin Press, 1939.

———. *The New Nation: A History of the United States during the Confederation, 1781–1789.* New York: Alfred A. Knopf, 1950.

Jillson, Calvin. "Constitution-Making: Alignment and Realignment in the Federal Convention of 1787." *American Political Science Review* 75 (1981), 598–612.

———. "Ideas in Conflict: Political Strategy and Intellectual Advantage in the Federal Convention." In *To Form a More Perfect Union: The Critical Ideas of the Constitution,* ed. Herman Belz, Ronald Hoffman, and Peter J. Albert. Charlottesville: University Press of Virginia, forthcoming.

Jillson, Calvin, and Thornton Anderson. "Realignments in the Convention of 1787: The Slave Trade Compromise." *Journal of Politics* 39 (1977), 712–29.

Jillson, Calvin, and Cecil Eubanks. "The Political Structure of Constitution Making: The Federal Convention of 1787." *American Journal of Political Science* 28 (1984), 435–58.

Johnson, Victor L. *The American Commissariat during the Revolutionary War.* Philadelphia: University of Pennsylvania Press, 1941.

———. "Fair Traders and Smugglers in Philadelphia, 1754–1763." *Pennsylvania Magazine of History and Biography* 83 (1959), 125–49.

Kenyon, Cecelia. "Men of Little Faith: The Anti-Federalists on the Nature of Representative Government." *William and Mary Quarterly,* 3d ser., 12 (1955), 3–43.

Kettner, James H. *The Development of American Citizenship, 1608–1870.* Chapel Hill: University of North Carolina Press, 1978.

Kramnick, Isaac. *Bolingbroke and His Circle: The Politics of Nostalgia in the Age of Walpole.* Cambridge, Mass.: Harvard University Press, 1968.

———. "The 'Great National Discussion': The Discourse of Politics in 1787." *William and Mary Quarterly,* 3d ser., 45 (1988), 3–32.

Lang, Daniel George. *Foreign Policy in the Early Republic: The Law of Nations and the Balance of Power.* Baton Rouge: Louisiana State University Press, 1985.

Larson, John Lauritz. " 'Bind the Republic Together': The National Union and the Struggle for a System of Internal Improvements." *Journal of American History* 74 (Sept. 1987): 363–87.

Lerner, Ralph. "Commerce and Character: The Anglo-American as a New-Model Man." *William and Mary Quarterly,* 3d ser., 26 (1979), 3–26.

Letwin, William. *The Origins of Scientific Economics: English Economic Thought, 1660–1766.* London: Methuen & Co., 1963.

Levy, Leonard, and Dennis J. Mahoney, eds. *The Framing and Ratification of the Constitution.* New York: Macmillan, 1986.

Lienesch, Michael. *New Order of the Ages: The American Constitution and the Making of American Republican Thought.* Princeton, N.J.: Princeton University Press, 1988.

Low, W. A. "Merchant and Planter Relations in Post-Revolutionary Virginia, 1783–1789." *Virginia Magazine of History and Biography* 61 (1953), 314–24.

Lynd, Staughton. "The Compromise of 1787." In *Class Conflict, Slavery, and the United States Constitution,* by Staughton Lynd, 185–213. Indianapolis: Bobbs-Merrill, 1967.

———. "The Mechanics in New York City Politics, 1774–1788." *Labor History* 5 (1964), 215–46.

McCoy, Drew R. *The Elusive Republic: Political Economy in Jeffersonian America.* Chapel Hill: University of North Carolina Press, 1980.

———. "James Madison and Visions of American Nationality in the Confederation Period: A Regional Perspective." In *Beyond Confederation: Origins of the Constitution and American National Identity,* ed. Richard Beeman, Stephen Botein, and Edward C. Carter II, 226–58. Chapel Hill: University of North Carolina Press, 1987.

McCusker, John J., and Russell R. Menard. *The Economy of British America, 1607–1789.* Chapel Hill: University of North Carolina Press, 1985.

McDonald, Forrest. *Novus Ordo Seclorum: The Intellectual Origins of the Constitution.* Lawrence: University Press of Kansas, 1985.

Macfarlane, Alan. *The Origins of English Individualism.* New York: Cambridge University Press, 1979.

McKendrick, Neil, John Brewer, and J. H. Plumb. *The Birth of a Consumer Society.* Bloomington: Indiana University Press, 1982.

Macpherson, C. B. *The Political Theory of Possessive Individualism: Hobbes to Locke.* Oxford: Oxford University Press, 1962.

Main, Jackson Turner. *The Antifederalists: Critics of the Constitution, 1781–1788.* Chapel Hill: University of North Carolina Press, 1961.

Marks, Frederick W., III. *Independence on Trial: Foreign Affairs and the Making of the Constitution.* Baton Rouge: Louisiana State University Press, 1973.

Marston, Jerrilyn Greene. *King and Congress: The Transfer of Political Legitimacy, 1774–1776.* Princeton, N.J.: Princeton University Press, 1987.

Martin, Margaret. *Merchants and Traders of the Connecticut River Valley, 1750–1820. Studies in History,* vol. 24. Northampton, Mass.: Smith College, 1938.

Matson, Cathy. "American Political Economy in the Constitutional Decade." In *The U.S. Constitution: The First 200 Years,* ed. R. C. Simmons and A. E. Dick Howard, 16–35. Manchester: Manchester University Press, 1989.

———. "From Free Trade to Liberty: New York City Merchants and the Reshaping of a Dissenting Economic Ideology." Manuscript in preparation.

―――. "Jealousy, Liberty, and Union: The New York Economy in the 1780s." In *New York in the Age of the Constitution*, ed. William Pencak and Paul Gilje. Charlottesville: University Press of Virginia, forthcoming.

―――. "Public Vices, Private Benefit: William Duer and His Circle, 1776–1792." In *New York and the Rise of American Capitalism*, ed. Conrad Wright and William Pencak, 72–123. Charlottesville: University Press of Virginia, 1989.

―――. "Reluctant Federalists: Lesser Merchants and Ratification in New York." In *The Reluctant Pillar: A Supplement*, ed. Stephen Schechter. New York State Commission: Albany (forthcoming).

Matson, Cathy, and Peter Onuf. "Toward a Republican Empire: Interest and Ideology in Revolutionary America." *American Quarterly* 37 (1985), 496–531.

Meek, Ronald. *Social Science and the Ignoble Savage*. Cambridge: Cambridge University Press, 1976.

Morgan, Edmund S. "The Puritan Ethic and the Coming of the American Revolution." *William and Mary Quarterly*, 3d ser., 24 (1967), 3–43.

Morris, Richard B. *The Forging of the Union, 1781–1789*. New York: Harper & Row, 1987.

―――. *Government and Labor in Early America*. New York: Columbia University Press, 1946.

Murrin, John. "The Great Inversion, or Court versus Country: A Comparison of the Revolution Settlements in England (1688–1721) and America (1776–1816)." In *Three British Revolutions, 1641, 1688, 1776*, ed. J. G. A. Pocock, 368–453. Princeton, N.J.: Princeton University Press, 1980.

Nash, Gary. *The Urban Crucible: Social Change, Political Consciousness, and the Origins of the American Revolution*. Cambridge, Mass.: Harvard University Press, 1979.

Nelson, John R., Jr. "Alexander Hamilton and American Manufacturing: A Reexamination." *Journal of American History* 65 (1979), 971–95.

Nettels, Curtis P. *The Emergence of a National Economy, 1775–1815*. New York: Holt, Rinehart, and Winston, 1962.

North, Douglas C. *The Economic Growth of the United States, 1790–1860*. Englewood Cliffs, N.J.: Prentice Hall, 1961.

Onuf, Peter S. "American Federalism and the Politics of Expansion." In *Essays on the Constitution*, ed. Hermann Wellenreuther. Forthcoming.

―――. "Anarchy and the Crisis of the Union." In *To Form a More Perfect Union: The Critical Ideas of the Constitution*, ed. Herman Belz, Ronald Hoffman, and Peter J. Albert. Chapel Hill: University of North Carolina Press, forthcoming.

―――. "Articles of Confederation." In *The Framing and Ratification of the Constitution*, ed. Leonard Levy and Dennis Mahoney, 82–97. New York: Macmillan, 1986.

―――. "Constitutional Politics: States, Sections, and the National Interest." In *Toward a More Perfect Union: Six Essays on the Constitution*, ed. Neil L. York, 29–58. Provo, Utah: Brigham Young University Press, 1988.

―――. "Liberty, Development, and Union: Visions of the West in the 1780s." *William and Mary Quarterly*, 3d ser., 43 (1986), 179–213.

———. "Maryland: The Small Republic in the New Nation." In *Ratifying the Constitution*, ed. Michael Gillespie and Michael Lienesch. Lawrence: University Press of Kansas, 1989.

———. *Origins of the Federal Republic: Jurisdictional Controversies in the United States, 1775-1787.* Philadelphia: University of Pennsylvania Press, 1983.

———. "Reflections on the Founding: Constitutional Historiography in Bicentennial Perspective." *William and Mary Quarterly*, 3d ser., 46 (Apr. 1989), 341-75.

———. *Statehood and Union: A History of the Northwest Ordinance.* Bloomington: Indiana University Press, 1987.

———. "State Sovereignty and the Making of the Constitution." In *Conceptual Change and the Constitution*, ed. Terence Ball and J. G. A. Pocock, 79-98. Lawrence: University Press of Kansas, 1988.

Onuf, Peter S., and Nicholas G. Onuf. "American Constitutionalism and the Emergence of a Liberal World Order." In *The Impact of the United States Constitution Abroad*, ed. George A. Billias. Westport, Conn.: Greenwood Press, forthcoming.

Paige, Jerome. "The Evolution of Mercantile Capitalism and Planter Capitalism and the Development of Economic Ideas." Ph.D. diss., American University, 1982.

Papenfuse, Edward, Jr. *In Pursuit of Profit: The Annapolis Merchants in the Era of the American Revolution.* Baltimore: Johns Hopkins University Press, 1975.

Pocock, J. G. A. *The Machiavellian Moment: Florentine Political Thought and the Atlantic Republican Tradition.* Princeton, N.J.: Princeton University Press, 1975.

Pole, J. R. *The Gift of Government.* Athens: University of Georgia Press, 1983.

Ragatz, L. J. *The Fall of the Planter Class in the British Caribbean, 1763-1833: A Study in Social and Economic History.* New York: Century Co., 1928.

Rakove, Jack N. "Articles of Confederation." In *Encyclopedia of American Political History*, ed. Jack P. Greene, 1:83-91. 3 vols. New York: Charles Scribner's Sons, 1984.

———. *The Beginnings of National Politics: An Interpretive History of the Continental Congress.* New York: Alfred A. Knopf, 1979.

———. "From One Agenda to Another: The Condition of American Federalism, 1783-1787." In *The American Revolution: Its Character and Limits*, ed. Jack P. Greene, 80-103. New York: New York University Press, 1987.

———. "The Great Compromise: Ideas, Interests, and the Politics of Constitution Making." *William and Mary Quarterly*, 3d ser., 44 (1987), 424-57.

Reid, John Philip. *The Concept of Liberty in the Age of the American Revolution.* Chicago: University of Chicago Press, 1988.

Renzulli, L. Marx. *Maryland: The Federalist Years.* Rutherford, N.J.: Fairleigh Dickinson University Press, 1972.

Rezneck, Samuel. "The Rise and Early Development of Industrial Consciousness in the United States, 1760-1830." *Journal of Economic and Business History* 4 (1932), 784-811.

Riesman, Janet A. "Money, Credit, and Federalist Political Economy." In *Beyond Confederation, Origins of the Constitution and American National*

Identity, ed. Richard Beeman, Stephen Botein, and Edward C. Carter II, 128–61. Chapel Hill: University of North Carolina Press, 1987.

Risjord, Norman. *Chesapeake Politics, 1781–1800.* New York: Columbia University Press, 1978.

Rives, William C. *History of the Life and Times of James Madison.* 3 vols. Boston: Little, Brown, 1866.

Roche, John F. *Joseph Reed: A Moderate in the American Revolution.* New York: Columbia University Press, 1957.

Roche, John P. "The Founding Fathers: A Reform Caucus in Action." *American Political Science Review* 55 (1961), 799–816.

Rothenberg, Winifred B. "The Market and Massachusetts Farmers, 1750–1855." *Journal of Economic History* 41 (1981), 283–314.

Royster, Charles. *A Revolutionary People at War: The Continental Army and American Character, 1775–1783.* Chapel Hill: University of North Carolina Press, 1979.

Schlesinger, Arthur M. *The Colonial Merchants and the American Revolution, 1763–1776.* New York: Atheneum, 1968.

Sekora, John. *Luxury: The Concept in Western Thought, Eden to Smollett.* Baltimore: Johns Hopkins University Press, 1977.

Setser, Vernon G. *The Commercial Reciprocity Policy of the United States.* Philadelphia: University of Pennsylvania Press, 1937.

Shaffer, Arthur H. *The Politics of History: Writing the History of the American Revolution, 1783–1815.* Chicago: Precedent Publisher, 1975.

Singleton, Esther. *Social New York under the Georges, 1714–1776.* New York: D. Appleton, 1902.

Skinner, Andrew S. "Adam Smith: An Economic Interpretation of History." In *Essays on Adam Smith,* ed. Andrew S. Skinner and Thomas Wilson, 154–78. Oxford: Oxford University Press, 1975.

Slaughter, Thomas P. *The Whiskey Rebellion: Frontier Epilogue to the American Revolution.* New York: Oxford University Press, 1986.

Spaulding, E. Wilder. *New York in the Critical Period, 1783–1789.* New York: Columbia University Press, 1932.

Steffen, Charles G. *The Mechanics of Baltimore: Workers and Politics in the Age of Revolution, 1763–1812.* Urbana: University of Illinois Press, 1984.

Storing, Herbert J. *What the Anti-Federalists Were For.* Vol. 1 of *The Complete Anti-Federalist.* 7 vols. Chicago: University of Chicago Press, 1981.

Stourzh, Gerald. *Alexander Hamilton and the Idea of Representative Government.* Stanford, Calif.: Stanford University Press, 1970.

———. *Benjamin Franklin and American Foreign Policy.* 2d ed. Chicago: University of Chicago Press, 1969.

Szatmary, David P. *Shays' Rebellion: The Making of an Agrarian Insurrection.* Amherst: University of Massachusetts Press, 980.

Thayer, Theodore. "The Army Contractors for the Niagara Campaign, 1755–1756." *William and Mary Quarterly,* 3d ser., 14 (1957), 31–46.

Tully, James. *A Discourse on Property: John Locke and His Adversaries.* Cambridge: Cambridge University Press, 1980.

Tyler, John W. *Smugglers and Patriots: Boston Merchants and the Advent of the American Revolution.* Boston: Northeastern University Press, 1986.

Ver Steeg, Clarence. *Robert Morris, Revolutionary Financier.* New York: Octagon Books, 1972; orig. pub. Philadelphia, 1954.

Watlington, Patricia. *The Partisan Spirit: Kentucky Politics, 1779–1792.* New York: Atheneum, 1972.

Weeden, William B. *The Economic and Social History of New England, 1620–1789.* 2 vols. New York: Houghton, Mifflin, 1899.

Weinberg, Albert K. *Manifest Destiny: A Study of Nationalist Expansionism in American History.* Baltimore: Johns Hopkins University Press, 1935.

Wiebe, Robert H. *The Opening of American Society: From the Adoption of the Constitution to the Eve of Disunion.* New York: Alfred A. Knopf, 1984.

Williams, Samuel Cole. *History of the Lost State of Franklin.* New York: Press of the Pioneers, 1933.

Wilson, Charles. *England's Apprenticeship, 1603–1763.* London: Longmans, 1965.

———. *Profit and Power: A Study of England and the Dutch Wars.* London: Longmans, 1957.

Winch, Donald. *Classical Political Economy and Colonies.* Cambridge, Mass.: Harvard University Press, 1965.

Winslow, Cal. "Sussex Smugglers." In *Albion's Fatal Tree: Crime and Society in Eighteenth-Century England,* ed. E. P. Thompson et al., 119–66. New York: Pantheon, 1975.

Wolin, Sheldon. *Politics and Vision: Continuity and Innovation in Western Political Thought.* Boston: Little, Brown, 1960.

Wood, Gordon S. *The Creation of the American Republic, 1776–1787.* Chapel Hill: University of North Carolina Press, 1969.

———. "Interests and Disinterestedness in the Making of the Constitution." In *Beyond Confederation: Origins of the Constitution and American National Identity,* ed. Richard Beeman, Stephen Botein, and Edward C. Carter II, 69–109. Chapel Hill: University of North Carolina Press, 1987.

York, Neil L., ed. *Toward a More Perfect Union: Six Essays on the Constitution.* Provo, Utah: Brigham Young University Press, 1988.

Young, Alfred F. "Conservatives, the Constitution, and the 'Spirit of Accommodation.'" In *How Democratic Was the Constitution?* ed. Robert Goldwin and William Schama. Washington, D.C.: American Enterprise Institute, 1980.

———. *The Democratic Republicans of New York: The Origins, 1763–1797.* Chapel Hill: University of North Carolina Press, 1967.

Zagarri, Rosemarie. *The Politics of Size: Representation in the United States, 1776–1812.* Ithaca, N.Y.: Cornell University Press, 1987.

Index